Switching to Cyber

Switching to Cyber

The Mid-Career Guide to Launching a Cybersecurity Career

Josiah Dykstra
Helen Patton

CISO DRG Publishing
P.O. Box 581
Paso Robles, CA 93447
<www.CISODRG.com>
info@cisodrg.com
ISBN 978-1-955976-26-8

DISCLAIMER: The contents of this book and any additional comments are for informational purposes only and are not intended to be a substitute for professional advice. Your reliance on any information provided by the publisher, its affiliates, content providers, members, employees, or comment contributors is solely at your own risk. This publication is sold with the understanding that the publisher is not engaged in rendering professional services. If advice or other expert assistance is required, the services of a competent professional person should be sought.

To contact the authors, write the publisher at the address provided above, "Attention: Author Services."

Edited by Bill Bonney
Artwork by Gwendolyn Peres
Copyediting by Nadine Bonney
Production by Last Mile Publishing

Acknowledgments

A book on cybersecurity careers by its nature draws heavily on collective experiences and connections across a lifetime. We have countless people to thank for influencing our thinking about this topic, including close friends and all those who responded to social media questions and questions!

We owe our gratitude to CISO DRG Publishing and especially Bill Bonney. Bill gave us helpful feedback, expert editing, and constant support throughout the writing and production process. Bill was the first one to see the potential and value in this book when our idea was still evolving.

To all those who offered reviews and comments on the draft, your input and suggestions made this a better book. Thank you to Rita Doerr, Wendy Nather, Tim Sexton, and Ed Skoudis.

Helen: First and foremost, thank you to my co-author Josiah, who approached me with the idea of writing this book and who was such a great writing partner. Also, to my husband, Darren, for always affording me the time to research and write; and to Bear, for helping me to write with heart.

Josiah: Huge thanks to Helen for agreeing to take on another book with me and being a fabulous co-author. Thank you to my wife, Alicia, for her unending love and support in writing, in work, and in life. I dedicate this book to my mother who was the source of endless love and pride for her children.

Table of Contents

Foreword

It is with great enthusiasm that I write this Foreword. The authors, Dr. Josiah Dykstra and Ms. Helen Patton, are two very well-regarded international professionals in the cybersecurity, network security, and enterprise management worlds. Their combined expertise makes this book, *Switching to Cyber*, uniquely different, and it certainly fills the void. One no longer must look any further, except to this outstanding book—really a tutorial—on how to break into the cybersecurity profession mid-career.

Both Josiah and Helen have graciously shared their unique perspectives and explain that "it's not you" but rather in cybersecurity you must just think a little bit differently, be a little bit more creative, in order to open the doors. And there is no better time than today! This is your time to embrace your future and dive in!

This book is not just a roadmap: it is a lantern for those navigating the uncharted pathway between established expertise and new beginnings. Like myself, Josiah and Helen are seasoned practitioners, authors, and celebrated mentors in the field that had varied experiences prior to full-time roles in cybersecurity, so they bring to these pages an understanding that is both practical and deeply empathetic. They recognize that mid-career professionals carry with them a wealth of skills—strategic thinking, leadership, adaptability—that are not only transferable but often essential to thriving in cybersecurity's dynamic environment.

What sets *Switching to Cyber* apart is its ability to speak to readers at multiple levels. For some, it is a gentle encouragement—a reassurance that the leap into cybersecurity is not only possible but also profoundly rewarding. For others, it offers tactical guidance: how to translate prior achievements into relevant competencies, how to cultivate a network in a new field, how to bridge knowledge gaps efficiently, and how to face the inevitable moments of self-doubt that accompany any career transformation.

The wisdom in these pages is grounded in real stories, practical frameworks, and candid reflections from professionals who have walked the path. Josiah and Helen's approach is refreshingly honest, acknowledging the challenges without glossing them over, yet always pointing toward the possibilities that lie ahead. They understand that career advancement is not a linear ascent but a series of intentional choices, each one a step toward a more fulfilling professional life.

Offering a few specific insights for you:

- Look at the layout of each chapter so it can be used like a textbook!

- Each chapter has its own theme and comes complete with a Chapter Summary and Chapter References; some also include Action Steps and Tips on how to roadmap your next five years.

- Please "tab" or use a highlighter to mark the areas that resonate with you!

- Undoubtedly, this book will become your "go-to" guide each time you think about embracing your next position or increase in responsibilities.

- We are all deliberate owners of our future. Both Josiah and Helen mention throughout the concept that yes, you do have control of your entrance into and your progression along the cybersecurity professional journey.

- Moving forward is all about being deliberate, so you are on the right path already by picking up this book.

- There are many notable words of wisdom throughout *Switching to Cyber*, such as interview skills and approaches, credentials, networking, negotiating, training, upskilling, mentoring, improving one's writing skills, gaining technical skills, and more, but the best takeaway of *Switching to Cyber* is that in its totality it will give you the confidence to move forward, embrace your passion, and defeat the adversary!

Readers will find value here not only in the actionable advice but also in the validation of their own aspirations. Whether you are contemplating cybersecurity as a new direction, seeking to deepen your engagement with the field, or simply in need of inspiration at a crossroads, this guide is a resource to return to again and again.

In closing, as we all know, the world of cybersecurity is as much about people as it is about technology. Most importantly, please know that you belong in cybersecurity. Its landscape is in constant motion, shaped by sophisticated evolving threats, emerging tools, mitigations, increasing adversaries, and—most crucially—you, the skilled individual who chooses to dedicate their talents to its cause, are vital.

It is precisely at this intersection of experience and ambition that Dr. Josiah Dykstra and Helen Patton's book, *Switching to Cyber,* becomes your indispensable companion. As you turn the pages of *Switching to Cyber*, my hope and anticipation is that you find the motivation, clarity, and courage to forge your own path forward, armed with the knowledge that your unique journey is not an obstacle, but the very foundation of your future success in cybersecurity.

Best to you all!

Welcome to our #cybercommunity! #youbelong

Diane

Dr. Diane M. Janosek, PhD, Esq, CISSP
CEO, Janos LLC
Dianejanosek.com

Many of life's most transformative opportunities come from unexpected moments—when the stars align just right. This book exists because of one such moment.

In the Spring of 2024, Josiah had just made a big leap, transitioning from 19 years in government service to a new role in the private sector. While the work was still in cybersecurity, it didn't take long to notice something significant. There were countless fabulous resources for people starting their first job in the field, including Helen Patton's book, *Navigating the Cybersecurity Career Path*. But there was surprisingly little guidance for those already deep into their careers, looking to shift gears or reimagine their professional journey. Aside from a lucky few with mentors to steer them, many were left navigating this transition alone.

The reality is clear: cybersecurity is a growing field with an insatiable need for skilled professionals. And it's not just for those "traditional" applicants who are fresh out of school or moving from one cybersecurity job to another. Many mid-career professionals in other fields are drawn to jump to or start a second career in cybersecurity for its dynamic nature, intellectual challenges, and the opportunity to make a real impact. We say: Hallelujah! We can't wait to have you!

Switching to Cyber is for you—the seasoned professional with a wealth of experience in any field, now eager to tackle a new challenge in cybersecurity. Whether you're looking for a career change, a fresh perspective, or a sense of purpose in this fast-growing domain, you're in the right place.

What follows is a guide born from personal journeys, lessons learned, and a shared passion for helping others succeed. We've been where you are, and we've designed this book to be the resource we wish had existed during our own transitions. We'll offer practical advice, actionable strategies, and plenty of real-world examples to help you land on your feet and thrive in this exciting field.

So, let's dive in—your new career in cybersecurity awaits!

Introduction

As the title suggests, this is a book for mid-career people. "Mid-career" is difficult to define precisely. We intend it to mean a professional stage in which someone has gained experience and expertise but still has many years left in their career. It's a time when they can continue to advance their skills and competencies and may pursue leadership roles, higher salaries, and more flexibility. Mid-career can also involve transitioning into a new field or profession.

Mid-career is not necessarily synonymous with midlife. One government study used age 35 as the start of mid-career, but this is a crude metric. Many of us will change jobs or fields multiple times across the entire spectrum of our working lives. So, mid-career is less about the number of jobs we've had and more about the time since we started working. Professions vary widely in when people start work and how long they work. Physicians may start working in their 30s after medical school and may be defined as "early-career" for their first five years.

Think of your life as a book with many chapters. Our careers are one part of our life story, but a career can have many chapters. For example, psychologists used to categorize personality by "fixed," lifelong traits such as introversion and agreeableness. New thinking acknowledges that we change over time. Who we are in our twenties may differ from who we are in our thirties or forties. Whatever your path has been thus far, it influences—but does not have to define or limit—the next chapter of your career.

Both of us (Helen and Josiah) are mid-career cybersecurity professionals. We've each had multiple employers and multiple jobs within those employers. Neither of us is planning to retire tomorrow. Looking back at the last decade, things have changed a lot: the world has changed, our lives have changed, and our passions and priorities have changed. When we all think about the next ten years, we should expect that change will continue. So, now could be the time for you to break into cybersecurity.

Josiah's first job after college required moving 1,036 miles across the United States, getting a new apartment, and adjusting to a new city. For him, the choice was influenced by a desire to work in national security and unconstrained by ties to a particular geographic location. Salary was a consideration but not the driving motivation. When he left government work 19 years later, he had built a wealth of technical expertise and contributions, gotten married, and settled into a comfortable home. The next job needed to accommodate those constraints and also be a fit for his level of seniority and desire for impact.

Helen's career is a story of luck, serendipity, and hard work. She started working before she started college and continued to work while pursuing bachelor's and master's degrees—neither in cybersecurity. She made the decision to stay based in Ohio—so when opportunities arose elsewhere, she decided to turn them down and focus on roles that were local. Now, with remote work, other opportunities present themselves. Salary and family circumstances have always been part of the decision equation, and now the opportunity to impact the community looms large in career decisions.

If you are reading this book, you are at least considering a move into cybersecurity. Great—we can't wait to have you in the field! You might still be working in another job or field at this moment. If so, it's not too early to begin preparing for the transition. Before you start applying for jobs, we will help you think about your existing skills, what to expert in cybersecurity, and how to succeed. In this book, we will give advice for finding a good job and preparing yourself for the move. If you've already transitioned, it's not too late. If you find yourself saying "what did I get myself into?" jump to Part 3 where we talk about thriving in cybersecurity.

Cybersecurity is a unique profession. This is an important consideration as you navigate into the field, and it is notably different than the surface differences of simply not being in the same role as your last job. One notable distinction is that cybersecurity has an active adversary. We are trying to protect against criminals and other attackers who aim to trick us or break into our accounts and steal things like money. This might be most familiar if you have worked in law enforcement, the military, or healthcare, where a physical-world thief or a biological virus, for instance, wanted to win and for you to fail. Like those fields, there can be serious consequences to safety and privacy and other values we cherish.

Whether or not we consider a job a "cybersecurity job" is open to some opinion and we'll draw the boundaries more precisely in Chapter 1. Security work involves protecting systems, networks, and data from unauthorized access, threats, and vulnerabilities, focusing on risk management and safeguarding information. It spans areas like encryption, incident response, and compliance, but excludes broader IT tasks like general system administration unless tied to security concerns.

A common area of misperception is worth correcting explicitly: not all technology jobs are cybersecurity jobs. Programmers write software and data scientists extract insights from data, but neither group is necessarily focused on security goals by default (though we'd appreciate it if everyone had security in mind!). More specifically, not even every IT and system administration job is a cybersecurity job. The world needs plenty of workers to help build, maintain, and operate the digital world around us; it just might be another person's role to focus on the confidentiality, integrity, and availability of the network and the data.

We can't anticipate all the reasons that you are getting into a cybersecurity job, but we do want you to be happy and fulfilled in it. In her book, *Job Therapy*, Professor of Psychology Tessa West discusses common sources of career frustration. Among them is career remorse. That is, the feelings of unhappiness and disenchantment that arise from a career that isn't what you wanted or expected. We hope that this book gives you an honest view of cybersecurity work, even if we can't shield you from a bad boss or an unforeseen company failure. Remember that a job is like a relationship and people have emotional connections to their work, hopefully more often positive than negative.

The good news is that there are things you can learn and do to get ready for a cybersecurity role while you have another job in your current field. You can assess your current skills (see Chapter 2) and start filling the gaps for a particular specialization (see Chapter 5). You can learn the lingo (Chapter 4) and study the market (Chapter 3). By the time you apply for a job and sit for an interview, you'll be a knowledgeable and competitive applicant.

How This Book Is Organized

The book is organized into five parts that progress roughly in the order you might need them in a new career. Yet, jumping around and reading the whole book before changing careers is also encouraged.

Part One is self-assessment. These chapters help reveal the relevant skills you already possess and how they will be valuable in cybersecurity. We also provide an overview of the cybersecurity profession with regard to the spectrum of job roles and job factors. Part Two is about how to take the leap of selecting a specialization, getting hired, and filling any gaps in your skillset. Once you know how to get established in the field, Part Three covers the topics of thriving and flourishing, such as staying ahead of changes and deepening your expertise. Part Four discusses career advancement including promotions and leadership roles. Finally, Part Five addresses specialized topics such as work-life balance, ethics, considerations for minorities, and the future of cybersecurity as a field.

Part 1

Self-Assessment

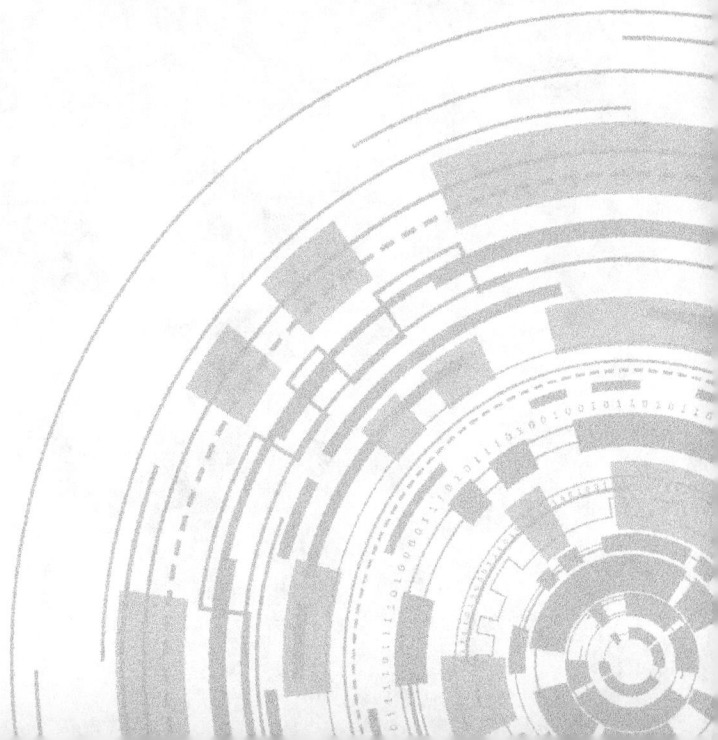

Chapter 1

Identifying Your Motivations and Goals

Is Cybersecurity Right for You?

Finding a path into cybersecurity starts with understanding yourself. Understanding what interests you about cybersecurity, what skills you bring to your first cybersecurity job, the kind of work you like to do, and the kind of place you like to work are all necessary before you start responding to your first job posting. The cybersecurity work and workforce are diverse and in need of many different skills and backgrounds. Whatever brings you here, it's important to have an idea of why you want to work in cybersecurity and the kind of cybersecurity work you want to do. Without a general plan for the kind of work you want to do, it is easy to get lost or discouraged by the technologies, practices, threats, vulnerabilities, laws, regulations, and all the other things that make up the cybersecurity landscape.

Although it may seem like a narrow specialty, the cybersecurity field is big and getting bigger. Check out Rafeeq Rehman's *CISO MindMap* to see all the functions managed by a Chief Information Security Officer (CISO) to get a sense of the kind of work covered by "cybersecurity." We used to consider cybersecurity a single discipline, a sub-function of what is called Information Technology (IT). Now, cybersecurity has become its own big, sprawling job family. Cybersecurity is a horizontal function touching every part of modern businesses. The good news is that cybersecurity has room for anyone with any kind of background. The harder part is deciding where to start and how to proceed.

For someone who already has some work experience—in any field!—identifying the cybersecurity work you want to do might be easier than for a person with little or no prior experience. Chances are you've had some opportunities to find out what you are good at (Customer service? Analysis? Leadership? Management?) and have an idea of what you don't like (Repetitive tasks? Public speaking? Administrative tasks?). Even better, you probably have an idea of or experience with a certain kind of industry or environment you may want to be part of (Retail? Finance? Education?) and the type of company that works best for you (International? Fortune 1000? Start-up? Privately-owned?). If not, don't worry—we'll cover this later in this chapter.

Take some time to jot down what you already know about yourself—strengths, weaknesses, likes, dislikes, experience—and we'll help you add to this as you go through the book. It will form the basis of your strategy to move into the cybersecurity profession and stop you from wasting time chasing poor leads and bad fits.

We recommend attending a low-cost, local cybersecurity conference to get a first-hand experience with the individuals, organizations, problems, and current focus areas in cybersecurity. BSides, for instance, is a community-driven event held in many cities around the world.[1] It is a great way to familiarize yourself with the profession.

What Is Cybersecurity?

A quick internet search will reveal numerous different definitions of cybersecurity. For the mid-career jobseeker, a solid definition is a reasonable place to start but not always helpful when trying to understand how the job market and profession really work. Instead of a standalone definition, we think it is useful to understand the evolution of cybersecurity—where cybersecurity started from and where it's going—so you can position yourself for your future career. What follows is a brief overview of the development of the cybersecurity profession. We encourage you to continue studying the history of the profession as you continue your career journey.

---

[1]   https://bsides.org/.

There are many insights to learn from the work of those who have gone before.

Before the 1990's

It may surprise some people to understand that people have been "doing" cybersecurity for a long time, even before the invention of computers. Ancient Egyptians used cybersecurity concepts like encryption, and people have added to them over the centuries.[2]

Computer passwords were first introduced in the early 1960's. The initial use was allowing multiple people to use a single computer at the same time (known as time-sharing). To keep each user's files and work separate, system designers implemented individual accounts protected by a password. This was the origin of the login-and-password model that became the standard for decades afterward.

However, the modern cybersecurity team as we know it today didn't exist before the 1980's. Instead, cybersecurity was included as part of someone's job in IT (usually the network engineer). Cybersecurity in this decade focused on identifying what assets an organization had, and how to ensure those assets supported the business. Jobseekers looked for IT jobs, not cybersecurity jobs, and people interested in security were more likely to be hacking on their own time than being paid to hack. For a great book on this, check out *Cult of the Dead Cow* (2019) by Joseph Menn.

The 1990's

With the rise of the networked PC, and the various worms and viruses that grew up to exploit the weaknesses of these new systems, the issue of cybersecurity started to emerge. If an organization had a dedicated security team (which was still less likely than you would think), they were focused on tools like firewalls, anti-virus, etc., and were concerned with preventing viruses and network attacks. They

---

[2] "A Brief History of Cryptography" (2006, Cypher Research Laboratories) https://www.cypher.com.au/crypto_history.htm.

were part of the IT organization, and usually a small part at that. In 1995 Citicorp named Steve Katz as the first known Chief Information Security Officer (CISO) (although certainly not the first security leader).[3] In this decade, cybersecurity focused on protecting on-premises assets from viruses and worms. Cybersecurity jobs were starting to pop up, usually in the form of network security engineering.

The 2000's

The rise of regulations and the influence of the Sarbanes-Oxley Act in the U.S. after major publicly traded company financial failures resulted not only in security teams that needed to understand what controls were in place and how to detect when defenses had failed, but also an ecosystem of internal and external technology auditors. Now security teams needed to have a security program and prove that the program was working. Nation-state attacks were growing, and national security organizations were starting to take notice. Cybersecurity was focused on detecting attacks and understanding when defensive measures failed. In fact, it was less likely that the security team and function was called "Cybersecurity," and more likely it was called "Information Security," encompassing the protection of all information and all systems that processed or stored information from any kind of attack. Jobs started to pop up not only in the security analyst/engineering functions but also in governance functions like third-party risk management, identity management, and security training/awareness.

The 2010's

This decade will be remembered for the rise of ransomware attacks—ones that not only resulted in data loss but also negatively impacted business operations and human life. The first documented ransomware attack occurred in 1989 and they continued to increase in scale and impact through the 2000's and

---

[3]   "Steve Katz Dies" (2023) Steve Zurier
      https://www.scmagazine.com/news/steve-katz-dies-cybersecurity-innovator-known-as-worlds-first-ciso.

beyond.[4] Companies were moving their workloads to the cloud, creating a shared risk model for cybersecurity. Privacy regulations requiring confidentiality security controls were proliferating. Nation-state and criminal attacks were on the rise, resulting in huge amounts of data theft. Security teams were growing, adding not only security operations functions but Identity and Access Management (IAM), Governance, Risk and Compliance (GRC), endpoint engineering, security awareness, and other functions. The security teams were starting to impact not just the IT organizations but other parts of the business. The industry recognized that guarantees of perfect defense were impossible; attention turned to proactively identifying weaknesses in defenses and improving detection/response capabilities. Cybersecurity now refined its focus to detection and response capabilities and proactive security controls. Cybersecurity jobs like Security Cloud Engineer and Penetration Tester started appearing.

The 2020's

Business leaders, from boardrooms to regulators, started taking notice of cybersecurity. The security team became more likely to split away from the IT reporting line and have its own functional domain, particularly in larger, more mature organizations. Regulators began scrutinizing how companies governed their cybersecurity risks, giving rise to more business-minded security leadership skills. Cybersecurity is now about cybersecurity resilience and improving the ability of an organization to recover from a cybersecurity event of any kind. The term "Information Security" is used less often now, as teams are focused on protecting against external attacks, and other business functions like data governance and privacy have assumed some of the other information protection capabilities.

What started in the 1980's as something IT people did when they had time has grown into a fully-fledged profession with its own

---

[4]   CSOOnline.com July 2020, Andrada Fiscutean
      https://www.csoonline.com/article/569617/a-history-of-ransomware-the-
      motives-and-methods-behind-these-evolving-attacks.html.

functional responsibilities that impact all aspects of an organization. For mid-career jobseekers, this means that opportunities to find roles that leverage your prior work experience are highly likely and that there is room for career growth once you find your first security role.

Why Do People Pick Careers in Cybersecurity?

Before you dive right into finding a cybersecurity job, it is helpful to consider why you're attracted to cybersecurity in the first place. Understanding what is appealing about the profession will help you target the kinds of jobs and roles that align with these interests. Here are some interests that people already in cybersecurity have expressed.

Potential Income

Most people consider cybersecurity to be a high-paying technology job. According to Payscale, a cybersecurity analyst in the United States in 2024 makes an average salary of approximately $81,000 a year, 25% more than the national average.[5] The most in-demand skills can pay much more. According to Cyberseek.org, organizations have multiple job openings for cybersecurity professionals (pay attention to the nuances here, there aren't shortages for entry-level security jobs!) across multiple industries and geographies. Jobseekers looking to maximize their earning potential and have some level of industry-level job security are attracted to cybersecurity for these reasons.

Being motivated to join cybersecurity for income and job security is completely valid, but, given the nature of cybersecurity work, it is unlikely that pay will be enough to sustain you when the job becomes difficult. Cybersecurity professionals have a high level of job stress and related burnout; this may come from long shifts supporting a security operations center, the increasing volume of regulations requiring audits and reviews, or the need to defend

---

[5]   https://www.payscale.com/research/US/Job=Cyber_Security_Analyst/Salary (retrieved November 2024).

against more and more attacks. The biggest source of security fatigue may be something closer to home: convincing non-security employees to take cybersecurity seriously and prioritize security actions over other priorities.

Look for other reasons to join cybersecurity that will sustain you during difficult times.

Interesting and Challenging Technology

At its heart, cybersecurity is a profession based on computing technologies. Even if you are interested in a job that isn't deeply technical on a day-to-day basis, such as cybersecurity law or marketing, there is a need to understand and appreciate a wide variety of technologies and security functions.

Some people are primarily attracted to the cybersecurity profession because they are interested in the wide variety of technologies involved. When you work in cybersecurity, you may go very deeply into a single technology (encryption, identity, networks, cloud) or you may work across broad swaths of technologies impacting all layers of the technology stack (users, data, networks, devices, applications) as well as people.

Being part of the cybersecurity profession means continuous learning of new technologies and security practices. If the idea of technology leaves you cold, reconsider cybersecurity as a career path. On the other hand, if you like "playing" with technology, this is a profession for you. We are among many cybersecurity professionals who thrive on the challenge of keeping up with ever evolving and exciting tech!

Defense Against the Dark Arts

There are many people working in cybersecurity who joined or stayed because they are driven to help organizations and people defend against cybersecurity attacks. It doesn't matter where the attack comes from—criminals, nation-states, insiders—the impact is negative, and cybersecurity professionals want to prevent or minimize these effects in the future. Cybersecurity is about helping to protect people and organizations from harm, and that feels great.

The cybersecurity profession has long attracted people who operate with a "mission" mindset, such as ex-military, emergency responders, healthcare professionals, and other like-minded people. This devotion to protection and service gives purpose to their work and helps them endure when the job gets stressful.

National Security

In 2019, Richard Clarke and Robert Knake wrote *The Fifth Domain*, a book which discusses the role of computing technologies on the national security landscape. Since that time, community awareness of the cybersecurity threat of nation-states has only grown. If you are motivated by a desire to help your country or to play a role in countermeasures against hostile nations, cybersecurity is one way to help.

It is an unfortunate reality that some nations conduct malicious cyber operations for financial gain, political leverage, and power and control. These days, nation-state attackers don't target only government or military targets, they also attack private companies. We saw this when North Korea attacked Sony in 2014. People who serve in military and government organizations are most aware of nation-state cyber threats, and the cybersecurity profession provides a logical place for them to continue their careers within their military organizations or in the private sector.

Additionally, most "critical infrastructure" organizations around the world are not run or protected by the military; instead, they are run by private and government organizations—so a partnership between critical infrastructure organizations and government agencies is required for a robust national cybersecurity defense.

Law and Order ("Dun-Dun")

There are many sources of cybersecurity incidents including nation-states, organized crime, malicious insiders, or even script kiddies. The "blast radius" of a cyberattack is felt regardless of the initial threat actor's motivation. A victim wants the harm and damage to stop, no matter where it came from. Many cybersecurity professionals come into or stay in the profession because it satisfies their sense of justice—that law and order are important and will prevail.

We might call cyberattack protection "Defense Against the Dark Arts." But this motivation goes further: to understand the methods and techniques used by the attackers, to identify the types of attackers using these techniques, and to work with the cyber community (and law enforcement) to identify and catch the people responsible. People motivated by law and order may choose roles such as computer forensics, security research, or other technically advanced roles.

I Didn't Pick Cybersecurity, It Chose Me

There is more than a passing chance that you didn't exactly pick cybersecurity as your career: it came in on its own. Jobs are continuously evolving and technology can be very disruptive, changing how we accomplish human goals. A large proportion of modern jobs that didn't used to be computer-related now require computers.

Perhaps your role has evolved to include more technology, and cybersecurity has become a new responsibility. Maybe you now must manage software developers for the first time, or you are responsible for keeping the office computers patched and up to date. This will feel new and uncomfortable. This book is also for you!

So What? (aka What Can You Do with This Information?)

As a mid-career jobseeker, you may already have a sense of what makes you tick: a need for financial security, variety in your work, providing a service, or something else. The suggestions above are just that—suggestions. You may see yourself in one of these groups.

If you do, great! Maybe there is something else that's interesting to you—wonderful!

If you can't think of anything compelling right now, but you still think cybersecurity could be a good place for you to work, don't give up. You can just start with "I want to try something new" and continue to experiment.

Either way, write it down somewhere, and we'll come back to it as we help you navigate the different kinds of roles in cybersecurity and how your motivations may align.

Choosing a Place to Work

Cybersecurity is a horizontal function. That is, we can find cybersecurity work in every industry and nearly every company. Even within a company, cybersecurity responsibilities should be woven throughout the organization's entire structure rather than relegated to a single department or team. However, the way cybersecurity is executed, and therefore the way cybersecurity jobs are done, has a lot to do with the type of business, the culture of the organization, and the size of the organization. The more resources an organization has, and the longer they have been in business, the more likely they are to have dedicated security roles. The term "cybersecurity poverty line" identifies the line below which an organization cannot be effectively protected and includes factors such as money, expertise, capability, and influence. Every industry has organizations above and below this line. When we think about the kind of cybersecurity we want to do, we should consider the company factors that will influence our work.

Industry

An industry is a group of companies and organizations that perform the same service or produce the same kind of goods. As with any worker in any profession, these companies exist for a purpose, and employees will want to ensure that purpose aligns with their personal values. A cybersecurity jobseeker should consider the business elements of an industry and how that impacts the security team so that the day-to-day work will be satisfying.

The good news for mid-career jobseekers is that they already have some experience in at least one industry. Some cybersecurity people work their entire career in an industry and have a deep technical and organizational understanding that assists their security skills. Some move around, bringing diverse learnings with them as they move. For jobseekers, it often makes sense to look for security jobs in the industry they already know—they have the inside track on industry context and networking contacts that makes landing the first job easier.

The main question is whether the industry typically supports security with resources: people, tooling, and organizational support. Table 1.1 compares these attributes across various industries.

Industry	Resource Support	Security Capabilities	Why?
Finance	High	High	Highly regulated; High profit margins
Technology	High	High	High profit margins; Inherent workforce expertise
Education	Low	Varies	Highly regulated; Complicated organizational structures and technologies
Healthcare	Low	Varies	Low profit margins; Complicated technologies
Manufacturing	Low	Low	Complicated technologies
Retail	Low	Low	Low profit margins
Government/ Public Sector	Low	Low	Highly regulated; Low/No profit margins; complicated technologies; distributed management
Hospitality	Medium	Medium	Moderately regulated

Table 1.1 –Various industries and their general levels of support and capabilities for cybersecurity.

Company Size and Age

More than the industry, the size and age of a company have a lot to do with how big the security team is and how much resource support it provides. Start-ups and small- to mid-size businesses are often below the cybersecurity poverty line because they don't yet have the financial bandwidth to support an effective security function. The more time, size, and maturity, the more likely it is that the company will have the will and resources to prioritize cybersecurity.

Ironically, mid-career jobseekers with multiple skills are more likely than entry-level individuals to find work in smaller companies. Smaller companies look for experienced candidates who can perform multiple security functions. For example, you may be responsible for conducting vulnerability scans, monitoring logs, creating policies, conducting training, and doing incident investigations.

The larger the company, the more the security roles are specialized into discrete functions. The helpdesk, for instance, might reset passwords for a user who is locked out of their computer but may not perform vulnerability assessment or digital forensics. A jobseeker in this environment can expect to learn a lot about a single function. Someone who knows what kind of security they want to do would fit well in a larger organization. For someone still experimenting with the kind of security they want to do, it might make more sense to look for security roles in smaller organizations where they can "wear many hats" and learn a broad swath of cybersecurity skills.

Regulatory Landscape

Laws, policies, and regulations exist to enforce various rules and standards that ensure safety and well-being, including throughout cybersecurity. Legal rules vary by region. In the United States, there are laws about encrypting health information and safeguarding credit card numbers. Healthcare and financial services are highly regulated, given the risks involved. Other industries, such as agriculture or entertainment, have their own regulations and compliance requirements.

As cybersecurity has developed as a profession, the industries subject to regulation (such as financial services) have advanced the fastest and furthest in cybersecurity and have the tightest connections to business leadership in an organization.

Cybersecurity professionals will insist that security isn't only a compliance function; it is much more of a risk management function, and compliance with rules and regulations shouldn't drive the security program. That's fair enough, but the business reality is that finance people are more likely to pay for the things they must do to avoid breaking laws and contracts than for future risks that aren't tied to a law.

If a jobseeker is looking for a company that funds security activities and has a big enough security team to support long-term career goals, it makes sense to look for companies in highly regulated industries. If a jobseeker is looking for an organization that grows quickly, innovates security tools and functions, and provides a technical learning experience, looking for a less-regulated industry (i.e., regulated to some degree) may make more sense.

Location

For mid-career jobseekers with established roots or local ties, it may be undesirable to uproot and move location. The types of available jobs and roles are impacted by geographic location. The contrast is most evident between large urban environments, which attract a diverse set of companies, and rural environments, where there are naturally fewer businesses. Even if there is a local bank or chain restaurant in a small town, they may not hire local cybersecurity staff. Post-pandemic, companies are making decisions about hybrid, fully remote, or on-premises working requirements. Not only will this impact the kinds of security jobs available to you (can you do your job from anywhere, or will you be tied to where you live?), but it also changes the security profile of the company (having remote workers increases the complexity of security processes, tooling, and risk profiles).

The physical footprint of a company influences the security team and the way security is done, primarily because of the variations in regulatory requirements. Working for a multinational organization will expose an employee to multiple country, state, local, and regulatory agency rules and regulations, some of which will conflict with each other. Alternatively, working for a company that is wholly within a given country will simplify the rules and regulations (somewhat).

Some jobseekers will see this complexity as a benefit; they will be exposed to a variety of requirements and ways of working; they will work with people from multiple countries or locations; and they will build a resume that will demonstrate a broad understanding of the industry. Others will see this as just another layer of administrative oversight that stifles creativity and diverts resources away from the truly risky pieces of the profession. For these jobseekers, look for companies that have a more confined footprint or are a start-up/mid-sized company.

Choosing How to Work: Security Personas

Jobseekers of any age or experience looking to enter the cybersecurity field would benefit from talking to people already in the industry. Find out why and how they joined and why they stayed. In doing so, you will find that there are some themes behind the security profession that we call "security personas." These are general categories of types of jobs, just as in healthcare there are surgeons and primary care doctors.

Figure 1.1 illustrates various types of jobs in cybersecurity. You can see that some roles overlap in the kind of work they include. Let's look at each role.

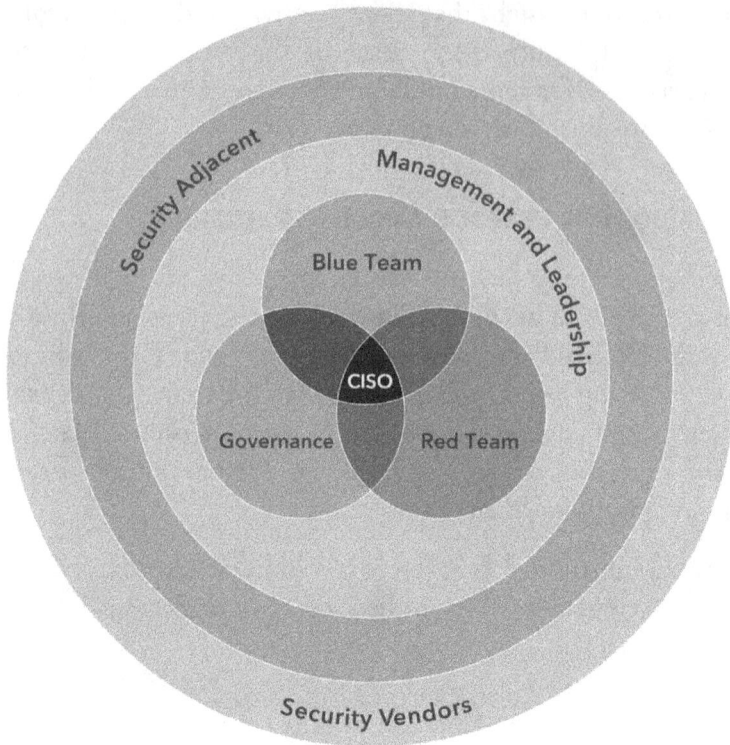

Figure 1.1 – Categories of jobs in cybersecurity.

Red Team

Red Teamers are professionals who emulate the attack tools and techniques of adversaries, using those skills to attack their own companies to find out where their company has security weaknesses. Professionals in this category also include hackers (aka security researchers) who may be employed by a company or may do their own research via bug bounty programs or others. This group of cybersecurity professionals are curious, creative, and have a highly technical skillset. Some have a military background. Many red teamers are competent software programmers and are well-versed in social engineering methodologies.

This kind of security persona is what most non-security people think of when they first think of cybersecurity professionals. "Entry level" positions in this area include security analysts who participate in penetration tests (pentests) and shadow more senior team members as they conduct offensive projects; however, being a red teamer assumes deep security experience and these "entry-level" roles are competitive, even for people with work experience in other domains.

Blue Team

Blue Teamers are part of the defense of an organization. Typically, these are security engineers, analysts, architects, compliance officers, and others who make up the bulk of an enterprise or product security team. This includes the incident detection and response team (often generalized as Security Operations Center staff), who are the first responders to a security incident for an organization. Defensive professionals provide strategic direction to the entire organization, as well as tactical functions that help the entire business secure its operations. Most possess a strong technical background in IT engineering and/or software development or a technical understanding that allows them to manage policies, security training, security compliance, or other governance functions.

People interested in blue teamwork are the most common of the security personas and often come to this work with a strong sense of justice/ethics/service. Mid-career jobseekers will find roles here where their existing work experience can augment the security program, even if their security work experience is limited.

Security Adjacent

Security teams of any moderate size and maturity will include support functions that help the security team operate more efficiently. People in these roles may be part of the security team, but their day-to-day roles look more like other functions: project management, communications, training, and so on. Security adjacent roles may also exist in other parts of the organization entirely—security liaisons, compliance officers, and others work closely with security in support of security efforts, but the primary purpose of these roles is not security.

Employees who support core security functions are critical to the running of the security program. These people enjoy working with security analysts and engineers, are immersed in security functions and processes, and have the same motivations as the other personas (curiosity, creativity, ethics, justice) but apply their non-security functional skills to support the security team.

Mid-career jobseekers often move into security adjacent functions as a first step towards moving into another security role. People who are project managers, HR partners, lawyers, purchasing managers, teachers, business analysts, or others can all find security-adjacent roles that open the door to the security profession. Some find that once they arrive there, they are very happy in these roles and look to advance their careers within the security support function.

Management and Governance

Governance (or lack of it) happens in any organization, even if there is no one definitively assigned to a governance role. Once organizations get to a certain size they will often create a governance team that is responsible for Governance, Risk and Compliance (GRC) activities. GRC roles ensure the business is complying with laws and regulations, decide which security frameworks to adhere to, track cybersecurity risks and risk mitigation activities, and work with internal and external auditors to ensure the business is meeting security objectives.

Management roles also happen in any organization, but the size and complexity of this function in security will depend on the particulars of the overall company, and the size of the security budget. Management roles include the CISO and deputy-CISO, Security Chief of Staff, Security Operations Officer, and other roles that require extensive security experience as a prerequisite to being in the role.

Vendors

There is a large ecosystem of vendors that provide security products and services to companies. These can include vendors that create security products, consultants, or managed security service providers (MSSP) that sell services.

In these organizations, security roles focus on helping customers buy and use security products and services and include security sales engineers, security salespeople, cybersecurity advisors, cybersecurity consultants, virtual CISOs, field CISOs, and others. These people work with the sales, customer success, and/or product teams to help customers test, select, and implement solutions or services in a secure way. Working for a security vendor will give a person broad exposure to multiple industries and customer types, which is a great place to learn the general profession.

Mid-career jobseekers who come from product, sales and marketing backgrounds can often transition into cybersecurity by taking sales engineering and architecture roles or working in a product security team. Security professionals in these roles are not just protecting their immediate company; they are also protecting/defending their customer organizations as well—potentially a much larger community impact than other roles.

To conclude, before you just jump into finding your first security job, it will save you time and effort to know a little bit about yourself (motivations, strengths, and weaknesses) and the kinds of security roles and companies that will suit you. The cybersecurity industry is relatively new and constantly changing. Ground yourself in your purpose before you begin looking for a job, and it will help you sell yourself to potential employers.

Chapter Summary

- Write down what you already know about yourself—strengths, weaknesses, likes, dislikes, experience—and keep adding to this as you move through your job search and your cybersecurity career.

- Before searching for a cybersecurity job, learn about the industry by brushing up on its history and talking to people who work in cybersecurity about their jobs and career paths.

- Mid-career jobseekers benefit from having already worked somewhere else. Use this knowledge to make informed decisions about the kind of cybersecurity work you want to do and where you want to do it.

- Consider the kind of work you like to do on a day-to-day basis (your "micro" work preferences). Not everyone wants to be in front of a computer all day, but others want nothing else!

- Choose an industry (or two) you would like to work in (or not); each industry has different ways of doing security.

- Understand that the size of the company you work for impacts the way you do security: big companies hire for specialized security roles, while small companies hire security generalists.

- Consider the kind of security persona that interests you most: blue or red teaming, security back office, or vendors. Depending on where you're starting from, some may be easier bridges into cybersecurity than others.

- Know why you are interested in working in cybersecurity in the first place (your "macro" work preferences). Understanding yourself will help narrow the field of potential roles and the paths you need to take to get there.

Chapter References

Clarke, Richard A. and Robert K. Knake (2020). *The Fifth Domain: Defending our Country, Our Companies, and Ourselves in the Age of Cyber Threats*. Penguin.

Menn, Joseph (2019). *Cult of the Dead Cow: How the Original Hacking Supergroup Might Just Save the World*. Hachette UK.

Rehman, Rafeeq (2024). "CISO MindMap." https://rafeeqrehman.com/ciso-mindmap/.

Chapter 2

Assessing Your Skills and Strengths

Alex, a seasoned logistics professional, has spent over 15 years navigating the complexities of supply chain management. As a Logistics Manager, Alex has been at the helm of operations, ensuring goods move smoothly from suppliers to customers while optimizing warehouse workflows and coordinating with a network of partners. While deeply committed to optimizing logistics processes, Alex has recently become increasingly intrigued by the world of cybersecurity. Seeing firsthand how the digital landscape has transformed logistics, Alex recognizes the growing importance of protecting supply chains from cyber threats and is eager to pivot to a career in cybersecurity. This new direction offers a chance to build on existing strengths while embracing a field crucial to the future of global operations.

Alex's situation illustrates a common challenge for mid-career professionals entering cybersecurity: recognizing that your existing expertise is actually your greatest asset, not a liability to overcome. As you consider a career transition into cybersecurity, you may wonder what skills you already possess can be applied to this new field. Perhaps you're thinking about your past experiences and trying to identify which ones will translate well to the world of cybersecurity. Or you may be feeling uncertain about how your existing skills will stack up against those required in the industry.

In this chapter, we'll look closer at assessing your skills and strengths. We'll explore what transferable skills you may have developed in your previous career that can be applied to cybersecurity and identify areas where you may need improvement or additional training. Before diving into the details, let's set the stage for why self-assessment is crucial in this transition.

When Alex—or any of us—is considering a major career change, like transitioning into cybersecurity, it's natural to feel overwhelmed. There are many unknowns, from learning new technical skills to navigating the industry's complex landscape. However, one thing that can give us confidence and direction is knowing what we have already brought to the table.

As someone with years of experience, you've likely developed a range of valuable skills that can be applied to cybersecurity. You may have honed your analytical thinking, problem-solving, or communication skills through various projects or leadership roles. These transferable skills are essential to success in any field, and cybersecurity is no exception. Given these assets, you should lean into what you know and are excited to do. That is, use the strengths you already have before worrying about filling in any gaps. Cybersecurity professionals are *always* learning new things but also building and expanding on core strengths.

In fact, many professionals who transition into cybersecurity from other domains find that their existing skills provide a strong foundation for their new careers. By recognizing what you already know and can do well, you'll be better equipped to:

- Identify areas where you may need additional training or development
- Focus your learning efforts on the most critical skills for success in cybersecurity
- Develop a personalized strategy for getting up to speed in the industry

The foundation of this self-assessment process lies in understanding transferable skills—the professional abilities you've already developed that will serve you well in cybersecurity. Of course, transitioning into any new field requires a willingness to learn and adapt. Cybersecurity is no exception. You must stay current with the latest technologies and recommended practices. But by acknowledging your existing strengths and weaknesses, you can build a stronger foundation for your transition.

In the last chapter, we delved into motivations and goals, helping you understand what drives your desire to switch to cybersecurity. In this chapter, we'll explore how to identify your transferable skills and recognize areas where you may need improvement or additional training. We'll also discuss ways to build and strengthen your portfolio, which will be essential in showcasing your skills and experiences to potential employers.

The Power of Transferable Skills

Transferable skills are the unsung heroes of career transitions. These are skills you've cultivated and refined throughout your personal and professional journey already, regardless of the specific industry. They encompass a broad spectrum, including:

- **Technical Skills:** These are the practical abilities you use to perform tasks. In your previous role, these might have been productivity software, data visualization, or website administration skills. While the technical expertise required may differ in cybersecurity, your foundational understanding of these principles will prove invaluable.

- **Professional Skills:** These interpersonal and communication skills form the bedrock of successful collaboration. Problem-solving, critical thinking, teamwork, communication, and adaptability are all crucial assets in the fast-paced world of cybersecurity.

- **Business Acumen:** This refers to your understanding of how businesses operate. Your experience analyzing budgets, managing projects, and navigating internal dynamics will prove highly beneficial as you contribute to an organization's overall security posture.

Imagine yourself as a skilled warrior. You've spent years training with different weapons—technical skills, professional skills, and business acumen. Now, it's time to pick up a new weapon—cybersecurity expertise. But don't forget the arsenal you already carry! Each skill you've honed will be invaluable in mastering the art of cyber defense.

Ironically, we often hear people saying, "I don't know what skills I have." We hear you. Self-reflection can be challenging, particularly when put on the spot to do so. We offer some exercises below that will guide you through this process. These exercises don't have to be completed in a single session. Over the next few days or weeks, keep adding to the lists.

Diversity of skills is an underappreciated asset in cybersecurity organizations. Research has proven time and time again that teams with a diverse set of backgrounds and skills outperform homogeneous teams. Your experiences will be valuable in cybersecurity. Author David Epstein wrote an entire book about the value of breadth.[6] He writes that "rather than hiding diverse experience, explain it," which you can do by mapping your skills to those needed in cybersecurity. He goes so far as to describe how "Research has established pretty firmly that diverse groups of people are better at innovation and problem-solving, but more recent research finds that diverse career histories within a single person can also benefit performance." A diverse career history is central to the value you bring.

Let's take a brief aside to peek at the skills and attributes of successful people currently working in cybersecurity. Seldom does a single human possess every skill an employer desires. What is more useful in our journey now is a frame of reference about what those skills are *in general*. If we wanted to get a job as an automobile mechanic or a landscape designer, knowing what kinds of people succeed in *those* jobs would also be helpful.

To help you visualize what cybersecurity professionals actually do day-to-day, let's examine the diverse skill sets that characterize successful practitioners in the field. Table 2.1 shows a very incomplete list of example skills among cybersecurity professionals. It's okay if items like SIEM or OSI don't make sense today. Note

6   Epstein, D. (2021). *Range: Why Generalists Triumph in a Specialized World.* Penguin.

that technical skills—the software, concepts, and know-how of using a computer—are only a portion of what characterizes our skillset. These are necessary but not sufficient to be a cybersecurity professional.

Technical Skills	<ul><li>Solid understanding of cybersecurity frameworks and methodologies (e.g., NIST Cybersecurity Framework, MITRE ATT&CK).</li><li>Experience with various security controls (e.g., firewalls, intrusion detection/prevention systems, data encryption).</li><li>Familiarity with different types of cyberattacks (e.g., phishing, malware, ransomware).</li><li>Knowledge of detection and response tools and processes.</li><li>Understanding of cloud security concepts and best practices.</li><li>Ability to stay current with evolving cybersecurity threats and trends.</li></ul>
Leadership and Management Skills	<ul><li>Strong leadership skills: Motivate and inspire a team of cybersecurity professionals.</li><li>Excellent communication skills: Clearly articulate complex technical concepts to technical and non-technical audiences.</li><li>Effective delegation and task management skills: Assign tasks efficiently and hold team members accountable.</li><li>Partnership Skills: Ability to build and maintain strong relationships with other departments (e.g., IT, HR).</li><li>Mentorship skills: Help junior team members develop their skills and knowledge.</li><li>Conflict resolution skills: Effectively resolve issues within the team.</li></ul>

Table 2.1 – Example skills for cybersecurity professionals.

Leadership and Management Skills	• Ability to develop and implement a cybersecurity strategy that aligns with business goals. • Risk management skills: Identify, assess, and mitigate cybersecurity risks. • Budgeting and financial management skills: Manage the cybersecurity team's budget effectively. • Understanding of compliance requirements and regulations relevant to cybersecurity and the relevant industry.
Personal Attributes	• Strong work ethic and commitment to cybersecurity recommended practices. • Excellent problem-solving skills. • Ability to work independently and as part of a team. • Adaptability and willingness to learn new things. • Strong self-awareness and ability to manage mental and physical health.

Table 2.1 – Example skills for cybersecurity professionals (continued).

While this table shows the breadth of relevant skills, it is important to understand that your existing abilities will translate to cybersecurity work in different ways, depending on how directly they align with security-specific needs. Some skills fall along a spectrum regarding how they directly transfer to cybersecurity. Here are a few that apply in cybersecurity quite well with little adaption needed:

- **Problem Solving and Analytical Thinking**. Cybersecurity professionals need to identify threats, analyze data, and develop solutions. Experience in any role requiring critical thinking—like data analysis, law, or even project management—translates directly to tasks like investigating security incidents or creating defensive strategies.
- **Attention to Detail.** Meticulous attention to detail is vital for identifying potential security breaches, conducting audits, or spotting patterns in large data sets. Professionals from fields like accounting, auditing, or quality assurance often possess this skill, which is highly applicable in cybersecurity.

- **Project Management.** Managing cybersecurity projects (e.g., rolling out new security policies or technologies) requires strong organizational and leadership skills. Project managers in other fields already possess the skillset to manage resources, timelines, and risks, making this a seamless transition.

- **Legal and Compliance Knowledge.** Many cybersecurity roles deal with regulatory compliance, such as the European Union's General Data Protection Regulation (GDPR) or the Health Insurance Portability and Accountability Act (HIPAA). Lawyers, compliance officers, and those with experience in regulated industries often have a strong foundation in understanding and interpreting regulations, which can be vital in governance, risk, and compliance (GRC) roles in cybersecurity.

Now consider a few skills that are certainly valuable in cybersecurity but may require some additional training or re-contextualization for cybersecurity:

- **Customer Service and Communication.** Effective communication with non-technical stakeholders is essential, whether to explain security policies or respond to incidents. Customer service professionals excel at understanding user needs and conveying information clearly, though they may need to learn the specific language of cybersecurity.

- **IT Support and System Administration.** People with general IT support experience or system administration roles have a good understanding of networks, operating systems, and troubleshooting, which are relevant to cybersecurity. However, they must adapt by learning security-specific tasks such as securing configurations, monitoring threats, and incident response.

- **Data Analysis and Statistics.** Cybersecurity roles like security analysts or threat hunters require analyzing logs and datasets to identify trends. People with a data analytics or statistics background can transfer these skills but may need additional knowledge of cybersecurity tools like SIEM platforms.

- **Teaching and Training.** Cybersecurity awareness training is critical, especially for promoting best practices in organizations. Teachers or trainers with good communication skills can adapt by gaining cybersecurity knowledge and focusing on educating non-technical staff about security risks and solutions.

Finally, consider a few skills that could be indirectly valuable in a cybersecurity job, but which don't have clear and strong applicability in cybersecurity:

- **Creative Fields (Art, Design, Music, etc.).** While creativity can be helpful in problem-solving, professionals with backgrounds in purely creative fields like graphic design or music may need to lean on other skills with a more direct correlation to cybersecurity. However, creative professionals possess a unique strength: visual communication and user experience understanding. This translates well into security awareness training design, where the ability to create engaging, visually compelling materials that change behavior is invaluable. Creative professionals can also contribute to user interface security, helping design secure login flows and authentication experiences that people use, rather than circumvent. Many find success in incident communication roles, crafting clear, non-panic-inducing messages during security events. To bridge into cybersecurity, creative professionals could start by creating security awareness content—videos, infographics, or training modules—while simultaneously building foundational security knowledge through certifications or coursework.

- **Physical Trades (Construction, Carpentry, etc.).** Manual or hands-on skills from trades like construction or carpentry don't have much first-order overlap with cybersecurity, but these professionals bring exceptional systems thinking and methodical troubleshooting abilities. This expertise becomes highly valuable in operational technology (OT) security, where manufacturing, utilities, and infrastructure need people who understand both industrial processes and cybersecurity threats. Tradespeople excel at understanding how failures cascade through interconnected systems— whether it is plumbing, electrical, or network infrastructure. Their systematic, step-by-step approach to diagnosing and fixing problems translates directly to cybersecurity incident response. Many find opportunities in physical security integration, where digital and physical security intersect, or in risk assessment roles where understanding system interdependencies is crucial. The bridge strategy involves focusing on OT security positions or physical security roles while building cybersecurity knowledge, as many utilities and manufacturers specifically seek candidates who understand operational environments.

- **Sales (Product Sales, Retail, etc.).** While sales skills may include valuable interpersonal and negotiation abilities, transitioning directly into technical cybersecurity roles can be challenging without additional training. However, sales professionals possess a deep understanding of human psychology and trust-building that proves invaluable in specific cybersecurity applications. Security awareness training delivery is a natural fit, as these roles require "selling" secure behaviors to reluctant employees using persuasion and communication skills. Sales professionals also excel in vendor risk management, where the ability to evaluate security claims from technology vendors and ask probing questions becomes essential. Many transition into cybersecurity sales engineering, helping organizations understand and purchase security solutions, or explore social engineering testing roles where understanding persuasion techniques helps organizations identify vulnerabilities. The most effective bridge strategy involves starting with security awareness roles or moving into cybersecurity vendor sales while systematically building technical knowledge through targeted training and certifications.

Bridging the Gap: Recognizing Your Strengths and Building on Them

The key to a successful transition lies in recognizing your transferable skills and bridging any existing gaps between your current knowledge and the requirements of a cybersecurity career. We will do this by diving deeply into your skillset, identifying its strengths, and pinpointing areas for potential development. Remember, your strengths will become the pillars on which you build your cybersecurity expertise.

This self-reflection process becomes most valuable when you apply it systematically. The exercises that follow will guide you through a structured assessment of your professional assets. Throughout this chapter, we'll provide practical exercises and strategies to:

- **Inventory Your Skills**: We'll equip you with techniques to brainstorm and identify all your existing skills across technical, professional skill, and business acumen categories.

- **Conduct a Skills Gap Analysis**: Learn how to compare your current skill set with the qualifications required for your target cybersecurity role.

- **Prioritize Learning Needs**: Develop a clear roadmap for skill development, focusing first on areas that will significantly enhance your candidacy.

- **Craft a Winning Portfolio**: Discover how to leverage your transferable skills and showcase your abilities in a compelling portfolio, even with a non-cybersecurity background.

This journey of self-assessment is empowering. By uncovering your hidden strengths and formulating a plan to bridge any skill gaps, you'll gain the confidence needed to navigate your successful transition into the exhilarating world of cybersecurity.

There's one thing we already know: You can do better than an entry-level cybersecurity professional, even if we have never met. As we mature, we get better and better at combining and applying complex ideas. You might think younger cybersecurity professionals would have a career advantage because they recently learned about the latest topics and technologies in school or with hands-on use. Those skills are, in truth, very powerful. But working on cybersecurity problems frequently benefits from using existing ideas. Psychological research shows this no matter our profession. We can call this skill wisdom.

Many relevant skills in other industries, such as problem-solving, analytical thinking, or project management, can be applied directly to cybersecurity roles. This means that professionals with experience in areas like IT, business analysis, or compliance can leverage their accumulated wisdom to adapt quickly to cybersecurity challenges. You may have also acquired domain-specific knowledge that applies to cybersecurity. For example, a former financial analyst might understand the importance of data integrity and security in financial transactions, which can be valuable in a cybersecurity role focused on protecting sensitive business information. Finally, you may have developed leadership and communication skills that are highly valued in cybersecurity teams. These skills can help you effectively manage projects, collaborate with colleagues, and communicate complex security issues to stakeholders.

In Chapter 4, "The Lay of the Land," we'll explore more deeply how to translate your current expertise—including wisdom—directly into valuable cybersecurity applications. But first, let's focus on what you already bring to the table.

So, take some time to reflect on your past experiences and skills. What have you accomplished in your previous career that can be applied to cybersecurity? What skills have you developed through education or training? And what areas do you feel uncertain about or need improvement?

As we explore this self-assessment process together, remember that it's not just about identifying your strengths and weaknesses—it's also about recognizing the value you bring to the table. You've already accomplished so much in your previous career; now it's time to leverage those skills to succeed in a new field like cybersecurity.

Identifying Your Transferable Skills

As discussed earlier, transferable skills are the unsung heroes of career transitions. In this section, we'll explore practical exercises and strategies to help you identify your transferable skills. By recognizing what you already know and can do well, you'll be better equipped to:

- Identify areas where you may need additional training or development

- Focus your learning efforts on the most critical skills for success in cybersecurity

- Develop a personalized strategy for getting up to speed in the industry

Exercise 1: Brainstorming Your Transferable Skills

Take some time to reflect on your past experiences and skills. Write down every skill you've developed, no matter how seemingly unrelated it may be to cybersecurity. Don't worry about categorizing them just yet; let your thoughts flow freely. Table 2.2 shows an example list of transferable skills for Alex, who we introduced at the beginning of this chapter.

Some questions to consider:

- What specific tasks did I perform in my previous roles?
- Which software or tools did I use regularly?
- How did I communicate with colleagues and stakeholders?
- Were there any specific projects or initiatives I led or contributed to?
- What kind of problem-solving or analytical thinking did I do?

As you brainstorm, don't be afraid to include skills that seem unrelated. You might be surprised at how they can be applied in new and innovative ways.

Potential Transferrable Skills
• Supply chain management understanding end-to-end flow of goods and materials.
• Inventory management ensuring timely fulfillment of customer orders.
• Warehouse operations overseeing the receipt, storage, and shipment of goods.
• Time management managing the workload to meet customer expectations.
• Budgeting for transportation, warehousing, and logistics.
• Risk management associated with operations (e.g., delivery delays).
• Cost control associated with logistics expenses.
• Contract management with suppliers, carriers, and other partners.
• Business acumen in the business goals and objectives of the organization.
• Customer service through timely communication and issue resolution.
• Data analysis interpreting data from logistics to information business decisions and optimizing operations.
• Route optimization using analytics to determine the most efficient routes for delivery drivers.

Table 2.2 – Example list of skills of someone with prior experience in logistics.

Exercise 2: Categorizing Your Transferable Skills

Now that you have a comprehensive list of transferable skills, it's time to categorize them. Divide your list into three categories:

1. Technical Skills
2. Professional Skills
3. Business Acumen

As you move each skill into its corresponding category, reflect on how it can be applied in the context of cybersecurity.

Here are some examples to get you started:

1. **Technical Skills:** Proficiency in Microsoft Office Suite (Word, Excel, PowerPoint), experience with project management tools like Asana or Trello, and knowledge of HTML and CSS.

2. **Professional Skills:** Strong written and verbal communication skills, ability to work effectively in a team, experience with conflict resolution.

3. **Business Acumen:** Budgeting and financial analysis, project management, stakeholder engagement.

Technical Skills	Professional Skills	Business Acumen
• Data analysis interpreting data from logistics to information business decisions and optimize operations. • Route optimization using analytics to determine the most efficient routes for delivery drivers.	• Customer service through timely communication and issue resolution.	• Inventory management to ensure timely fulfillment of customer orders. • Warehouse operations overseeing the receipt, storage, and shipment of goods. • Contract management with suppliers, carriers, and other partners. • Risk management associated with operations (e.g., delivery delays) • Supply chain management understanding end-to-end flow of goods and materials • Budgeting for transportation, warehousing, and logistics. • Business acumen in the business goals and objectives of the organization. • Cost control associated with logistics expenses. • Time management managing the workload to meet customer expectations.

Table 2.3 – Example categorization of skills of someone with prior experience in logistics.

Exercise 3: Prioritizing Your Transferable Skills

Now that your transferable skills are categorized, it's time to prioritize them. Which skills do you think would be most valuable in a cybersecurity role?

Now, consider the specific requirements of your target role and how your transferable skills can be applied.

Some questions to consider:

- Which skills would give you a competitive edge in the job market?
- Are there any skills that are directly applicable to the job description?
- Are there any gaps in skills that need to be addressed?

Identifying Gaps and Opportunities

As you prioritize your transferable skills, remember that it's not just about identifying your strengths—it's also about recognizing areas where you may need additional training or development.

As we embark on this journey to assess your skills and strengths, it's essential to recognize that many skills you've developed in your previous career can be applied to cybersecurity. Cybersecurity is an industry that heavily relies on professionals from various backgrounds bringing their unique skill sets to the table.

Let's take project management as an example. If you have experience managing IT projects, you may not realize how much of that expertise translates to security project management. Effective communication, stakeholder engagement, and risk assessment are crucial in both cases. Your ability to prioritize tasks, allocate resources, and manage timelines can be applied directly to cybersecurity projects, where you'll need to oversee incident response efforts, coordinate with teams, and ensure compliance with regulatory requirements.

Another example is analytical thinking. As a professional in another field, you may have honed your analytical skills by identifying patterns, analyzing data, and drawing conclusions. These same skills are essential in cybersecurity, where you'll be tasked with analyzing network traffic, identifying anomalies, and developing strategies to mitigate threats. Your ability to think critically and creatively can help you stay one step ahead of attackers and protect organizations from cyber-attacks.

Communication is another critical skill that transfers well to cybersecurity. As a professional in your previous field, you've likely developed strong verbal and written communication skills essential for collaborating with cross-functional teams, stakeholders, and executives. In cybersecurity, clear and concise communication is vital when explaining complex technical concepts to non-technical stakeholders or presenting findings to leadership.

In addition to these transferable skills, your experience in other fields can provide a valuable industry perspective. For instance, professionals from the financial sector may understand regulatory compliance, while those from the healthcare industry may be familiar with HIPAA regulations. This domain-specific knowledge and expertise can be applied to cybersecurity roles, such as risk assessment, threat intelligence, or compliance management.

It's also worth noting that many cybersecurity roles require a unique blend of technical and business skills. For example, security architects must balance technical requirements with organizational goals and stakeholder expectations. Your experience in other fields has likely honed your ability to navigate complex organizational structures, prioritize competing demands, and make informed decisions—all essential skills for a successful cybersecurity professional.

As you continue assessing your skills and strengths, remember that the goal is not to recreate yourself entirely but to build upon your existing expertise. You may find that certain aspects of your previous career are more relevant than others or that new areas require additional development. This self-assessment process will help you identify areas where you can leverage your transferable skills and pinpoint growth opportunities.

In the next chapter, we'll explore how to understand the market landscape and identify potential entry points in the cybersecurity industry. But before we dive into that, take some time to reflect on your own experiences and skills. What transferable skills do you bring to the table? How can you apply them to a new field like cybersecurity? The answers may surprise you, but they'll also provide a solid foundation for transitioning into this exciting and rewarding industry.

Building and Strengthening Your Portfolio

So far, we've talked about listing your transferable skills. That list is useful to you because it helps identify relevant job leads. It's also useful to you when creating your resume or portfolio and when talking to recruiters and future colleagues in cybersecurity. This section will explore ways to highlight your relevant skills effectively and make your portfolio stand out.

A portfolio is a critical tool to showcase professional experience and is one of the most important reasons you will or won't get a particular job. Modern application systems parse and automatically analyze applications by looking for keywords and alignments with the job role and company values. So, clearly describing skills, experiences, and achievements is essential to a faithful representation of your professional identity.

Let's look at an example of someone coming into cybersecurity and how to present past work and transferable skills effectively in a portfolio for a new cybersecurity role.

Rowan, a retired Sergeant First Class with two decades of service as an IT Specialist in the Army, was eager to describe a career's worth of experience and skills as highly relevant to a new cybersecurity career. Rowan brought a unique blend of technical expertise and leadership experience that paints the picture of an attractive candidate in cybersecurity. Twenty years in the Army had honed Rowan's ability to think critically and strategically while working under pressure to resolve complex problems and protect sensitive information. This work also helped Rowan develop proficiency in networking, computer systems administration, and software development, which had laid a solid foundation in understanding network architectures, vulnerabilities, and security protocols. Additionally, leading teams of junior soldiers and contractors had taught the importance of effective communication, collaboration, and project management—essential skills for success in cybersecurity, where situational awareness and decision-making under uncertainty are paramount.

When applying for cybersecurity jobs, Rowan will need a resume that communicates this value to hiring managers. Rowan might represent his skills with bullets such as:

- Served in the U.S. Army for 20 years, utilizing expertise in cybersecurity, network administration, and software development to protect sensitive military information and networks.

- Demonstrated exceptional leadership skills, leading teams of 50 junior soldiers and contractors on high-priority projects.

- Utilized technical expertise in network design, implementation, and maintenance to set up and troubleshoot complex computer networks, often under operational pressure.

- Applied knowledge of local area networking (LAN), wide area networking (WAN), and internet protocol (IP) fundamentals to install, configure, and optimize computer networks for high-priority government systems.

- Utilized expertise in network architecture, including topologies, protocols, and devices (e.g., routers, switches, firewalls), to design and implement secure, high-performance networks that met specific government requirements.

These descriptions of past non-cybersecurity work are strong for a cybersecurity application because they speak to the technical, professional, and business skills relevant to cybersecurity. Rowan's past job was in IT, and these bullets convey those accomplishments clearly, highlighting cybersecurity-relevant potential.

Now, imagine that you have experience managing complex projects in another environment, such as logistics or manufacturing. This is a potent asset in the cybersecurity realm. Consider how you've orchestrated multi-faceted initiatives. You can frame this experience as the equivalent of managing a cyber incident response plan. Emphasize your skill in coordinating diverse teams, setting clear objectives, and adhering to strict timelines. This mirrors the demands of leading a cybersecurity team during a breach. Your experience in budget allocation can be directly translated into resource management within a security operations center (SOC). Highlight your ability to prioritize expenditures, optimize costs, and measure ROI. This demonstrates your financial acumen, a crucial aspect of cybersecurity strategy.

Moreover, analytical skills are invaluable in cybersecurity. If you've ever delved into data analysis, explain how you identified trends and patterns. This skill set is directly applicable to threat intelligence analysis, where professionals sift through vast datasets to uncover potential vulnerabilities. Your experience in risk assessment, perhaps from a financial or operational perspective, can be reframed as risk management in cybersecurity. Showcase your ability to evaluate potential threats, prioritize risks, and implement mitigation strategies. This demonstrates your understanding of the core principles of cybersecurity.

Your communication prowess is another transferable skill. If you've excelled in presenting complex information to diverse audiences, emphasize your ability to articulate technical security concepts to non-technical stakeholders. This is a highly sought-after skill in cybersecurity as it's essential for building trust and support for security initiatives. Additionally, your experience building relationships and influencing decision-makers can be framed as stakeholder management in cybersecurity. Highlight your ability to collaborate with different departments, address concerns, and gain buy-in for security projects.

Remember to quantify your achievements whenever possible. Instead of simply stating that you managed projects, specify the size and complexity of the projects, the budget involved, and the outcomes achieved. Use concrete examples to illustrate how your skills have been applied in previous roles. For example, saying "managed a team of 50 high-performing junior staff" is more impactful than the ambiguity of "Led teams on various projects, provided guidance and support to other soldiers." By effectively communicating your transferable skills and accomplishments, you can position yourself as a valuable asset to a cybersecurity organization, even without direct experience in the field.

Building and Strengthening Your Portfolio

Let's look at an example of someone coming into cybersecurity from a completely different field and how to present past work and transferable skills effectively in a portfolio for a new cybersecurity role.

Maya, a former retail district manager with twelve years of experience overseeing store operations, loss prevention, and staff training across multiple locations, was ready to translate her expertise into a cybersecurity career. Her background had given her deep experience in risk assessment, crisis management, and training reluctant employees on security protocols—skills that would prove invaluable in cybersecurity roles focused on governance, awareness training, and operational security.

When applying for cybersecurity jobs, Maya will need a resume that communicates this value to hiring managers. Maya might represent her skills with bullets such as:

- Managed comprehensive loss prevention programs across eight retail locations, reducing inventory shrinkage by 35% through systematic risk assessment and implementation of physical and procedural security controls.

- Developed and delivered security awareness training to 150+ employees quarterly, achieving 95% compliance with cash handling and theft prevention protocols in high-turnover environment.

- Led incident response efforts during security breaches and theft events, coordinating with law enforcement, documenting evidence, and implementing corrective measures to prevent recurrence.

- Conducted regular security audits and vulnerability assessments of store locations, identifying procedural gaps and technology weaknesses that could impact operational security.

- Analyzed point-of-sale system logs and transaction data to identify patterns of fraudulent activity, preventing an estimated $75,000 in losses annually.

These descriptions of past non-cybersecurity work are strong for a cybersecurity application because they speak to the technical, professional, and business skills relevant to cybersecurity. Maya's past job involved risk management, security awareness, incident response, and data analysis—core cybersecurity functions translated through retail operations.

Conclusion

Identifying your transferable skills is a crucial step in your career transition journey. By recognizing what you already know and can do well, you'll be better equipped to focus your learning efforts on the most critical skills for success in cybersecurity. Remember to prioritize your transferable skills, considering their direct applicability to the job description and their potential to give you a competitive edge in the job market.

In the next section, we'll explore how to translate your current expertise directly into valuable cybersecurity applications. But first, let's focus on crafting a winning portfolio that showcases your transferable skills and demonstrates your value as a candidate in the cybersecurity job market.

Chapter Summary

- Assess Your Existing Skills: Take stock of the technical, professional, and business skills you've developed in your previous career that can transfer to cybersecurity.

- Create a Skills Inventory: Conduct a thorough self-assessment to document your skills, strengths, and areas that need improvement for your career transition.

- Perform a Skills Gap Analysis: Compare your current skill set with those required in cybersecurity to pinpoint areas for improvement or further training.

- Leverage Your Transferable Skills: Identify and capitalize on existing skills such as problem-solving, project management, and communication, which are highly valuable in cybersecurity.

- Focus on Transferable Skills: Identify how skills like problem-solving, analytical thinking, and communication can be directly applied to cybersecurity roles.

- Recognize the Value of Diverse Experience: Emphasize the importance of your unique career history, as diversity in experience is a strength in cybersecurity.

- Use Professional Skills to Your Advantage: Skills such as teamwork, adaptability, and project management are crucial in cybersecurity and should be leveraged.

- Prioritize Learning New Technical Skills: Focus on developing cybersecurity-specific technical skills like understanding security controls and frameworks.

- Highlight Transferable Skills in Your Portfolio: When building a cybersecurity portfolio, showcase how your prior experience and skills directly apply to cybersecurity challenges.

Chapter References

Brooks, A. C. (2022). *From Strength to Strength: Finding Success, Happiness, and Deep Purpose in the Second Half of Life.* Bloomsbury Publishing.

Epstein, D. (2019). *Range: Why Generalists Triumph in a Specialized World.* Riverhead Books.

Graham, D. (2018). *Switchers: How Smart Professionals Change Careers and Seize Success.* AMACOM.

West, T. (2024). *Job Therapy: Finding Work That Works for You.* Portfolio.

Chapter 3

Understanding the Market Landscape

What Differentiates a Mid-Career Jobseeker?

When you were 10 years old, what did you want to be when you grew up? Did you dress up as an astronaut for Halloween like Josiah, dreaming that you would one day go to space? It seems like those childhood fantasies sometimes come true, but other times change dramatically. Some people seem to have decided their career path in preschool. Others chose their career in college after falling in love with chemistry or computer science. Some people are close to retirement and still haven't settled on just one area of interest and work. Regardless, here you are now! You've worked somewhere already, maybe in more than one place. For any number of good reasons, you're thinking about a move to cybersecurity, away from something you already know (at least a little bit). You're wondering how you can make this move without giving everything up and starting from scratch.

The good news is that your previous experience will make you more valuable to hiring managers if you know how to leverage it for your benefit (and theirs).

The Benefits of Being a Mid-Career Jobseeker

Functional Experience

Before I (Helen) landed my first cybersecurity job, I had worked paid jobs for 10 years in no less than seven industries: banking, food service, retail, administrative services, manufacturing, healthcare, hospitality, and IT. I knew what it was like to face down angry customers who didn't like the food I had served them, deal with manufacturing supply chain issues, manage a help desk, and run night shifts in a hotel.

At first glance, these roles had nothing to do with cybersecurity. In practice, it was exactly these experiences that helped me land and be successful in my first security job. This might sound surprising, so let's look at a few examples:

- **As a bank teller,** I participated in multiple physical security tests to prepare against bank robberies… which helped me later understand cybersecurity tabletop exercises, which assess environments for digital vulnerabilities and threats.

- **As a food service worker,** I often dealt with upset customers who didn't like their food… which helped me develop conflict resolution skills necessary for advocating for cybersecurity resources.

- **As a payroll clerk,** I learned that attention to detail was key to delivering great service… which helped me develop this attention to detail in evaluating security compliance requirements.

- **As a healthcare receptionist,** I learned the importance of taking care of customers, and how health issues make for a stressful environment… which helped me appreciate the impact that cybersecurity has on people's personal lives and how to have empathy for the stakeholders we work with.

You may not have had a role that explicitly looks like a cybersecurity role, but don't think for a second that the roles you have already performed haven't prepared you for, and given you experience in, the cybersecurity profession.

If you're not sure how your experience can relate to a cybersecurity role, find someone working in cybersecurity and ask them to review your resume, specifically looking for common skills and experiences like the examples above. Then re-write your resume with these thoughts in mind.

Industry Experience

The way security teams work is hugely impacted by the industry they are in. Some companies are in highly regulated industries (e.g., finance, healthcare) which requires them to spend a lot of resources on governance, risk, and compliance functions. Other organizations are public sector or government organizations which come with their own rules of engagement and execution that often baffle people from the private sector. Some companies work in industries with very low profit margins (including retail) that force security teams to squeeze every penny out of their teams, while other companies have big profit margins (think investment banking) that allow security teams the freedom to invest more liberally in tools and people.

Think of the businesses you have been a part of. Which industry(s) were they in, and how did that impact the kind of roles you have had?

As a mid-career jobseeker, having industry experience gives you two advantages:

> You are likely to know security people in your industry (if you don't know who does security for the company you currently work for, go make friends with them!) and can network with those people to learn about security while understanding the broader business they work in. Sometimes it can be easier to find a security job in your current company—working and building experience with that security team—than starting outside your company.

> You can leverage your industry experience in another kind of role to land a cybersecurity role in the same industry because you understand the nuances of that industry already. Don't try to change jobs *and* change industries at the same time unless you really must do so: leverage what you already know to be a more attractive cybersecurity candidate.

The Drawbacks of Being a Mid-Career Jobseeker

Think back to what it was like to come straight out of high school or college and start your first job. If you were like most people, you were likely single with no kids and limited debt (OK, maybe some student loans, but probably not yet a mortgage), and ready to take on the whole world. Maybe!

A mid-career jobseeker with five or more years under their belt probably has a few more obligations (kids, spouse, car loans, mortgage?) and is a bit more locked into commitments outside of work that must be considered as they consider switching careers. Let's talk about these.

Compensation Expectations

No one wants to take a pay cut and go back to entry-level wages when they switch careers. Not only are we likely to be accustomed to our current lifestyle funded by our current income, but we have people counting on us to continue to provide an income that supports their expectations too. Even if this isn't you, there are few people who feel comfortable taking a considerable pay cut just because they change careers even if they are moving to a more junior role. Shouldn't your previous experience count for something?

The good news is that the cybersecurity profession pays well compared to a lot of other professions. Most jobs in cybersecurity offer a salary as opposed to hourly pay. As of July 2024, the average salary of an entry-level cybersecurity specialist in the United States is between $92,000 and $120,000.[7] This figure varies by location, industry, and company. Compare that to the National Educator Organization (NEO.org), who show the average starting teacher salary is approximately $46,000, and the average entry-level physician salary is $113,000. Even if a mid-career person gets an

---

[7] See https://www.salary.com/research/salary/posting/entry-level-cyber-security-analyst-salary and
https://www.cybersecurityeducation.org/degree/salary/.

"entry-level" cybersecurity role, they can often expect a well-paying job with high growth opportunities.

Consider your minimum salary requirements (considering total compensation, including salary, bonuses, healthcare, stock grants, and other elements) and know what you need. Often, you will find lateral roles in cybersecurity that will offer what you need—assuming you have put in some pre-work to set yourself up for a lateral move. Table 3.1 explains compensation elements to consider as you move into security. Note that not all elements will be offered, particularly for public sector roles.

Compensation Element	Description
Base Salary	Most security roles are salaried, not hourly, and described in annual terms ($X/yr), which means you are not eligible for overtime pay.
Annual Cash Bonus	Most often paid annually, a bonus is typically paid based on a combination of employee and organizational performance.
Equity	Equity is most often paid in the form of Restricted Stock Units (RSUs) or other forms of stock. Typically, this is paid to mid- or senior-level roles, based on employee performance.
Signing Bonus	Negotiated for mid-or senior-level people joining a new organization. Typically paid out over multiple years.
Retention Bonus	Paid by companies looking to keep talent for a given amount of time (for example, a project, or through a merger.) Typically paid out in a lump sum to existing employees in critical roles.
Longevity Bonus / Long-Service Leave	Some companies will pay a one-time bonus or offer additional paid time off when an employee reaches a duration milestone (e.g., five or ten years). These are less common than other bonus types.
Paid/Vacation Time Off (PTO/VTO)	Companies will offer a certain number of "Paid Time Off" days, to be used for vacations or other personal reasons. Time off accrues as you work, and if you leave with unused time, you can receive this in a lump sum payment. Companies may have a "use it or lose it" policy forfeiting any unused accrued PTO/VTO. There is a trend for companies to move to "unlimited" vacation days, without accruing any time away, and taking time when needed. For the on-call security practitioner, it can be challenging to take enough time off.
Other Benefits	Consider retirement, health, life insurance, employee purchase plans and other benefits as part of your total compensation package.

Table 3.1 – Compensation elements of cybersecurity jobs.

Consider, too, the longer-term growth opportunities of a cybersecurity role compared to your current professional experiences. Even if you take a slight step backwards to move into cybersecurity, there is a high likelihood that you will progress into a role that will pay more than your current role within two to three years. A step backward now may pay off in the long run.

Non-Work Commitments

A mid-career jobseeker is typically older than the typical just-out-of-school candidate, which means you have commitments outside of work, like family, community organizations, hobbies, and the like. You can't as easily pick up and move, work long hours, commit to after-hours training, or travel frequently for work.

While every cybersecurity job will be different, in general, the cybersecurity profession offers jobs that have flexibility in where and when you work, which is a huge perk. Yes, there are jobs that require the employee to work nine to five at a dedicated on-site location. Many cybersecurity roles also have peak work times such as responding to an incident or completing an audit or helping a customer after hours, so hiring managers will expect some flexibility from you too.

If you need a job that is predictably eight hours a day, cybersecurity is likely not your profession of choice. On the other hand, as you negotiate with hiring managers, make sure you are clear on your needs regarding flexible hours or work conditions, so you can manage the non-work commitments you likely have. Hiring managers are likely to be willing to negotiate and compromise with you on this, so don't hesitate to negotiate your needs into your contract.

Professional Trends

Before you begin your job search, it is helpful to understand some professional trends that have been brewing in the cybersecurity industry for the last few years. These trends are impacting the kind of roles hiring managers are trying to fill, how in-demand certain roles are, and what kind of companies will have the roles you're looking for. Awareness of these trends will also prepare you to demonstrate your knowledge during the interview process.

Regulations

Countries have the incentive to protect their safety, security, and economy and, thus, direct regulatory agencies to oversee various aspects related to cybersecurity. In the United States, there are multiple federal agencies and multiple state and local governments that pass laws that directly or indirectly impact cybersecurity. For example, the Department of Health and Human Services establishes guidelines about the security and privacy of health data. Sometimes regulations between countries align and sometimes they contradict each other.

International regulators created most cybersecurity-impacting regulations more for privacy than for cybersecurity, focusing on data theft of personal information. The European Union's General Data Protection Regulation (GDPR) is a prime example of this kind of regulation. In the United States, there is no single federal regulation for privacy, but different agencies have their own versions (HIPAA for Healthcare, FERPA for Education, etc.), and every state has their own version.

Some regulations focus on data and computer theft, such as the U.S. Computer Fraud and Abuse Act (CFAA), which makes it a crime to attack or steal a computer or data without authorization. These laws and regulations emerged mostly in the 1980's and 1990's when regulators became alarmed at the potential for data theft and operational disruption for governments and companies.

With the rise of ransomware, which is impacting not just companies but consumers and entire supply chains, we are seeing a change in the focus of regulations from privacy and data theft to requiring companies to have incident detection and response capabilities. Organizations must have continuous threat monitoring and response capabilities and appropriate governance to manage incidents when they occur. Governments across the planet are starting to require companies to report cybersecurity incidents (reporting could be to multiple agencies as well as law enforcement) and to declare their response actions and defensive capabilities.

For jobseekers, regulation means that jobs in the detection/response/recovery functions will be more in demand than defensive/protective functions for the foreseeable future. There are two other regulatory trends worth noting: Security by Design and Accountability.

Security by Design

Governments recognize that products being used by companies and consumers are being created without cybersecurity protections in place—the burden is on customers/consumers to manage the security risk. This is not only impossible for most consumers but costly for vendors. As a result, there is regulatory pressure to ensure manufacturers of devices/hardware/software are implementing products that are "secure by design." According to the Cybersecurity and Infrastructure Security Agency (CISA), this means:

> *"Products designed with Secure by Design principles prioritize the security of customers as a core business requirement, rather than merely treating it as a technical feature. During the design phase of a product's development lifecycle, companies should implement Secure by Design principles to significantly decrease the number of exploitable flaws before introducing them to the market for widespread use or consumption. Out-of-the-box, products should be secure with additional security features such as multi-factor authentication (MFA), logging, and single sign-on (SSO) available at no extra cost."* [8]

In practice, this means that any vendor that creates a product must incorporate secure manufacturing/coding practices and provide low-friction ways to keep their products secure once they are sold.

Secure-by-design is relatively new for most industries, so roles are being created to make these changes. Jobseekers should consider this trend as they look for their next cybersecurity job. Most will be in the software/development/engineering functions but can also include software-focused elements of GRC such as regulatory compliance, training/awareness, and third-party risk management.

---

[8] https://www.cisa.gov/securebydesign.

Accountability and Governance

The other major trend impacting security teams is a regulatory move towards demanding cybersecurity accountability for boards of directors and C-suites. In the United States, this is being driven by the Securities and Exchange Commission (SEC), which is requiring leaders of publicly traded companies to embrace the ownership of security risk in their organizations. This trend is impacting other companies too as regulatory bodies put more emphasis on company governance to manage cybersecurity risk to consumers and shareholders.

What does appropriate governance look like?

- Board-Level
    - Hiring directors with cybersecurity expertise
    - Creating committees focused on cybersecurity and technology risk
    - Regular interactions with the CISO to understand a company's risk profile

- C-Suite
    - CISO reporting directly to the CEO, instead of the CIO/CTO
    - CISO being directly engaged in company strategic planning
    - Security with its own budget instead of being part of Information Technology

The NIST Cybersecurity Framework 3.0[9] introduced "Governance" as a function for the first time in 2024 (Figure 3.1). Jobseekers interested in understanding how Governance is changing and maturity models for cybersecurity oversight should read this document. Governments outside the United States have implemented similar frameworks.

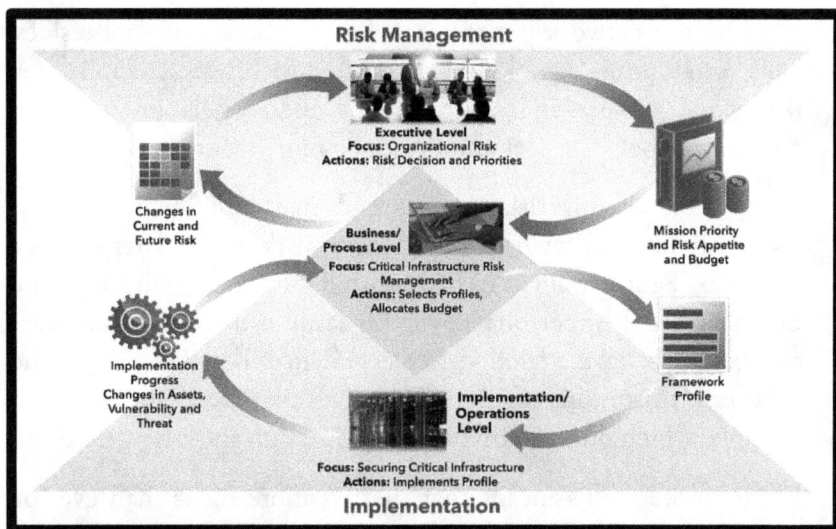

Figure 3.1: The NIST CSF 3.0 governance framework communication flow.[10]

For jobseekers, the trend towards better governance means that there may be more organizational support for the cybersecurity function, which may result in more funding and roles to enable the cybersecurity program. This isn't only about GRC roles, it has the potential to grow the overall cybersecurity function from top to bottom. It will likely start in publicly traded companies first, then move to private enterprise-sized organizations down to mid-size businesses. So, consider the size and type of company you are applying to with this trend in mind.

Identity Management

Not long ago, organizations had an easily defined perimeter that distinguished the boundary inside, which contained everything needing protection, from sensitive data to user accounts. We often depicted this as a castle with various protections around it, including a moat. As organizations have embraced remote work and cloud computing, the role of the local network as ground zero for security protection has changed. Now, security professionals

---

[10] Framework for Improving Critical Infrastructure Cybersecurity, available here: https://www.nist.gov/system/files/documents/cyberframework/cybersecurity-framework-021214.pdf.

consider the network perimeter to be anywhere that data resides. This can mean any kind of device (hardware), application (software), or person (process). The industry is interested in anything to help the user and device be more secure.

Layered on to this risk is the trend that individuals expect a consumer-like experience when they work with enterprise IT solutions. People want it to be easy to log in, use applications and browsers, use their personal devices as easily as their corporate ones, and generally have a friction-free experience. For the security and IT teams, this means offering IT services that are as easy to use as possible, which often counters an organization's security needs.

For jobseekers, this means that there is more focus than ever on how companies identify and track assets, how processes are designed with the user experience in mind, what security training and awareness looks like and what topics are covered, and how to monitor a variety of identities (human, software, and machine) for security threats. Roles in security teams that cover Identity and Access Management (IAM), Security Awareness, Endpoint Engineering, and others will continue to be in high demand.

National Security

The last couple of decades have seen a rise in the awareness of nation-state cyber-attacks, and governments have responded to this by investing in cybersecurity. Unlike other military theaters, cybersecurity and the protection of national critical infrastructure are partnerships between the military, law enforcement, domestic agencies, and the private sector. National security is a complex web of organizations and security roles, which increasingly overlap.

National security jobs exist in many places, even outside the government. The U.S. Department of Defense and its supporting agencies, such as the National Security Agency and U.S. Cyber Command, have many jobs that directly support national security. It can be powerfully fulfilling to know that your work directly defends your country from cyber-attacks. Other government jobs in national security include CISA and the Federal Bureau of

Investigation (FBI). The Defense Industrial Base (DIB) is another category of private-sector companies with government contracts that contribute to national security. These include Lockheed Martin, Boeing, RTX, General Dynamics, and Northrop Grumman. Although you may not consider Google or Meta to be focused on national security, even they have jobs that combat misinformation and fraud which benefit national security.

Public/Private Partnerships

The evolution of technology has always been a joint effort between the private sector and governments. The internet was created by a partnership between the military and academia, and it wasn't long before private companies sprang up to create web content. Applications for use in corporations are created by private companies and used by organizations that run our public infrastructure.

Governments and industry recognize that in order to maintain a safe digital environment we need to collaborate. As a result private, public, and non-profit groups such as InfraGard,[11] CISA's Joint Cyber Defense Collaborative,[12] and Information Sharing and Analysis Centers,[13] are focused on improving knowledge and sharing between these organizations.

For mid-career jobseekers, partnerships provide opportunities to bring non-cybersecurity skills to the cybersecurity industry. For example:

- Military personnel find a natural fit working with detection/response/investigative cybersecurity teams to assess nation-state threat actors, prepare organizations for incident response, and participate in incident response roles.

---

[11] https://infragard.org.
[12] https://www.cisa.gov/topics/partnerships-and-collaboration/joint-cyber-defense-collaborative.
[13] https://www.nationalisacs.org/members.

- Public policy analysts play a crucial role in translating between governments and the private sector, guiding cybersecurity policy initiatives, and assessing the effectiveness of government cybersecurity initiatives and regulations.

- From kindergarten to university, teachers use their teaching experience to help create curriculums and awareness programs that train cybersecurity workforces for the government and the private sector.

- Law enforcement (police, investigators, U.S. Secret Service, etc.) transfers into cybersecurity roles such as forensics, fraud, or auditing, and leverages those skills to help governments and private organizations detect and respond to nation-state threats.

Critical Infrastructure

Most governments prioritize the protection of critical infrastructure as one of their primary concerns. Critical infrastructure consists of sectors that governments consider "so vital…that their incapacitation or destruction would have a debilitating effect on security, national economic security, national public health or safety, or any combination thereof."[14] All things being equal, the government will help defend and restore these over the entertainment or hospitality sectors.

Various countries have their own definitions of critical infrastructure, as show in Table 3.2.

---

[14] https://www.cisa.gov/topics/critical-infrastructure-security-and-resilience/critical-infrastructure-sectors.

Sector	USA	UK	AUS	EU
Chemical	X	X		
Commercial Facilities	X			
Communications	X	X	X	
Critical Manufacturing	X			
Dams	X			
Defense Industrial Base	X	X	X	
Emergency Services	X	X		
Energy	X	X	X	X
Financial Services	X	X	X	X
Food and Agriculture	X	X	X	X
Government Services and Facilities	X	X		X
Healthcare and Public Health	X	X	X	
Information Technology	X	X	Data Storage and Processing	Digital Infrastructure
Nuclear Reactors, Materials and Waste	X	Civil Nuclear		
Transportation Systems	X	X		X

Table 3.2 – Critical infrastructure sectors by country.

When thinking about critical infrastructure, most people think about utilities such as water or power—and they are definitely critical! The U.S. government defines 16 industry sectors as critical, including finance, communications, and emergency services. The concern is that a cyber-attack on a critical infrastructure sector would be catastrophic for people in that country—impacting the health, safety, and economic security of residents.

In recent years, there have been rising numbers of attacks on critical infrastructure, and governments and the private sector are taking notice. For the jobseeker, this can be another opportunity to find roles that are in demand and meaningfully contribute to their community. Anecdotally, companies who experience a cybersecurity event will, in the short term, increase cybersecurity hiring. Companies such as Target, Equifax, and Okta increased hiring (exact numbers are kept confidential) post-event. Almost every type of cybersecurity job can be found in protecting critical infrastructure, and seekers with experience in these sectors will be in high demand. If you have experience in a health clinic or hospital, for instance, that will be immensely valuable if you transition to doing cybersecurity in healthcare.

Security Vendors

The security market (vendors who sell security solutions and services) has exploded over the last decade. As of this writing, the global market is estimated to be $194 billion.[15] Vendors emerge as start-ups to solve a specific niche security problem, then (hopefully) grow to a point where they stand alone as a market-dominant vendor or are acquired by another security vendor and absorbed into that vendor's portfolio of products. This trajectory of growth and acquisition is common in cybersecurity. Kevin Mandia, a former United States Air Force officer, started the cybersecurity firm Red Cliff Consulting in 2004. He rebranded it as Mandiant which was acquired by FireEye in 2013 for $1 billion and acquired again by Google in 2022 for $5.4 billion.

Larger security vendors try to solidify their market share by offering cybersecurity "platforms"—suites of cybersecurity tools and services covering many security program needs. This generates a lot of industry discussion regarding "platform vs. best-of-breed" solutions—but for a jobseeker, understanding who has the most common platforms can be a way to quickly learn technical and tool skills that are in demand by hiring organizations. An internet search of "largest cybersecurity companies" will reveal the current list of vendors who likely have a platform solution and product certifications and other training for jobseekers and practitioners.

---

[15] https://www.fortunebusinessinsights.com/industry-reports/cyber-security-market-101165.

Mandiant's website, for instance, distinguishes between their platform and their products and services.

Emerging Technologies

Entering the cybersecurity profession is like trying to jump onto a moving train—things are constantly changing, and it can be hard to know where to start, let alone how to keep up. History shows that technology trend cycles tend to happen over a three- to five-year period; that is, it takes three to five years before a new technology emerges, is understood, then is operationalized into everyday job roles. We saw this when cloud computing exploded in the 2010's and we are experiencing it now with generative AI.

A jobseeker should understand the current and emerging technology trends influencing the cybersecurity profession, enabling them to prepare and look for roles that are in higher demand. Knowing technology trends will also ensure any training or preparation can be sustained in the next few years, making the time and resource investment in training more valuable.

Cloud Technologies

Although we've put this topic in the "emerging" section, cloud technologies have been around for a while. Cloud computing is a model where companies, such as Amazon Web Services and Microsoft, offer compute services for a pay-as-you-go model, ranging from file storage to speech-to-text translation. You use cloud if you have iCloud or Google Drive and if you use Alexa or Siri. Understanding that most organizations have at least some of their infrastructure and applications in a cloud environment is important for jobseekers—you will need to understand how cloud works, as well as the current security methodologies to manage cloud-related risks.

When considering a cybersecurity career, it is useful to think of cloud in two ways:

- **Cloud Infrastructure:** Understanding how cloud is architected, how companies connect to cloud ecosystems, and how companies use cloud services to provide infrastructure is an important part of the Security Engineer and Security Analyst roles.

- **Software-as-a-Service (SaaS) Applications:** These applications run in clouds. Security professionals must understand how to connect to, monitor, and manage them.

A company that uses cloud (which is most of them) needs to understand the security risks and operational trade-offs involved— that's where the security team comes in. Newer companies are typically "cloud native"—their entire technology footprint is in the cloud. Older companies are trying to move as much as possible to the cloud but are usually in a hybrid state: some on-premises, some in the cloud. Using the cloud influences every part of a cybersecurity program, so jobseekers should have at least a basic understanding of this technology.

Jobseekers wishing to get familiar with cloud and cloud security can look at the resources in Table 3.3.

Resource	Purpose
Online Training such as: • LinkedIn Learning (https:// www.linkedin.com/learning/) • Coursera (https:// www.coursera.org/) • AWS (https:// aws.amazon.com/training/) • Microsoft (https:// learn.microsoft.com/en-us/training/azure/) • Google (https:// cloud.google.com/learn/training/)	Learn the basics of cloud architecture and configuration, how to secure cloud environments and applications.
Cloud Standards and Frameworks: • Cloud Security Alliance (https:// cloudsecurityalliance.org/) • OWASP Top 10 Cloud Security (https:// owasp.org/www-project-cloud-native-application-security-top-10/) • NIST Cybersecurity Framework (https:// nvlpubs.nist.gov/nistpubs /CSWP/ NIST.CSWP.29.pdf) • Center for Internet Security (CIS) Benchmarks (https:// www.cisecurity.org/cis-benchmarks)	Standards and frameworks provide guidance for understanding and securing cloud environments and applications.

Table 3.3 – Resources for learning about cloud computing.

Generative Artificial Intelligence (GenAI)

Jobseekers should understand that security vendors are incorporating AI into security tooling as quickly as possible given its hype and potential. Such integrations include:

- An AI-powered assistant that will assist SOC analysts to interrogate data to find intrusions
- Use of AI-powered search engines for research

- Using AI to understand security contract obligations in vendor contracts
- Using AI to test other AI Learning Language Models

It is important for any jobseeker to have a basic understanding of how AI operates, appreciation for how it is being used in the security industry, and knowledge about where it is appropriate to allow unsupervised AI. However, AI is changing rapidly; there are not yet widely accepted rules on how to use, protect, or defend against rogue AI. Expect to get questions about AI during job interviews, but don't expect that you must have all the answers, either. In fact, a good answer is to acknowledge that a company should be proactive but appropriately skeptical about the benefits of AI. We will discuss the security challenges of AI in more detail in Chapter 17.

Resource	Purpose
Online Training such as: • LinkedIn Learning (https://www.linkedin.com/learning/) • Coursera (https://www.coursera.org/learn/ai-for-everyone • AWS (https://aws.amazon.com/training/learn-about/machine-learning • Microsoft (https://learn.microsoft.com/en-us/ai/) • Google (https://cloud.google.com/learn/training/machine-learning-ai/)	Learn the basics of AI terminology, how to use AI for different purposes, how to do prompt engineering.
AI Standards and Frameworks: • OWASP AI Exchange (https://owaspai.org/) • OWASP Top 10 for Large Language Models (https://owasp.org/www-project-top-10-for-large-language-model-applications/) • NIST AI Risk Management Framework (https://nvlpubs.nist.gov/nistpubs/ai/nist.ai.100-1.pdf) • MITRE Adversarial Landscape for AI Systems (https://atlas.mitre.org/)	Standards and frameworks guide understanding and securing AI environments.

Table 3.4 – Resources for learning about artificial intelligence.

At a minimum, jobseekers should consider becoming familiar with the recent developments in generative AI and know how to use commercially available GenAI assistants such as ChatGPT or Claude for research, writing, and other content creation. Bonus points if you learn the basic concepts around securing AI (see Table 3.4). More bonus points if you take the time to understand current international, national, and state policies.

Ransomware

Organizations are facing all kinds of external threats all the time, but none are getting more publicity and attention than ransomware. Why? Because a ransomware event has the potential to hit an organization in multiple ways:

- **Operational disruption.** Computers may be "bricked"—made inoperable—and stop the organization from conducting its mission until services are restored.

- **Data theft.** Ransomware operators take ownership of the data, requiring companies to notify regulatory groups, customers, and partners of a data breach.

- **Extortion.** Ransomware groups have been known to extort the company, even after a ransom is paid, threatening to expose the data if a second payment isn't made. Some even extort the individuals whose data has been stolen, making it a reputational challenge for individuals and companies.

Many companies can weather the impacts of data theft, regulatory scrutiny, and brand damage. However, they can't easily handle operational disruptions. In some industries, such as healthcare, ransomware can lead to patient death—the worst-case scenario for any organization.

Organizations have dealt with this new risk by investing in detection and response capabilities, email security, endpoint detection, multi-factor authentication, security awareness training (don't click on that link!), and other controls to minimize the ransomware threat.

For jobseekers, the effects of ransomware present opportunities to focus on the security functions receiving company attention. Understand how organizations protect and respond to ransomware and consider learning the skills to fill those roles.

Understanding the Job Market

Before you jump into actively looking for cybersecurity roles you need to understand the current state of supply and demand in cybersecurity. By "current state" we mean the prevailing environment of the 2020's where information about job availability and candidate demand is often confusing.

Be aware that job postings in cybersecurity, especially desirable mid-career positions, may only remain publicly advertised for a few days due to high demand and rapid applicant response. However, this initial speed often contrasts sharply with the actual hiring process, which frequently takes six to eight weeks or longer to complete, involving multiple interview rounds, technical assessments, and internal approvals. Plan your application strategy and manage expectations accordingly.[16]

Because of the high stakes and sensitivity in cybersecurity roles, many organizations lean toward internal candidates or those with established trusted relationships. These individuals often come with a known track record, familiarity with the company's culture, and a demonstrated commitment to its mission—all of which reduce the perceived hiring risk. For external candidates, this means you must clearly communicate not only your technical abilities, but also your alignment with the organization's values and mission. Hiring managers consistently favor applicants who show practical, real-world experience alongside collaborative problem-solving skills. Demonstrating how you've worked across teams to navigate complex challenges can often carry as much weight as technical credentials.

Supply: Security Workers

The Nuance Around Worker Vacancies in Cyber

Higher education and private companies have learned that there is money to be made by offering cybersecurity training and degrees. Governments are funding this training, recognizing the need for a cybersecurity-ready workforce. As a result, many people are entering the cybersecurity profession as "entry-level" workers with

---

[16] For more, see https://cyberflorida.org/the-search-for-the-cyber-unicorn/.

some kind of education credential. According to 2024 reporting,[17] there is a 12% surplus of workers seeking entry-level jobs but that supply only supports 77% of jobs requiring more than two years of experience. The shortage is even more significant for senior and very technical roles.

The Myth of "Entry-Level"

What is "entry-level" anyway? Some define "entry-level" as a job requiring minimal skills or prior work experience. If we use this definition, there are very few "entry-level" cybersecurity jobs. Most cybersecurity jobs require a functional understanding of technology (jobseekers can specialize, such as operating systems, mobile, application development, etc.). This is a good thing for mid-career jobseekers—the work you've already done (even in a different industry) contributes to your prior experience and puts you in the market for mid-level experience.

On-The-Job Experience

Jobseekers have a "chicken-and-egg" problem: they need on-the-job technology skills to get a cybersecurity job but can't get a job without the skills. Training companies such as SANS[18] and HackTheBox[19] are trying to correct this by offering training that simulates on-the-job experiences, using cyber ranges for realistic exercises, conducting capture the flag (CTF) competitions, and offering internships and student co-operatives. If you have no employment-based technology experience, look for "skills-based" training options if you are choosing to take a class or complete a certification.

Diversity in Cybersecurity

The cybersecurity industry has two worker problems: there aren't enough people to fill demand, particularly at more senior levels, and

---

[17] https://lightcast.io/resources/research/quarterly-cybersecurity-talent-report-june-24.

[18] https://sans.org.

[19] https://HackTheBox.com.

the current workforce lacks people from diverse backgrounds. For jobseekers looking to move into cybersecurity mid-career, this presents an opportunity to look for programs designed to fast-track someone with your background and work with those groups.

Look for companies who offer resources or employee resource groups, such as:

- General diversity in cybersecurity
- Military and veteran groups
- Women in cybersecurity
- LGBTQ+
- Non-White
- Neurodiverse
- Financially disadvantaged regions

Demand: Hiring Organizations

Yes, there is a demand for cybersecurity workers. Demand for cybersecurity professionals rises and falls by industry after a big cyber incident, a technological change, or when regulations change. Hiring managers are often inundated with candidates for entry-level roles but can wait months to find the right person with the right skill set, particularly for mid- and senior-level roles. Why is that?

Because there are no industry standards for roles, skills, or job requirements, it is up to each organization to create their own job descriptions—and those descriptions vary widely in terms of titles, required education, and skills. Almost every technology job desires some experience with security, even if it's not a security-first job. So, using search terms on job boards results in lots of postings, but it makes it challenging to find the right kind of role. Imagine that you search for "cybersecurity jobs" and see one called Systems Architect. Is this role a "technology" role with a bit of security or a "security" role focused on a bit of technology?

Hiring managers who have been in the industry for ten or more years most likely learned their skills "on the job," because there were no formal cybersecurity career paths or training when they started. When selecting a candidate, they look for on-the-job experience as a primary and preferred attribute, making it more difficult for people outside the industry to break in. They want this experience to ensure a new hire has a high likelihood of success and effectiveness in their new role. This bias towards on-the-job experience serves a valid purpose but also makes it harder for people outside the security/technology sector to enter the profession.

There is a lot of noise about high-paying cybersecurity jobs, and it's true that, as an industry, the average compensation is higher than some other roles, but there is a lot of variability in compensation packages. Candidates should consider the total compensation, which includes salary, annual bonuses, health insurance, retirement contributions, restricted stock, signing bonuses, and retention bonuses. Keep in mind that:

- Publicly traded companies will often offer bonuses and restricted stock as part of the package.

- Public Sector (Government) organizations rarely offer bonuses and never stock. The base salary is often 20-30% lower than other industries, but the public sector often hires entry/junior level staff and invests in training.

- The more regulated the industry, the more likely they will pay compensation at or above market rates.

- Location always impacts total compensation, with bigger cities paying more than rural locations, including remote workers. Your compensation package will reflect where you are, not where the company is headquartered.

Given these considerations, jobseekers are left to sift through multiple security postings and hope they are applying to the right kind of jobs. It means that jobseekers self-select out of applying for poorly written job postings that require too many pre-requisite skills. It means that the hiring process is inefficient and frustrating. Consider the example job posting in Table 3.5.

Job Description Items	Description Analysis
Job Title: Senior Security Architect (Cloud and On-Premises)	**Job Title:** Architects are "senior" by definition, so what does "senior" mean? Look to their "years of experience" requirements to find out.
Location: Mountain View, CA (with option to work remotely or from other Corporate offices)	**Location:** Looks like it's remote-friendly, but may require easy access to an office location - hybrid?
About Us: Cloumera is committed to building a safer and more secure online experience for our users. As a Senior Security Architect on our team, you will play a critical role in designing and implementing secure architectures that protect our infrastructure, services, and data.	**About Us:** Looks like a tech start-up, perhaps? Needs more context on age/maturity of organization.
Job Summary: We are seeking an experienced Security Architect to join our team, focusing on the design and implementation of secure cloud and on-premises architectures for Cloumera's global operations. The ideal candidate will have a deep understanding of security principles, architecture patterns, and industry best practices.	**Job Summary:** How does this "team" fit into an organization's hierarchy? "Design" and "Implementation" are two very different things - seek more clarity about time spent in each space.
Responsibilities: • Design and implement secure architectures for cloud and on-premises environments • Collaborate with engineering teams to integrate security into product development and infrastructure planning • Develop and maintain security policies, procedures, and standards • Conduct risk assessments and provide recommendations for mitigation • Work with cross-functional teams to ensure compliance with regulatory requirements and industry standards (e.g., SOC 2, PCI-DSS) • Stay up-to-date with emerging threats and technologies, and advise on potential impacts to Cloumera's infrastructure	**Responsibilities:** Is there anything this role DOESN'T do? If you assume these points are in order, how much time do they expect a person to spend in each of these areas? Does this align to the kind of work you want to do on a daily basis? Do policies, procedures and standards not already exist? Would you be creating these from scratch, or building on what already exists? Which cross-functional teams would you engage with?

Table 3.5 – Example job description and key content for jobseekers to consider.

Job Description Items	Description Analysis
Requirements: • Bachelor's degree in Computer Science or related field; Master's degree preferred • Minimum 8 years of experience in security architecture, engineering, or a related field • Proven track record of designing and implementing secure architectures for large-scale systems • In-depth knowledge of cloud security platforms (e.g., AWS, GCP), on-premises infrastructure (e.g., VMware, Cisco), and security technologies (e.g., firewalls, VPNs) • Experience with security frameworks (e.g., NIST, ISO 27001) and compliance regulations (e.g., GDPR, HIPAA) • Strong analytical and problem-solving skills Excellent communication and collaboration skills	**Requirements:** Degree requirements are restrictive. If you have the experience, but not the degree, consider applying anyway, but know you might not make it past the recruiting filters. If your experience is in "a related field", but not security, apply anyway - and pull examples where your designs were secure (regardless of job title). Consider highlighting training/certification for knowledge of cloud security platforms, etc., instead of on-the-job experience. Get ready to translate your existing analysis/problem-solving/communications skills into a security setting.
Nice to Have: • Experience with DevOps practices and tools (e.g., Jenkins, Docker) • Familiarity with containerization (e.g., Kubernetes, Docker) • Knowledge of machine learning and AI security considerations	**Nice to Have:** Be familiar with these terms - they'll come up in an interview, but if you don't have them don't worry.
What We Offer: • Competitive salary and benefits package • Opportunity to work on complex, high-impact projects that drive Cloumera's growth and innovation • Collaborative and dynamic work environment with a talented team of engineers and security professionals • Access to cutting-edge technologies and training opportunities • Flexible work arrangements (remote or in-office) and flexible hours	**What We Offer:** This environment will assume you can self-sustain your work and learning. Look for words like "complex", "innovation", "dynamic", "cutting edge". If this excites you, great.
How to Apply: If you're passionate about building secure systems and want to join an innovative company that's making a difference, please submit your resume and cover letter through our online application portal. We can't wait to hear from you!	

Table 3.5 – Example job description and key content for jobseekers to consider
(continued).

There is some hope to fix these problems.

- NICE has established a cybersecurity job framework that maps roles and skills to jobs.[20] Although it is not yet widely used by hiring managers it is gaining popularity as it matures.

- Groups such as The Aspen Institute provide research and tools for hiring managers to better position themselves in the hiring market.[21]

- The education/training sector is moving away from theory-only learning to "skills-based" learning models, simulating real environments for "on-the-job" training.

- There is a movement towards apprenticeship training models, not just short-term internships, that allow deeper training while earning a paycheck.

Jobseekers can take advantage of these changes:

- Reference the NICE framework to understand the role/skill/certification mappings. Use this as a guide, not an authoritative text—but it can help you better articulate your value proposition to hiring managers.

- Look for training/certification programs that lean into skills-based learning methodologies.

- Consider recommended practices for creating a job description (JD) and look for JDs that follow those principles. Recognize when a JD *doesn't* follow those principles and adjust for that as needed.

- Investigate apprenticeship/internship programs—not necessarily to participate in one (although that's an option, too!) but to understand how they plan for skills/experience acquisition and how to map that to your journey.

---

[20] https://niccs.cisa.gov/workforce-development/nice-framework.
[21] https://www.aspeninstitute.org/wp-content/uploads/2018/11/Aspen-Cybersecurity-Group-Principles-for-Growing-and-Sustaining-the-Nations-Cybersecurity-Workforce-1.pdf.

To sum up, the cybersecurity market is a continually changing thing and understanding where it is and where it is headed will help you choose where to invest your efforts to train for and land a position. Understanding what jobs are available, and how to be a preferred candidate, will help you transition successfully into the profession.

Chapter Summary

- Mid-career jobseekers have industry experience that can help with a job search, but they must be clear with themselves and hiring managers about salary and seniority expectations.

- Leverage your professional networks, starting with your existing company, to find contacts who will refer you to cybersecurity roles.

- Regulations, "security by design," and accountability/governance trends are changing the jobs that are in demand. Jobseekers should be aware of these trends and look for roles that leverage this need.

- Identity Management remains a strong focus of technology and design trends in the market.

- Public/Private partnerships, particularly for critical infrastructure sectors, are driving a lot of job demand.

- Emerging technologies like cloud, AI, and ransomware are driving demand for workers who can secure them.

- There are few "entry-level" jobs, and the supply of workers for these jobs is high. Demand exists for mid- and senior-level roles. Mid-career jobseekers should look for these roles.

- Hiring managers prefer people with "on-the-job" experience, particularly with technologies relevant to the job. If you don't have this experience, look for "skills-based" training options.

- Candidates from underrepresented groups, such as veterans and women, can work with organizations that support these groups, to find roles and network.

- Hiring managers struggle to write job descriptions and postings. Know what to look for in a cybersecurity job description and what to ignore!

Chapter References

Aspen Institute. Principles for Growing and Sustaining the Nation's Cybersecurity Workforce 2018: https://www.aspeninstitute.org/wp-content/uploads/2018/11/Aspen-Cybersecurity-Group-Principles-for-Growing-and-Sustaining-the-Nations-Cybersecurity-Workforce-1.pdf

Cybersecurity and Infrastructure Security Agency. *Critical Infrastructure Sectors* 2024: https://www.cisa.gov/topics/critical-infrastructure-security-and-resilience/critical-infrastructure-sectors

Cybersecurity and Infrastructure Security Agency. *Secure by Design* 2024: https://www.cisa.gov/securebydesign

Fortune Business Insights. Cybersecurity Market Size, Share and Industry Analysis, By Component (Solutions and Services), By Deployment (On-premises and Cloud), By Security Type (Network Security, Cloud Application Security, End-point Security, Secure Web Gateway, Application Security, and Others), By Enterprise Size (Small and Medium Enterprises (SMEs) and Large Enterprises), By Industry (BFSI, IT and Telecommunications, Retail, Healthcare, Government, Manufacturing, Travel and Transportation, Energy and Utilities, and Others), and Region Forecast, 2024-2032, 2024: https://www.fortunebusinessinsights.com/industry-reports/cyber-security-market-101165

Lightcast. The Lightcast Quarterly Cybersecurity Talent Report 2024: https://lightcast.io/resources/research/quarterly-cybersecurity-talent-report-june-24

National Initiative for Cybersecurity Careers and Studies Workforce Framework for Cybersecurity (NICE Framework) 2024: https://niccs.cisa.gov/workforce-development/nice-framework

National Institute of Standards and Technology. *The NIST Cybersecurity Framework (CSF) v2.0* 2024: https://nvlpubs.nist.gov/nistpubs/CSWP/NIST.CSWP.29.pdf

Part 2

How to Break into Cybersecurity

Chapter 4

The Lay of the Land

Stepping into the world of cybersecurity can feel like entering a bustling city for the first time—full of unfamiliar landmarks, complex pathways, and a language that seems entirely its own. To effectively navigate the dynamic environment of cybersecurity, you need to understand the lay of the land. In this chapter, we'll guide you through the essential terminology, communities, and professional norms that shape cybersecurity. By familiarizing yourself with these elements, you'll gain confidence in your ability to communicate and contribute within this space, making your transition smoother and more impactful.

Essential Language and Jargon of Cybersecurity

Try reading the following sentence that might be heard among cybersecurity colleagues:

> "To mitigate the risk of a zero-day exploit, we need to implement robust IDS/IPS solutions, ensure proper RBAC for all users, and conduct regular pentesting to identify vulnerabilities in our DMZ, while also leveraging SIEM for real-time threat intelligence and anomaly detection to protect against APTs and minimize the attack surface in our hybrid cloud environment."

If that sentence is impossible to decipher, we understand. Don't be scared or deterred! Cybersecurity has a lexicon and language unto itself. This happens in many specialties, from medicine to the military, and we want to give you a jump start. There are far too many words and phrases for us to introduce here, but Table 4.1

provides a sense of the terminology you will encounter and need to learn to succeed.[22]

The essential language, acronyms, and jargon of cybersecurity are vast and constantly expanding. Even long-time experts in the field are continually learning, so you're not alone in the struggle to keep up. Try reading some cybersecurity articles and then look up the words and acronyms you don't recognize.

One tip is to be cautious in assuming that the use of a *common* word means the same in cybersecurity as in another use. Cybersecurity has borrowed words such as "virus" and "firewall" from their non-technical origins. Oftentimes, these words share attributes in common with the first use, but the analogies and metaphors are imperfect. If you *think* you know what the word means, look it up to see what the differences are. For instance, in building construction, a firewall is used to physically block the spread of fire while in cybersecurity it digitally blocks unauthorized access to a network and allows authorized traffic to flow through.

---

[22] An extensive glossary can be found at https://csrc.nist.gov/glossary.

Word/Phrase	Description/Explanation
Firewall	A network security device that monitors and controls incoming and outgoing network traffic based on rules.
VPN (Virtual Private Network)	A service that encrypts your internet connection to provide privacy and security while using the web.
IDS/IPS (Intrusion Detection /Prevention System)	Tools that monitor networks for suspicious activity and can prevent attacks.
Phishing	A type of social engineering attack where criminals try to trick you into sharing sensitive information.
Malware	Software designed to damage or gain unauthorized access to a computer system.
Zero-Day Vulnerability	A security flaw that is unknown to the software vendor and actively exploited before a fix is available.
SIEM (Security Information and Event Management)	Software that collects and analyzes log data to detect security incidents.
Encryption	The process of converting information into a code to prevent unauthorized access.
RBAC (Role-BasedAccess Control)	A method for managing user access to resources based on their role in the organization.

Table 4.1 – Common words and phrases in cybersecurity with their definitions.

Word/Phrase	Description/Explanation
Pentesting (Penetration Testing)	Simulated attacks on a system to find vulnerabilities before an actual attacker does.
APT (Advanced Persistent Threat)	A prolonged and targeted cyberattack, usually conducted by a group, aiming to steal data.
DDoS (Distributed Denial of Service)	An attack that overwhelms a service with traffic to make it unavailable to users.
Vulnerability Management	The process of finding, assessing, and fixing weaknesses in a computer system.
MFA (Multi-Factor Authentication)	A security system that requires more than one form of identification to access something.
Data Breach	An incident where sensitive, confidential, or protected data is accessed without permission.
Social Engineering	A tactic attackers use to trick individuals into revealing confidential information.
DMZ (Demilitarized Zone)	A part of a network that is exposed to the internet to add an extra layer of security to internal networks.
Honeypot	A decoy system designed to lure attackers and detect unauthorized access attempts.
PII (Personally Identifiable Information)	Data that can identify an individual, such as name, address, or social security number.
Threat Intelligence	Information gathered to understand potential cyber threats and how to defend against them.

Table 4.1 – Common words and phrases in cybersecurity with their definitions (continued).

A Day in the Life

To provide a sense of what a workday is like for someone in cybersecurity, consider the following vignette. It is meant to be representative despite the differences among individual roles, industries, and circumstances.

Sarah arrives at her downtown office around 8:30 a.m., settling into an open-plan workspace filled with monitors displaying real-time security alerts, network traffic visualizations, and system health metrics. As a cybersecurity analyst at a financial services company, she works alongside a diverse team of fellow analysts, each specializing in different aspects of security monitoring and incident response. The morning begins with a quick stand-up meeting where the night shift hands over any ongoing incidents or suspicious activities they've been tracking. Today, they flag unusual login patterns from several corporate accounts that began in the early hours.

Throughout the day, Sarah alternates between proactive threat hunting and responding to security alerts generated by their detection systems. She investigates the suspicious logins from the morning report, methodically analyzing login timestamps, IP addresses, and user behavior patterns. When she discovers that several accounts were accessed from an unusual geographic location, she coordinates with the identity management team to force password resets and escalates the incident to senior analysts for further investigation. Between incidents, she reviews and tunes detection rules, documenting her findings and updating the team's knowledge base with new threat indicators she's identified.

The afternoon brings a different challenge when a marketing manager urgently requests temporary access to a restricted system for a deadline-driven project. Sarah carefully evaluates the request against security policies, consults with her team lead, and works to find a secure solution that meets both security requirements and business needs. Later, she joins a virtual meeting with the development team to review security requirements for a new customer-facing application, translating complex security concepts into actionable guidance. As she wraps up her shift around 5:30 p.m., she updates the incident tracking system, prepares handover notes for the evening team, and sets up automated alerts for several suspicious patterns she wants to monitor overnight.

Switching Industries

People switch to cybersecurity from nearly every other field. We've known musicians, graphic designers, athletic trainers, police officers, and on and on who have successfully transitioned to cybersecurity roles. In this section, we won't cover the nuances of every type of switch but will address some of the most common fields from which people transition into cybersecurity: IT and engineering, military and law enforcement, and risk management (including finance and auditing).

Switching from IT and Engineering

For those transitioning from IT and engineering roles into cybersecurity, the shift can be both exciting and challenging. While your existing technical skills will undoubtedly be valuable, there are key differences to consider.

First, the mindset in cybersecurity is often more focused on threat detection, prevention, and response than on building and maintaining systems. This involves a deeper understanding of the methods that attackers use to break into systems (we call them attack vectors), vulnerabilities (security weaknesses or flaws), and malicious actors. You'll need to develop a proactive approach to security, rather than simply reacting to issues as they arise. Additionally, the regulatory landscape in cybersecurity is constantly evolving. Staying up to date with compliance standards and industry best practices will be crucial.

Second, the skills required for cybersecurity can be quite diverse. Your technical expertise in areas like networking, systems administration, and programming will be tremendously valuable. But you may also need to delve into areas like digital forensics, incident response, and security architecture. Professional skills, such as problem-solving, critical thinking, and communication, are also highly valued in this field.

While the technical nature of cybersecurity may seem familiar to those coming from IT and engineering, the pace and pressure can be significantly higher. Cyber threats are constantly evolving, and security professionals must be able to adapt quickly to new challenges. The potential impact of a security breach can be severe, making it essential to maintain a high level of focus and diligence.

Despite these differences, there are many similarities between IT or engineering and cybersecurity roles. Both fields require a strong foundation in technology, a passion for problem-solving, and a commitment to continuous learning. By leveraging your existing skills and knowledge, and by acquiring the necessary cybersecurity expertise, you can successfully transition into this exciting and rewarding career path.

Switching from Military and Law Enforcement

If you are coming from the military or law enforcement, you will find familiarity in cybersecurity with the defensive mission. These fields share a focus on protecting assets and mitigating threats, which can give veterans and former officers a natural advantage in understanding the security mindset. However, there are significant differences in approach, tools, and day-to-day operations that you'll need to navigate as you make the switch.

One of the most valuable assets you bring from military or law enforcement experience is your understanding of risk assessment and threat management. Whether you've been trained to secure physical spaces, manage crises, or analyze intelligence, these skills translate well to cybersecurity. In cybersecurity, the threats are digital, but the core principles of identifying vulnerabilities, anticipating attacks, and responding decisively are highly applicable. Your ability to remain calm under pressure and think critically during high-stakes situations is an invaluable asset in roles like incident response and threat hunting.

That said, the cultural shift between military or law enforcement and cybersecurity can be significant. While both fields value discipline and hierarchy, cybersecurity teams often operate with more fluid structures and collaborative environments. You'll need to adapt to a workplace culture that may place less emphasis on traditionally rigid chains of command and more on teamwork, problem-solving, and innovation. Cybersecurity is also a field that rewards curiosity and continuous learning, so be prepared to embrace a mindset of exploration and adaptability.

Another area to focus on is the technical skill set required in cybersecurity. Military and law enforcement professionals often have exposure to technology, such as secure communication systems or surveillance tools, but cybersecurity requires deeper expertise in areas like network security, cryptography, and ethical hacking. While these skills can be learned, it's important to assess your current technical knowledge and identify gaps that need to be addressed. Certifications like CompTIA Security+, Certified Ethical Hacker (CEH), or Certified Information Systems Security Professional (CISSP) can provide a structured pathway to acquiring the foundational knowledge you'll need.

Understanding the legal and regulatory landscape is also crucial. While your previous career may have involved enforcing laws or understanding rules of engagement, cybersecurity requires familiarity with frameworks like GDPR, HIPAA, or NIST standards. In some cases, especially in government or defense-related cybersecurity roles, your background in handling classified or sensitive information will give you an advantage. However, you'll need to adapt to the specific compliance requirements and privacy considerations of the digital domain.

Cybersecurity roles also demand a shift in how you perceive and address threats. Unlike in military or law enforcement roles, where adversaries are often visible or tangible, in cybersecurity, attackers are typically invisible, working remotely through digital means. This requires you to develop skills in threat intelligence, forensic analysis, and understanding the methods hackers use to exploit systems. A proactive, rather than reactive, approach to identifying and mitigating these threats is essential.

One key advantage of transitioning from the military or law enforcement is the potential for leveraging your existing security clearances. Many cybersecurity roles, particularly those in government, defense, or critical infrastructure, require clearances that can take years to obtain. If you already hold an active or easily reactivated clearance, this can open doors to highly specialized roles that others may find difficult to access.

Finally, while the technical and operational aspects of cybersecurity are critical, don't underestimate the value of your professional skills. Communication, leadership, and the ability to build trust with colleagues and stakeholders are just as important in this field as in your previous role. Cybersecurity professionals often need to explain complex threats or technical solutions to non-technical audiences, making clear and effective communication a vital skill.

By building on your strengths in threat management, discipline, and risk analysis, and by committing to acquiring the technical knowledge and cultural adaptability needed for cybersecurity, you can make a smooth and successful transition into this growing and dynamic field.

Switching from Risk Management

Professionals transitioning from risk management roles in finance, auditing, or compliance into cybersecurity bring a wealth of experience that will be relevant and familiar in cybersecurity. These fields share a focus on identifying vulnerabilities, enforcing controls, and ensuring adherence to standards—all key components of cybersecurity.

One of the strongest assets you bring to cybersecurity is your expertise in assessing risk. In finance or auditing, you're already accustomed to evaluating vulnerabilities, whether in financial processes, operational systems, or regulatory compliance. Cybersecurity requires a similar mindset but applies it to digital assets and networks. Your ability to assess threats, prioritize risks, and recommend controls will directly translate to roles such as risk analyst, compliance officer, or cybersecurity governance specialist.

Another area where you're well-prepared is regulatory compliance. As someone experienced in navigating frameworks like SOX, ISO 27001, or financial audit standards, you likely have a strong foundation in ensuring organizational adherence to rules and regulations. Cybersecurity involves a similar focus, but the frameworks may shift to include HIPAA, GDPR, California Consumer Privacy Act (CCPA), or NIST. Your ability to interpret regulatory requirements and apply them effectively will make you a valuable asset, especially in roles that involve policy development or compliance auditing.

However, transitioning into cybersecurity also means adapting to a more dynamic and fast-paced environment. While finance and auditing often operate on scheduled cycles or predictable timelines, cybersecurity requires constant vigilance and adaptability. Threats evolve daily, and professionals must stay ahead of emerging risks. This can mean reacting quickly to incidents, staying informed about the latest attack vectors, or integrating new security measures on short notice. Cultivating agility and a proactive mindset will help you thrive in this new landscape.

The technical aspects of cybersecurity may also require a learning curve. In risk management, you're likely accustomed to assessing processes, systems, or financial controls, but cybersecurity adds layers of complexity with concepts like cryptography, network security, and vulnerability management. While you don't need to become a technical expert in all areas, gaining foundational knowledge in key cybersecurity domains will enhance your credibility and effectiveness. Certifications like CompTIA Security+, Certified Information Systems Auditor (CISA), or Certified Information Security Manager (CISM) can provide a structured path for building these skills.

Collaboration with technical teams is another area to prepare for. In cybersecurity, risk management often intersects with IT, engineering, and legal teams to ensure a holistic approach to security. Your ability to communicate risk clearly and translate complex regulatory requirements into actionable tasks will be critical. This may involve creating policies, conducting security awareness training, or working with IT to implement technical controls.

Your analytical and detail-oriented mindset will also serve you well in cybersecurity. Whether analyzing data breaches, identifying suspicious activity, or reviewing system logs for anomalies, the skills you've honed in risk management directly apply. Additionally, your experience in creating and presenting reports to stakeholders or leadership will be invaluable in conveying the importance of cybersecurity initiatives to decision-makers.

Finally, your career in finance, auditing, or compliance has likely instilled a sense of accountability and integrity—qualities that are highly prized in cybersecurity. Organizations need professionals who can handle sensitive information, maintain trust, and ensure ethical practices in their security operations. By building on these strengths and expanding your technical knowledge, you'll be well-equipped to transition into a rewarding and impactful cybersecurity career.

Whether you are transitioning from IT, military service, law enforcement, or risk management, the key to success lies in recognizing that your previous experience isn't a hurdle to overcome—it's an asset to leverage. Each background brings unique perspectives that cybersecurity teams desperately need. The field's complexity requires professionals who can think beyond purely technical solutions, communicate across diverse stakeholders, and apply hard-won wisdom to emerging challenges. As you navigate this transition, remember that cybersecurity isn't just looking for people who fit a predetermined mold. It's looking for professionals like you who bring depth, maturity, and fresh thinking to persistent problems.

Affinity Groups

The cybersecurity community recognizes the value of diverse backgrounds and has created numerous support networks to help professionals succeed in leveraging shared experiences, backgrounds, and identities to provide support, mentorship, and opportunities for growth. These groups are especially important in a field as dynamic and challenging as cybersecurity, where professionals often navigate complex technical landscapes and career transitions. For example, groups for women, veterans, and former government employees create spaces to address unique challenges and leverage strengths specific to these communities. By fostering inclusion and building supportive networks, affinity groups help individuals adapt, thrive, and contribute diverse perspectives that drive innovation and resilience in the cybersecurity industry.

Some affinity groups are also minority groups. We will return to minorities in Chapter 15. Here, we want to introduce you to specific considerations for cybersecurity careers among people with shared attributes. Note that larger employers may have group structure for these and other affinity groups. Google, Netflix, Apple, and others call them Employee Resource Groups (ERGs). Ask if your candidate companies have them, too.

Women in Cybersecurity

Women have historically been underrepresented in cybersecurity, making up only about a quarter of the workforce, despite their vital contributions to the field. This disparity has sparked the growth of organizations and initiatives designed to empower women, foster inclusion, and bridge the gender gap. Groups like Women in CyberSecurity (WiCyS) and Girls Who Code provide valuable resources, including mentorship programs, scholarships, networking opportunities, and community support.[23] [24] These organizations help women develop the skills and confidence needed to succeed in a male-dominated industry while advocating for systemic change to make the field more inclusive.

One of the challenges women often face in cybersecurity is overcoming stereotypes and biases that may exist in the workplace. For example, they may encounter skepticism about their technical abilities or find fewer women in leadership roles to look up to as mentors. Affinity groups play a crucial role in addressing these issues by connecting women with peers and role models who have navigated similar challenges. Events like the Grace Hopper Celebration, specifically focused on women in tech, offer

---

[23] https://www.wicys.org/.
[24] https://girlswhocode.com/.

opportunities to learn, network, and celebrate achievements, inspiring the next generation of female cybersecurity leaders.

Women may also bring strengths to cybersecurity, including strong communication, collaboration, and problem-solving skills, which are increasingly recognized as critical for success in the field. These qualities enable them to excel in roles like incident response, threat analysis, and governance, where the ability to work across teams and explain complex issues to non-technical stakeholders is essential. By participating in affinity groups and leveraging these skills, women can not only advance their own careers but also contribute to shaping a more diverse, equitable, and innovative cybersecurity landscape.

Neurodiversity in Cybersecurity

Neurodiversity in cybersecurity has emerged as a significant strength for the industry. Many organizations recognize that neurodiverse professionals—such as people with ADHD, autism, or dyslexia—often possess exceptional pattern recognition, detail orientation, and problem-solving abilities that are invaluable in threat detection and analysis. Affinity groups provide spaces where neurodiverse professionals can connect with mentors who understand their unique perspectives, share workplace accommodation strategies, and discuss how to leverage their distinct cognitive approaches in security roles. These communities help members translate their natural abilities into successful cybersecurity careers, such as sustained focus on complex systems, ability to spot anomalies, and innovative thinking.

For career changers, neurodiversity affinity groups offer particularly valuable insights into company cultures and hiring practices that support neurodiverse professionals. Members share experiences about employers with inclusive interview processes, flexible work arrangements, and sensory-friendly office environments. These groups often maintain relationships with organizations that have neurodiversity hiring programs, helping connect qualified candidates with positions that match their strengths. Additionally, many groups offer workshops on professional communication, executive functioning strategies, and career advancement specifically tailored to neurodiverse professionals in technical fields, making them an essential resource for those navigating both a career transition and workplace dynamics.

Veterans in Cybersecurity

Veterans are uniquely positioned to succeed in cybersecurity thanks to the skills and experiences they bring from their military service. Traits such as discipline, leadership, adaptability, and the ability to perform under pressure align closely with the demands of cybersecurity roles. Having (or having had) a security clearance is an asset. Additionally, veterans often have experience with risk assessment, securing sensitive information, and responding to threats—skills that translate directly into areas like incident response, threat hunting, and governance, risk, and compliance (GRC). Organizations such as VetSec, CyberVetsUSA, and the Department of Defense SkillBridge program help veterans transition into the cybersecurity workforce by providing tailored training, mentorship, and job placement opportunities.[25] [26] [27]

While veterans bring many strengths to cybersecurity, adapting to a civilian workplace culture can sometimes be a challenge. The collaborative and less hierarchical environments typical of tech industries may differ significantly from the structured chain of command in the military. Affinity groups and mentorship networks for veterans can ease this transition by providing a supportive community where individuals can share experiences, seek advice, and build connections. By combining their military-honed skills with new technical expertise and professional support, veterans can successfully transition into cybersecurity roles and make significant contributions to securing the digital frontier.

---

[25] https://vetsec.org/.
[26] https://www.cybervets.org/.
[27] https://skillbridge.osd.mil/.

Former Government Employees in Cybersecurity

Former government employees transitioning into cybersecurity bring a wealth of experience, particularly in areas like regulatory compliance, intelligence analysis, and risk management. Their familiarity with working under stringent protocols and handling sensitive or classified information aligns well with cybersecurity's emphasis on protecting data and adhering to legal standards. Many government roles, especially those related to defense, homeland security, or intelligence, provide a foundation in assessing threats, implementing controls, and understanding adversarial tactics—all of which are directly applicable to cybersecurity. Organizations like InfraGard and cybersecurity-focused professional networks offer resources to help former government employees leverage these skills as they enter the private sector.

The cultural shift from government to private-sector cybersecurity, however, can be a key adjustment. Private organizations typically operate with more flexibility and faster decision-making processes than government agencies. Former government employees may also encounter differences in resource allocation, where private-sector budgets and timelines might be less constrained but also more results-driven. Affinity groups and professional organizations can help bridge this gap by providing connections to peers who have successfully transitioned and offering advice on navigating corporate dynamics.

Balancing Tactical Work with Overhead

If there is one adjective to describe the work of cybersecurity, that word might be: tactical.

People describe cybersecurity work as "tactical" because it often involves immediate, hands-on actions to address specific threats, mitigate risks, and respond to incidents. Furthermore, professionals frequently deal with situations that demand quick thinking and problem-solving under pressure. If there is a malware infection or active phishing attack, response is needed immediately. Actions such as isolating compromised systems are also short-term measures compared to broader strategic goals like designing long-term security architectures.

A specific cybersecurity job may be attractive specifically because of the hands-on technical or operational work. For instance, daily tasks like running scans and analyzing logs are direct and technical. Even in those roles, almost everyone has overhead. Overhead, in this context, refers to the necessary but non-tactical tasks and activities that support an employee's ability to perform their core technical duties. It encompasses everything required to maintain personal and organizational functionality, from attending meetings to preparing reports.

Cybersecurity involves a significant amount of administrative work, often overshadowing the hands-on technical tasks that draw many professionals to the field. The more senior people become, the more administrative work tends to be involved. Beyond responding to threats and managing systems, cybersecurity practitioners are responsible for maintaining documentation, such as incident reports, compliance records, and risk assessments. They must attend meetings to coordinate with other departments, align with organizational goals, and communicate technical findings to non-technical stakeholders. Policy development, user training, and vendor evaluations also fall under the administrative umbrella. Compliance with regulations such as HIPAA, GDPR, or the Payment Card Industry Data Security Standard (PCI DSS) often requires meticulous tracking and reporting. While administrative work can feel removed from the action, it plays a critical role in building a robust security posture, ensuring accountability, and enabling seamless operations during high-pressure incidents. Balancing this workload requires both organizational skills and a clear understanding of priorities.

Because we don't go into a job because of the overhead, it feels like a painful burden. How can you find a balance? Overall, prioritize and streamline non-technical tasks. Start by identifying which overhead activities directly support or enhance your core responsibilities, such as documenting incident responses to improve future workflows. Next, use tools and automation to reduce repetitive tasks, like creating templates for reports or scheduling recurring meetings during low-productivity times. Practice boundary setting by respectfully declining non-essential activities that don't align with your role's objectives. Finally, adopt a mindset that sees overhead as an opportunity to amplify impact—framing reports as a chance to communicate value or meetings as platforms to gain support for necessary resources. This approach not only reduces the pain of overhead but also ensures it contributes to long-term career success.

> ### Case Study: Penetration Testing
>
> Carlos works for a company that provides services in penetration testing. When a business wants to know how an attacker might try and break in, they hire a penetration testing firm who emulates those attackers but, instead of causing damage, delivers a report about where and how to strengthen the client's security.
>
> Carlos works regular 8-hour days. While there are busy times and slow times, on average he spends 4 hours per day on the actual technical work of the job. He spends 1 hour on preparation (reviewing notes and making plans for the work), 1 hour on wrap-up (analysis and documentation), and 2 hours in meetings and email.

What Is Stressful about Working in Cybersecurity?

Here are a few statements that you might hear from people doing their cybersecurity jobs:

- "What is going on with our systems? If we don't get back online the business is going to fail."
- "This situation is so complex I can't get my head around it."
- "I've been staring at this problem for days and just can't figure it out."

Those statements can be motivational for people who love challenges. For others, they are stressful. It depends on you and your mentality. Many people have described cybersecurity as solving puzzles. Others describe it as a drug!

First, all stress is subjective. People experience stress differently and have different capacities for handling stressful situations. Stress management can be learned, and we encourage you to make that part of your self-improvement.

You can be better prepared for the stress of a cybersecurity role with a few simple rules. Remember that cybersecurity is not an end state, but instead a continual process. That context means there we always end up leaving a to-do list when we stop working each day. A related area of stress (and burnout) is appreciating our value and worth. When the problems of cybersecurity seem never-ending—like one incident after another—it's natural to think, "What difference does it make... there's just going to be more...?" But this work does matter, and every attack prevented and problem resolved helps people and organizations protect the things they value.

Many security professionals eventually encounter the frustration of trying to advocate for essential security measures while facing resistance from management or colleagues who view security as an obstacle rather than a necessity. This challenge becomes particularly acute when dealing with stakeholders who not only lack understanding of security principles, but actively resist learning about them, often dismissing security concerns as overly paranoid or viewing security teams as the "Department of No" despite the fact that we are trying to protect both them and the organization from very real threats.

Finally, remember that important parts of cybersecurity success are out of our control. An elite athlete can control their diet and study the competition, but they cannot control the weather. Similarly, we cannot fully control when or how an attacker decides to target us. This is frustrating! In psychology, *locus of control* describes a large field of knowledge and research about the stress that comes when we don't have the power to change our circumstances. We can combat this by focusing on the things within our control, like how we spend the next hour of our day.

In Chapter 14 "Maintaining Work-Life Balance" we will explore additional ways to find balance and resilience for stress.

Chapter Summary

- Cybersecurity is a unique field with its own language. Understanding the jargon and acronyms of cybersecurity is essential for effective communication and confidence.

- Transitioning into cybersecurity builds on existing skills. Your background in IT, engineering, military, law enforcement, or risk management provides a strong foundation for cybersecurity roles.

- A proactive mindset is critical in cybersecurity. Cybersecurity demands anticipating and preventing threats rather than reacting to problems after they arise.

- Affinity groups can accelerate your success. Joining communities like Women in Cybersecurity or VetSec can provide mentorship, support, and professional growth opportunities.

- Expect a mix of tactical work and administrative tasks. Cybersecurity combines technical problem-solving with responsibilities like documentation, compliance, and reporting.

- Cybersecurity roles require continuous learning. The field evolves rapidly, so staying current with new threats, tools, and frameworks is essential for long-term success.

- Stress management is part of cybersecurity. Challenges like evolving threats and incomplete control require resilience and a focus on what you can manage.

- Your work in cybersecurity has real impact. Preventing attacks and resolving issues protects people, organizations, and critical systems, making your efforts highly meaningful.

Chapter References

Carey, M. J. and Jin, J. (2019). *Tribe of Hackers: Cybersecurity Advice from the Best Hackers in the World.* John Wiley & Sons.

CybersSeek (2025). https://www.cyberseek.org/pathway.html

Cyberwire (2024). Career Notes Podcast. https://thecyberwire.com/podcasts/career-notes.

Chapter 5

Choosing a Specialization

Why Specialize?

In previous chapters we have helped you think about your motivations, how your skills align to a cybersecurity career, what the market looks like, and how to understand what your daily work might entail. It's time to put all those things together and decide what kind of cybersecurity role you want to pursue so you can efficiently navigate referral networks, companies, and industries.

Even though you are still working through a broad move to cybersecurity, there are many advantages to considering specialization:

- Articulating where your interests lie will help you find mentors and advocates who can prepare you for the kind of role you want to have, without wasting time drinking beverages with people doing work you don't care about.

- Understanding where you want to specialize will help you assess your skills, identify any gaps, get training where needed, and generally prepare yourself for the role.

- Knowing your focus areas will help you write your resume and target companies who do interesting work in the function of your choice—leading to longer term career satisfaction. You will also show up more prepared for interviews and more ready to take on a cybersecurity job.

The career progression of most cybersecurity professionals involves starting in a place where there is a single focus. It might be a technology type (networks, cloud, IoT devices), or a functional focus (identity management, risk management, vulnerability management). Once a person learns the security of that first area, they then choose how to expand. This could be becoming a deep subject matter expert in that same area, branching out to adjacent security fields, or even applying the same security function to a different industry. The progression from single focus to broad/deep focus is a mark of a mature security professional. For jobseekers, then, it makes sense to think about that first steppingstone—where you want to start, as a springboard to the rest of your career.

Find a Problem to Solve

In his blog "Unsupervised Learning," Daniel Miessler writes about identifying a "problem to solve"[28] as a way of approaching the cybersecurity industry. Focusing on a problem instead of a job role will help you identify areas of passion/interest and help you think broadly about all the functional stakeholders involved in solving that problem, giving you more than one role to consider as your entry point into the industry.

When I (Helen) was working as an IT manager in the early 1990's, my company was constantly suffering disruptions due to internet worms and viruses. I was not only annoyed that my daily plans were being upended, but I was offended that someone could get away with it. My problem to solve was how to design our technology so the number of unplanned interruptions were minimized. Trying to solve this problem took me first to business continuity management, and later to third party risk management, and later still to cybersecurity policy think tanks. "Availability" is a core security tenet, and also the reason I started in (and stay in) the security profession.

What problems are you curious about? Table 5.1 shows some suggestions to get you thinking (and to add to your journal).

---

[28] https://danielmiessler.com/p/plan-career-around-problems.

Circumstance	Problem To Solve	Possible Cybersecurity Roles
My company was hit by ransomware and it hurt	Companies need help preparing for and responding to ransomware events	Incident Response SOC Analyst/Manager Incident Manager Business Continuity/Disaster Recovery BC/DR Planner Security Engineering Email Security Endpoint Security Identity and Access Management (IAM) Governance Risk and Compliance (GRC) Cyber Lawyer Cyber Insurance Agent Security Analyst Cybersecurity Auditor
Family members have been tricked by online fakes and scams	People need help identifying deep fakes and online security	Training and Awareness Trainer Cybersecurity Analyst Security Engineering Identity and Access Management AI Cybersecurity Analyst Web Designer Threat Detection and Response
A local emergency services center was disabled due to a cyber event	Critical Infrastructure organizations require cybersecurity support	Security Engineering Operational Technology (OT) Security Network Security Endpoint Security Threat Detection and Response Cybersecurity Analyst Cybersecurity Policy Analyst

Table 5.1 – Example circumstances of problems to solve and possible cybersecurity roles.

Circumstance	Problem To Solve	Possible Cybersecurity Roles
Logging into consumer websites is really annoying	Improve the consumer IAM experience	Identity and Access Management IAM Engineer Authentication Engineer Access Operations Analyst Website Management Web Designer Application Security Engineer
I completed my military service and....	Defend the country against nation-state cyber attacks	Incident Response SOC Analyst/Manager Incident Manager Threat Detection & Response Cybersecurity Analyst Cybersecurity Policy Analyst Business Continuity/Disaster Recovery BC/DR Planner Incident Manager
The pandemic changed how and where people work	Making identification and authorization easier in a remote/hybrid working environment	Identity and Access Management JAM Engineer Authentication Engineer Access Operations Analyst Security Engineering Network Security Endpoint Security

Table 5.1 – Example circumstances of problems to solve and possible cybersecurity roles (continued).

Exploring Security Domains

Unfortunately, there is no authoritative map of the security profession. In order to work out where to specialize, you'll need to cobble together a number of ways of thinking about security to create your own map. Having mental models that focus on functional areas, or "jobs to be done,[29]" or technologies to manage, may be a way to slice the cybersecurity profession into manageable, bite-sized chunks.

NIST Cybersecurity Framework

The most common functional framework for security is the NIST Cybersecurity Framework (CSF).[30] The CSF defines six functional domains for security, with associated subcategories. These are summarized in Table 5.2.

---

[29] The phrase "jobs to be done" is commonly used in the world of innovation, including by Clay Christensen. One article writes that "'Job' is shorthand for what an individual really seeks to accomplish in a given circumstance." For more, see https://hbr.org/2016/09/know-your-customers-jobs-to-be-done.

[30] NIST Cybersecurity Framework v2.0: https://nvlpubs.nist.gov/nistpubs/CSWP/NIST.CSWP.29.pdf.

Function	Description	Subcategories
Govern	The organization's cybersecurity risk management strategy, expectations, and policy are established, communicated, and monitored.	Organizational Context Risk Management Strategy Roles, Responsibilities, and Authorities Policy Oversight Supply Chain Risk Management
Identify	The organization's current cybersecurity risks are understood.	Asset Management Risk Assessment Improvement
Protect	Safeguards to manage the organization's cybersecurity risks are used.	Identity Management, Authentication, and Access Control Awareness and Training Data Security Platform Security Technology Infrastructure Resilience
Detect	Possible cybersecurity attacks and compromises are found and analyzed.	Continuous Monitoring Adverse Event Analysis
Respond	Actions regarding a detected cybersecurity incident are taken.	Incident Management Incident Response Reporting and Communication Incident Mitigation
Recover	Assets and operations affected by a cybersecurity incident are restored.	Incident Recovery Plan Execution Incident Recovery Communication

Table 5.2 – The NIST Cybersecurity Framework.

For example:

- Problem: Identifying deep fakes
- NIST Function(s): Protect or Detect
- Sub-Categories/Possible Roles: Identity Management; Awareness and Training; Adverse Event Analysis

Or:

- Problem: Critical Infrastructure Protection
- NIST Function(s): Govern; Identify; Protect; Detect; Respond; Recover

- Sub-Categories/Possible Roles: Policy; Supply Chain Risk Management; Risk Assessment; Technology Infrastructure Resilience; Continuous Monitoring; Incident Management; Incident Recovery Plan Execution

In the second example, you can see that the problem statement is so broad that it potentially covers every functional area. A jobseeker addressing this problem might consider narrowing the problem statement or simply focusing on one of the functional areas ("I'd rather be a protector than a responder").

NICE Work Role Categories

The U.S. federal government's National Initiative for Cybersecurity Careers and Studies (NICCS) has created a NICE Workforce Framework for Cybersecurity jobs.[31] Written primarily for government security jobs, it can be a useful reference for mid-career jobseekers looking to understand how skills and jobs fit together. The NICE Framework breaks the cyber workforce into seven categories (see Table 5.3) with 52 related work roles, then links those to skills and competencies.

---

[31] https://niccs.cisa.gov/workforce-development/nice-framework.

Category	Description
Oversight and Governance	Provides leadership, management, direction, and advocacy so the organization may effectively manage cybersecurity-related risks to the enterprise and conduct cybersecurity work.
Design and Development	Conducts research, conceptualizes, designs, develops and tests secure technology systems, including on perimeter and cloud-based networks.
Implementation and Operation	Provides implementation, administration, configuration, operation and maintenance to ensure effective and efficient technology system performance and security.
Protection and Defense	Protects against, identifies and analyzes risks to technology systems or networks. Includes investigation of cybersecurity events or crimes related to technology systems or networks.
Investigation	Conducts national security and cybercrime investigations, including the collection, management and analysis of digital evidence.
Cyberspace Intelligence	Collects, processes, analyzes and disseminates information on all sources of intelligence on foreign actors' cyberspace programs, intentions, capabilities, research and development, and operational activities.
Cyberspace Effects	Plans, supports, and executes cyberspace capabilities where the primary purpose is to externally defend or conduct force projection in or through cyberspace.

Table 5.3 – NICE Framework workforce categories.

Each category contains work roles, and each work role contains task, knowledge and skill statements. For the uninitiated, the amount of information here can be overwhelming. Remember that:

- This is meant to be a framework and guide that is still under development, not a list of must-have skills and experiences.

- It is focused on government cybersecurity jobs, so security-adjacent roles like sales or project management or security training/awareness aren't included.

Consider this a reference to help organize your thoughts. Read the skills needed for each role, and the kind of knowledge you might need. If it fits what you're looking for, or your background—great! If not, move on. For example:

- Problem: Protecting Critical Infrastructure
- NIST Function(s): Protect
- NICE Work Category: Protection and Defense
- Possible NICE Work Roles: Defensive Cybersecurity; Infrastructure Support; Threat Analysis; Vulnerability Analysis

Certifications

Another way to explore the cybersecurity field is to investigate the different kinds of certifications, and understand the topics included in each certification. An internet search of "Cybersecurity Certifications [current year]" will give you a list to start with. Completing this as an image search will reveal a number of charts that show the breadth of certifications available.

For example, the Certified Ethical Hacker[32] certification from EC-Council includes the following topics:

Introduction	Footprinting and Reconnaissance	Scanning Networks	Enumeration
Vulnerability Analysis	System Hacking	Malware Threats	Sniffing
Social Engineering	Denial-of-Service	Session Hijacking	Evading IDS, Firewalls, and Honeypots
Hacking Web Servers	Hacking Web Applications	SQL Injection	Hacking Wireless Networks
Hacking Mobile Platforms	IoT and OT Hacking	Cloud Computing	Cryptography

Table 5.4 – EC-Council Certified Ethical Hacker certification course outline.

As you can see from Table 5.4, being an ethical hacker requires a deep understanding of technology (although to get the certification

---

[32] https://www.eccouncil.org/train-certify/certified-ethical-hacker-ceh/.

the providers recommend only two years of prior IT experience). If you have spent time in the IT domain already as a systems engineer or other hands-on technology role, ethical hacking may be a security function for you to pursue. If not, keep looking.

Alternatively, you might look at Governance, Risk, and Compliance (GRC) certifications. For the ISC2 CGRC certification, the learning topics include the following.[33]

- Security and Privacy Governance, Risk Management, and Compliance Program
- Scope of the System
- Selection and Approval of Framework, Security, and Privacy Controls
- Implementation of Security and Privacy Controls
- Assessment/Audit of Security and Privacy Controls
- System Compliance
- Compliance Maintenance

Here, there is still an assumption of technical knowledge, but the coursework is more about applying frameworks and risk assessments to technology than hands-on technology activities. This kind of focus may be more appropriate for someone who has less (but not zero!) technical acumen and is more interested in governance and organizational design for a day-to-day job.

Choosing a Function

Another way to choose where to start is to consider the functional areas of a cybersecurity team and choose a role that aligns to your interests and the hiring market. When taking this approach, you must first realize that the size of the organization is the primary determinant of the size of the security team, and the functions included within it. According to a 2024 Security Benchmark Study by IANS Research, most organizations have small teams with only

---

[33] https://www.isc2.org/certifications/cgrc.

the large publicly traded companies being big enough to support multiple security functions.[34]

Type	Security FTE	Security budget range and median	Annual revenue range and sample median	Security characteristics
Fortune-size organizations	Range: 50+ Median: 88	Range: $10M+ Median: $40M	Range: $6B+ Median: $2.5B	• Highly complex security initiatives • Large, specialized security workforce covering comprehensive security measures • Adhering to a complex set of local, national and international laws, regulations and governing bodies
Large organizations	Range: 10-50 Median: 22	Range: $2.5M-$10M Median: $7M	Range: $400M-$6B Median: $2.5B	• Moderate to substantial security requirements • Dedicated security team responsible for a range of security functions
Midsize organizations	Range: <15	Range: $1M-$5M Median: $1.4M	Range: $50M-$400M Median: $300M	• Limited security requirements • Small, focused security team handling essential security measures

Table 5.5 – IANS Research and Artico search – types of security organizations.

This means that jobseekers pursuing small organizations will find roles that are generalist, doing essential security functions such as vulnerability management, detection and response, endpoint management, etc. Job roles are usually advertised as "security analyst" or "security engineer" but often show up as "network engineer" or "identity engineer," with only a part of the role being security-focused (these can be terrific "bridge" jobs into cybersecurity for those with a technical background).

Most enterprise security organizations start small and grow, so most organizations will start with these essential functions then add more as the organizations grow, as shown in Table 5.6.

---

[34] https://www.iansresearch.com/resources/ians-leadership-organization-benchmark-report.

Organization Size	Typical Security Functions
Small Organizations	May have no dedicated security teams. Functions are often blended with other IT roles • Heavy use of managed security service providers (MSSPs) and other external support
Mid-Size Organizations	Security Operations Vulnerability Management Cross-functional analysts, engineers Governance, Risk and Compliance
Large-Size Organizations	Mid-Size functions, plus: • Architects and Engineers • Identity and Access Management • Application Security • Adjacent Functions (e.g., project management, communications, etc.)
Publicly Traded Organizations	Large-Size Functions, plus: • Product Security • Sub-Business Security Teams (distributed security) Limited use of MSSPs

Table 5.6 – Typical security functions based on size of organization.

The security team in any organization should be aligned to the business needs of the organization it supports, so every organization will have slightly different functional roles. For example, a large company involved in a lot of mergers and acquisitions may include a dedicated security function for evaluating and managing companies that are to be acquired. An organization that sells products to government clients may have a dedicated team that ensures products are certified to meet regulatory requirements. Understanding the industry of an organization, not just the size, will help a jobseeker identify the kinds of functions available.

Remember in the first part of the book we asked you to consider the kind of organization you wanted to work for? Here is why it matters—if you want to work for a start-up, the security roles will likely be generalist roles, or you may even find work with an MSSP supporting multiple startups. If you want to work for a publicly traded organization, there are likely to be many kinds of security functions available to consider. This may also be the place where people with less technical backgrounds can find functional areas to match their professional skills.

Choosing a Technology Function

A jobseeker may choose to start their cybersecurity career by focusing on different parts of the technology stack (there are different stacks for different purposes!) and looking to understand the threats and vulnerabilities of that technology, and how to protect or attack that piece of technology. At its most simplistic, you may consider:

- Users
- Data
- Networks
- Applications
- Devices

If you have already worked in a technology job, this might be an easy choice. Worked as a network engineer? Start by working in securing networks. Application developer? Move into a security team as an application security engineer. Worked as a business analyst? Consider protecting users as a security trainer, or identity management analyst.

If there are no technology jobs on your resume, consider the technology you use every day. If you're heavy into using Microsoft Office at work, perhaps considering data security is a place to start. If you play a lot of computer games, consider application security. If you can't stay off your mobile phone, perhaps learning mobile device security would be something to consider.

A way to think about this is to use Sounil Yu's Cyber Defense Matrix, which combines the five NIST functional areas with the five technology asset types (Figure 5.1).[35]

	Identify	Protect	Detect	Respond	Recover
Devices					
Applications					
Networks					
Data					
Users					
Degree of Dependency	Technology		Process/Govern		People

Figure 5.1 – Cyber defense matrix.

You can see from this chart that the "Identify" and "Protect" functions rely more heavily on technology, whereas the "Respond" and "Recover" functions rely more on people and processes. In the matrix, the governance function crosses all technologies. You'll notice that it is its own functional area in the NIST framework—Sounil created the matrix when Version 1 of the CSF existed, and governance wasn't a distinct function in Version 1—an example of how quickly things change!

If you already have a technical background, considering a role that is an engineering or analyst function for any of the technical asset types might be a good fit for your current skills. If not, consider working in governance, business continuity, disaster recovery or

[35] https://cyberdefensematrix.com/.

other incident response functions, learning about your technology of choice as a focus, might be a useful place to start. Typically, you will have, for example, a security operations team that is responsible for detection/response activities across the entire technology stack. Or you will have an application security team, but that team will *also* need to understand how the applications interact with networks, devices, and data. There will be, perhaps, an identity management team—and they will cover all kinds of identities, not just user identities.

One of the few exceptions to this is people who secure operational technologies (OT). OT is the hardware and software that monitors and controls devices, processes, and infrastructure. Typically found in manufacturing or critical infrastructure organizations, OT security engineers would focus on all NIST functions but only for OT devices. So, while it can help frame your thinking to consider which technologies you may want to focus on first, this is only to get entry into an operational team where you will apply your functional understanding across all technology types.

Choosing an Operational Function

In practice, most security organizations are organized by function, not by technology type. Teams are also not cleanly organized by NIST functions like Protect or Detect but instead by functions that deliver a security outcome. Security teams are always influenced by the nuances of their age, industry, regulatory profile and so on, but there are common functions to look for. Here are a few operational functions and their associated work.

Governance Functions

In order to be successful in a governance role, you must have a basic level of technology knowledge. However, the majority of the workday is spent focusing on people, processes, and organizational management. Typically, we classify all kinds of governance into the GRC function: governance, risk, and compliance, even though each of these functions are slightly different.

- *Governance teams* focus on setting and enforcing security policies within an organization. They understand security frameworks like NIST, OWASP, and others, and determine which frameworks need to be in place to support the business. For example, if you were working for a hospital you may be asked to develop, enforce, and audit security policies that align with HIPAA. Analysts in the GRC function are primarily translators between regulatory requirements and the way an organization conducts business, so there is a high need for empathic individuals who can creatively apply regulations and enforce organizational change.

- *Risk teams* align with governance and compliance teams but work to determine resource priorities and strategic remediation projects. Much of this work involves data analytics and the creation of management reporting that will allow leadership to make business decisions about risk management. In larger organizations they may also partner with other kinds of risk managers who make up an enterprise risk management function, so they are not only managing cyber risk but are negotiating with other kinds of operational risk functions to determine prioritization across the entire organization. In a hospital, you might be responsible for assessing and prioritizing cybersecurity risks to the network, then working with IT to mitigate threats to patient data and hospital operations.

- *Compliance teams* may reside within the security team, or often they may exist in the legal/compliance teams. They partner with governance and risk teams to ensure the organization meets legal, contractual, and regulatory requirements. This function has a very close relationship to privacy management, often sharing responsibilities with the privacy function. A hospital compliance team would monitor adherence to HIPAA, conduct internal audits, and prepare for external audits.

As you can see, there is significant overlap between these three sub-functions. In small- to mid-size organizations a single team may cover all of these sub-functions simultaneously.

Governance functions are often considered a good place for mid-career jobseekers to begin their security careers if those seekers come from less technical roles. Business analysts, project managers, teachers/trainers, logistics experts, lawyers, and others can often find complementary skills in the GRC function.

Identity Management

Identity management is like having a super organized clubhouse. Everyone who wants to get in has to show a special pass that proves who they are (identity), and the clubhouse rules decide which rooms they can go into (access). It helps keep the clubhouse safe and makes sure only the right people can use the right spaces. Identity management is a function that is fundamental to securing an organization and has both technical and non-technical components. In fact, because it has close procedural ties to groups like human resources and purchasing, it may not sit in the security team at all. Of all the security functions, this one is the most visible to the non-technology parts of an organization. Every employee or customer must interface with this team's processes at some point so the ability to work with multiple stakeholders is very important. Identity management has a number of sub-functions, including but not limited to:

- *Access Management* (AM): Where an operations team determines the level of privileges assigned to people in an organization and implements these privileges in applications and other technology systems. These teams work closely with application development teams to ensure the lifecycle of access across an employee's work life is efficiently and effectively managed. The work of individuals does not require deep technical experience, but people who work in these teams learn technical skills quickly due to the nature of the job.

- *Privileged Account Management* (PAM): Understanding and managing accounts that have extra "privilege" in an organization. This is usually a heavily technical role, managing authorization and authentication for people, applications, and devices that require administrative privileges beyond those of a typical user.

- *Identity and Access Management* (IAM): Identities could be internal (employees, contractors) or external (customers, consumers, partners). This function may also include managing identity systems such as the central identity database, multi-factor authentication, and password management. These roles are technical, and partner closely with systems and application teams.

People coming into cybersecurity with a strong understanding of business processes can often find roles in the access management function, because they not only understand the applications used in an organization but *why* and *how* those applications are used, which are important skills for AM analysts.

Software developers and systems integrators can find roles in the PAM and IAM spaces, where they engineer processes to manage authentication and authorization systems.

Vulnerability Management

Most security teams include a vulnerability management (VM) function. At its most basic, VM includes scanning the technology stack for vulnerabilities, ranking those vulnerabilities in order of risk, ensuring known vulnerabilities are remediated or risk is appropriately accepted, and reporting to management about the state of vulnerabilities in the environment.

In practice, the VM team is most involved in scanning and reporting—it is the general IT teams that are responsible for patching or otherwise managing the vulnerabilities in the environment. The security team members need to have a technical understanding of the hardware and software environments they scan, and act as advisors and engineers to the rest of the IT organization to help them mitigate their vulnerabilities.

Security Operations

Most jobseekers think of the Security Operations function when they first think about a security career. While every organization has slightly different security operations functions, "SecOps" usually includes:

- Security Monitoring, which may be done by an internal team or an outsourced contracting team. Security Operations Centers, or SOCs, are the place where systems are monitored in real-time to detect and respond to security incidents. SOC Analysts are a common entry-level role for cybersecurity professionals.

- Incident Response teams, which activate when a security incident or major vulnerability event occurs. This team may be part of the SOC, or a stand-alone team. Companies that sell software products may have incident response teams for their central company as well as incident response teams for individual products they sell.

- Vulnerability Management, as described previously. In some organizations the VM function is part of, not separate from, the Security Operations team.

For mid-career jobseekers who have a background in IT, the SecOps function can be a great place to start a cybersecurity career. The roles are operational—there is a requirement to be consistently available, follow prescribed playbooks and processes, and be on-call most of the time. Ex-military jobseekers can often find compatible skills in incident response and monitoring functions, even if they have less IT experience.

Application Security

For companies that have their own software development teams, the security team needs to include professionals that enable secure software development. "AppSec" teams enable development teams to securely code, test, deploy, and manage software.

Joining an application security team requires a background in software development. Jobseekers who have on-the-job experience with any kind of coding or development can move into these roles, even if their particular language or software background isn't exactly the same as the target company—but it does make it easier if you have matching software languages and testing tooling. Some people pursue coding bootcamps or other academic learning pathways to get the application development experience needed to move into these roles—but the job is more than just coding. Security team members must understand the software development lifecycle, testing techniques and best practices.

Security Engineering

Sometimes security engineering can be part of an operations team. Other times, it is its own function. Security engineers work to secure devices, networks, servers, operational technologies, and other asset types.

Often, people move into security engineering from other IT fields. Network engineers become security network engineers. Help desk technicians become security engineers for mobile devices or servers. To work in this field, expect to understand how these devices work, what makes them vulnerable to attack, and what kinds of security controls are used to mitigate those vulnerabilities.

Security engineering can also be a function of a sales organization— particularly for companies that sell security products and services. Security sales engineers help customers assess, procure, design, and implement security solutions, so they need a strong technical and customer service background.

Security Adjacent Functions

In large- to enterprise-size companies, a security team is usually big enough to not only have the core functional areas discussed above, but supporting functions that make the team work more effectively. These could be roles such as:

- Project and Program Management
- Chief of Staff
- Marketing
- Product Management
- Finance/Business Management
- Training and Awareness
- Business Analysts

These wouldn't necessarily be in their own teams. Instead, they may be blended into other teams in single contributor roles.

These kinds of positions are terrific for people who have similar backgrounds in other disciplines. For example, you may have done a traditional finance or accounting job elsewhere, but can move to the security team and work directly with that team. The proximity will allow you to continue using the skills you have while learning more about the security function and gaining on-the-job experience alongside the other functional security teams.

The goal with specialization is to take your experience, skills, and interests and align them to the closest available security role. Doing this will allow you to find the fastest path into the cybersecurity world, from which you can then move about as your career develops. Doing this upfront work will save you a lot of time while job searching and will help you be successful once you land a role.

What About Generalists?

The larger the organization, the more likely it is to find people who specialize in a particular security function, however, most security teams are small - less than ten people, and workers in these teams are, by necessity, generalists. Their day-to-day jobs may include working on governance frameworks, monitoring the technology environment, or giving security awareness training to co-workers.

As people progress through their security career, they can choose to go deeply in one specialization, but many people will go broadly understanding how all the component parts of security and business work together. This is another form of generalization that allows senior management to be relatively well-versed in a lot of security functions, enabling them to orchestrate larger teams.

Our suggestion to consider a specialty is a technique to help you know where to start but will likely not be where you finish. Instead, it's a launch point that can allow you to use one kind of cybersecurity role to better understand and utilize all the others, progressing you from junior - or mid-level roles to senior ones.

Chapter Summary

- Why Specialize? Choosing a specialization allows you to focus your networking, training, and job-seeking energy into roles that best suit your existing skills and experience.

- Choose a Problem to Solve: By identifying a problem to solve you can target the kinds of security disciplines that are most interesting to you.

- Review Security Frameworks: These will help you understand how the security profession thinks and how it is organized.

- Learn About Security Functions: Talk to people in the different functional areas to get a feel for what they do and how your skills may transfer over.

- Begin With a Specialization: Use your specialization to find a way into cybersecurity, then move upwards or outwards from there.

Chapter References

Miessler, Daniel, (2024). "Plan Your Career Around Problems." https://danielmiessler.com/p/plan-career-around-problems.

Chapter 6

Getting Hired

As a mid-career professional, you've already worked in at least a couple of places, have a feel for the kind of organization that will work best for you, and know the kind of manager you need (or want to be). Every job has the capacity for positive and negative stress; cybersecurity is no different. Where you work will have a huge impact on your stress levels. Choosing the right company and manager will help you transition successfully into cybersecurity. In this chapter, we'll talk about what a security professional should look for in a hiring organization, manager, and team so that you can maximize the chance of landing a role that works for you long term.

What to Look for in a Hiring Organization

When interviewing for a cybersecurity role, a jobseeker should assess the culture of the overall organization, including to understand if cybersecurity is supported. No company is perfect, but taking time to assess the following attributes will allow you to be prepared for the culture of the organization you are joining and help you mitigate any red flags (or walk away completely). Cybersecurity employers expect you to have a list of questions. Include these topics in your list for hiring managers and other people you interview about a company.

Attribute #1: A Learning Organization

Because cybersecurity evolves so quickly, cybersecurity professionals must have the time and space to learn about new technologies, tactics, techniques, and procedures at a minimum. Very few things remain constant in this field, and your company should understand and support you in your continuous learning journey.

There are several ways to keep learning. Consider:

- Self-paced training: Does the company pay for subscriptions to learning tools, solutions, or vendor training, such as Udemy or SANS, that you can use as part of your role?

- Reference items: Does the company have access to digital libraries (e.g., Safari Books Online), or will they reimburse you for books and other resources?

- Certifications: Will the company pay for you to prepare for testing for certifications? Will they pay for annual membership fees for certification organizations or professional societies such as ACM? Will they cover the cost of tests and continuing education requirements?

- Conferences: Will the company cover the cost of registrations and travel to industry conferences?

- Mentoring: Does the company provide a mentoring program or encourage mentoring relationships?

Remember that training isn't only about cybersecurity skills (although, in the beginning, this should be your primary focus). Training on industry trends, professional skills such as communications or leadership, and other business-related training should be part of the continuous learning you do in your career. For instance, every cybersecurity professional should know the latest trends in cybercrime and ransomware technology.

Attribute #2: Flexible Work Hours

The nature of cybersecurity work is that some weeks require less effort, and some weeks require lots of effort and hours. Consider that in addition to the day-to-day requirements of a cybersecurity job, there may *also* be the following peak activities:

- A SOC analyst responding to a cybersecurity incident may be asked to contribute round-the-clock support while in the early days of an incident investigation.

- A GRC analyst responding to an external audit may be asked to put in long hours against an arbitrary deadline to provide evidence of controls to a third party.

- A pentester may work multiple consecutive hours to test the controls of a target.

- A cybersecurity sales engineer may put in long hours against a looming deadline, designing security architecture as part of a "request for proposal" to submit to a potential client.

- A cybersecurity product manager may need to work long hours in a short timeframe to meet a deadline committed to the market to release a new security feature.

The reality is that an employee can't put in a regular work week and also respond to emergencies, fires, or high-volume commitments. Not without burning out, at least. A jobseeker should ask:

- How does a company manage the peak workloads that come along with this cybersecurity job?

- What paid time off or other time off policies are acceptable (not just what is a policy) to the organization?

- How does that organization approach work-life balance?

A person looking for a cybersecurity job should expect that the role will come with some amount of high-hour work—but you should also expect that the company has considered how to manage employees so that a person isn't continuously working a full-time schedule *plus* high-volume periods. They should have the flexibility for the cybersecurity team to manage the peaks and the associated recovery times. Often, this will not be a company-wide policy but will come down to the individual manager of the cybersecurity team—so remember to ask these questions not just of the hiring manager but of the recruiter and anyone else you get to interview to see what the overall culture of the organization accepts.

Attribute #3: Operational Maturity

Mature companies are ones where day-to-day processes are well-documented, understood, monitored, and optimized. Operational maturity typically happens when an organization is bigger and older than its peers. But even within a big company there may be some pockets that are very mature, while others are less so. Smaller companies and start-ups are the least likely to be operationally mature.

Why should a cybersecurity jobseeker look for this quality in a company? In most cases, the cybersecurity professional is asked to implement security controls on top of existing company processes—the security team is rarely part of the initial planning and design of a process. To do the job well the company needs to have solid processes, particularly around technology processes like asset management, technology governance, change management, software development, and the like. When an organization lacks operational maturity, the job of the cybersecurity professional is so much more difficult.

On the other hand, a cybersecurity professional can make a big difference in helping an organization mature its operational processes—but it would mean the individual would be spending less time on cybersecurity and more on IT or business operations.

Jobseekers should ask about the maturity of IT and business operations in the recruiting organization. Immaturity isn't immediately a disqualifier but should be well understood before taking on a role, particularly a mid-career or management role, where your success will be measured by how much you impact the rest of the organization.

What If You're Seen as Overqualified?

Mid-career professionals may face a surprising barrier when transitioning into cybersecurity: being perceived as *overqualified*. Even when you're willing to take a junior or entry-level role to break into the field, hiring managers may hesitate. They worry you'll be bored, expect too much autonomy, reject basic tasks, or leave quickly for a more senior position. These concerns aren't personal they're risk calculations made to protect team cohesion, onboarding investment, and long-term retention.

Understanding this perception is key to overcoming it. The burden is on you to **reframe your experience as a strength** rather than a mismatch. In your resume and interviews, emphasize:

- **Your enthusiasm for learning and growth**, not just what you already know
- **Your respect for the complexity of the new role**, even if it seems more junior
- **Your track record of being coachable, collaborative, and adaptable**
- A clear explanation of why you're pursuing cybersecurity now, and how it fits into your longer-term goals
- **Your commitment to the organization's mission**, not just the job title

A well-framed narrative shows that you're not "settling" you're making a deliberate, strategic move. When done effectively, your prior experience becomes a differentiator, not a deterrent.

Attribute #4: Security Culture

In any organization, culture starts at the top. What do the organization's leaders say and do about cybersecurity? Do they talk about it at all? If they talk about it, do they support the cybersecurity team's goals? Do they encourage the rest of the organization to consider security as part of their core functions? Most cybersecurity professionals want their leadership to be more proactive about cybersecurity objectives. Pragmatically, cybersecurity is rarely a primary business objective but something that needs to be done so other business objectives can get done.

For jobseekers, assessing the security culture of the prospective organization is very important. If cybersecurity is under-valued at an organization, it can mean that funding won't be available to do security the way it needs to be done, that the security team will be treated as purely a back-office cost center, that security activities will be deprioritized against other goals. In short, a poor security culture will make your job much, much more difficult. Even if you are seeking a "front office" cybersecurity role, like a cybersecurity sales engineer, or as a cybersecurity consultant, the security culture of your company will impact how successful you can be in your role.

In your job interviews, consider asking:

- What is the most senior security role in the company, and how much access does that person have to the leadership team and the board (or other governing body)?

- Who controls the cybersecurity budget, and who must approve it?

- What kind of awareness training do non-security staff do, and how often?

- In the past year, how were the security teams recognized/thanked for performance by non-security leaders/teams?

- How would the interviewer describe the relationship between the security teams and non-security teams?

- What do the company leaders say about cybersecurity?

Attribute #5: Familiarity

When looking for your first cybersecurity role, try to find a company that has some familiar elements to you. Familiarity will help ease the transition and make you more immediately successful when you are already dealing with a new role. Don't simply look at a job title to see if it's the kind of job you want—make sure the sub-elements of the job match your background, too.

The first consideration is the industry. If you have already worked in a particular industry (retail, healthcare, finance, etc.), it may be useful to look for security roles in the same industry, so your learning curve isn't so steep. You're likely already familiar with the business models, regulations, and major applications used in an industry, and you're likely to have networking contacts in the industry. Make your job search easier by starting where you already are!

The second consideration is the technology being used. Hopefully by now you have learned some level of technology skills as a user or as an administrator—Windows, Macs, Linux, mobile, networks, browsers, software languages, etc. You may also have taken training using certain kinds of security solutions. Look for jobs where the same technology you're familiar with is being used. Again, this will help flatten your learning curve and set you up for early career success.

The third consideration is location. Try to find a company that has a physical footprint nearby, preferably with the security team members. Remote work is great, and for some of us it is the only option, but it is still easier to build networks and relationships in person, even if you don't see those people every day. Finding a company with a cultural connection to your home can make moving to a new role easier.

There will be plenty of new things for you to learn as you transition into cybersecurity, and if you are coming to cybersecurity from some other function the initial learning curve will be steep. Control for the things you can by selecting companies that match your experience to date and choose organizations that will maximize your opportunities for success.

Attribute #6: Security Team

In your first cybersecurity job, it's very helpful to have team members who have the knowledge and time to invest in you. It's not just about your manager (we'll talk about them next); it's also about the team members you work with. It would be great if they:

- Have time to train you on the tools, techniques, and procedures that the team follows.

- Have good retention. This means they stay in a role for a good amount of time—they don't leave too soon (which would indicate organizational problems) and don't stay too long (not always a bad thing, but can indicate stagnation and lack of growth opportunities).

- Have someone on the team with at least five years in cybersecurity to help you understand what is currently happening, as well as the history of how you got there.

- Have someone on the team who is a couple of years ahead of you in their career so you can watch and learn from their journey.

- Are active in the broader cybersecurity community so you can learn fresh new ideas.

- Are responsible for at least a couple of security functions, so you can learn more than just your immediate job and have room to grow.

You're looking for a team that will help you settle into the profession, learn something useful, and optimally offer opportunities for growth. As you interview, ask for details about the team to get a sense of their capabilities. If you have the time, interview people who are on the team outside of the formal interviewing process—find them on LinkedIn and ask questions.

Attribute #7: Hiring Manager

As a mid-career jobseeker you have already had a manager or two. You know that the right manager can make the difference between a successful career and a terrible experience. In security it is no different.

If you are transitioning into an organization's cybersecurity team from another profession, you will likely get a manager who is solely responsible for a cybersecurity function, either for the entire team or a particular piece of the security team. They are likely there because they have a number of years working in that part of the industry (operations, identity, application security, etc.) and have proven themselves to be a competent technical leader. This is a great person to learn from—*if* they have the time and skill to work with you. You need to be on the same page as them regarding the expectations of your job, how to communicate with each other, and how much authority/independence you will have. Just because you are new to cybersecurity doesn't mean you are a junior worker who must be micromanaged—unless you want to be. As you interview with the hiring manager, ask them:

- How do you like to communicate with your team (in person, email/messaging, phone, other)?

- Have you worked with other people who have transitioned into cybersecurity from another function? What worked, and what didn't?

- How often and in what ways do you meet with your existing team?

- Do you do a lot of coaching/mentoring now? What does this look like for you?

- What will I need to be focusing on in the first 30/60/90 days, and how will you like me to communicate my progress to you during that time?

Set the expectation early that while you have some level of experience because of your previous jobs, you will need guidance around the cybersecurity-specific aspects of your new role. Sometimes, managers are ignorant of their own strengths and weaknesses, so, if possible, talk to other team members about their experiences working with this person. Finding a manager who can help mentor and coach you as you transition into this role is extremely important. Finding a manager who has done this with other people is even better.

Many jobseekers have trouble landing their first cybersecurity job, so they aren't picky about the organization, team, or manager that is offering a role. This is completely understandable and also dangerous. Landing in an organization that doesn't support your needs as a mid-career jobseeker can make your first role much more challenging and make it difficult to progress from that first job. Ask questions, consider the responses, and do your best to find roles that match your needs well. If you do end up in a role that has a lot of red flags, consider the kind of support you will need to be successful in the role—outside mentoring, further personal investment in your development, etc.—and continue looking for the next role.

Sidebar: Flip the Script Putting the Burden Back on the Hiring Manager

Traditional job hunting involves scouring through job descriptions, matching your resume to specific qualifications, and hoping to check all the right boxes. But cybersecurity's persistent talent shortage creates an unusual opportunity: You can turn the tables on employers. As a mid-career professional, your diverse skills and experience already hold substantial value. Rather than guessing how you might fit an employer's rigid expectations, invite them to identify the roles they need filled. Consider using this provocative but powerful approach in conversations and interviews:

"I bring years of experience in [your domain—healthcare, finance, law, education, management], along with proven skills in [project management, compliance, training, leadership, etc.]. Rather than guess how I might fit your existing job descriptions, why don't you tell me where your greatest pain points are? I'd love to talk about how my background and strengths could address your most critical security or compliance needs."

This strategy accomplishes three important things:

1. Demonstrates confidence and self-awareness: You're aware of your value and willing to challenge the usual script.
2. Encourages real dialogue: Instead of superficial checklists, you spark deeper discussions about actual challenges the hiring manager faces.
3. Highlights your true strengths: It frames your existing skills as solutions to their pressing needs rather than forcing yourself into a narrow mold.

Hiring managers are often so busy solving urgent problems that they may overlook non-traditional talent proactively. This simple conversational pivot helps them imagine exactly how your experience can immediately help their organization.

Landing an Interview

Plenty of people are looking for their first cybersecurity role, so how do you stand out enough to get to the interview? The best way to get an interview is to be known before you start to apply for positions. Let's discuss what it takes to get known in a new career.

Informational Interviews

These are interviews where you meet with people in the career you're interested in so you can learn about them, their company, and their career path. Taking time to do informational interviews will prepare you for the real thing and enable you to make connections to people who can boost your reputation with hiring managers. You can talk to:

- People in your organization: If you are already working in an organization, start by reaching out to the people in your security team and asking to meet.

- Cybersecurity professionals at a local security meet up or conference: Specifically, schedule follow-up meetings to discuss further and to help them remember you.

- Recruiters working for hiring organizations: Not just for senior executives, talk to people at cybersecurity staffing agencies to find out what's happening in the market.

- Social media connections: If you follow people who might be able to refer you to hiring managers, these are great people to ask for an informational interview.

Once you decide who your targets will be, reach out and invite them to meet with you. In person is best, online (with camera on!) is fine, purely phone call is a last resort. The purpose here is twofold: to learn about them, and to impress them so they make recommendations to other hiring managers.

When you meet, remember to:

- Thank them for taking the time to meet with you.

- Give them a two-minute overview of your background and emphasize why you are interested in a cybersecurity role, and the kind of role you are looking for.

- Ask them about their experience in cybersecurity, and what their "why" is.

- Remind them of the skills you would bring to the kind of role you're looking for.

- Ask them if there is anyone else you should talk to, to whom they can make an introduction.

- Ask if there is anything you can help them with.

After the meeting, send a thank you message. If they refer you to someone else, thank them after that meeting happens. Even better, once you land an interview (even if it doesn't result in a job) drop them a line to let them know of the developments in your job search. (Keeping a list of who you meet, who referred you, and the outcome of the meeting is a great job search tracker to have!).

Very few security people will turn down a request to discuss security, so don't be nervous about making this request!

Finding Job Postings

According to Dawn Graham in the book, *Switchers: How Smart Professionals Change Careers and Seize Success*, you should approach the job market in the following order:

- Networking
- Internal company posting
- Directly to a company website
- Online job board

Knowing someone who is hiring and having the inside scoop on job openings is great, but for most mid-career jobseekers you will need to pursue a "quantity over quality" approach to land your first cybersecurity job. This means identifying online job postings and applying to as many as possible. Let's discuss how to find appropriate online job postings that are worth investigating.

Remember that most job postings are created by hiring managers with basic training on how to write a job posting and are managed by HR/recruiting teams that know next to nothing about cybersecurity jobs. The result is that there is no objective standard about what makes a quality job posting, and most postings will have some flaws. However, there are some things to look out for:

- It explains how the security team fits in the organization (who they report to, who their primary clients are, etc.).

- It is clear on the core skills and experience needed to perform the role, without including any extraneous requirements.

- The experience/qualifications requirements match the level of the job (i.e., it doesn't ask for an advanced degree for a junior level role).

- There is a description of the day-to-day responsibilities of the role (which makes clear that the role is a security role, not an IT role that includes security stuff on the side).

- It includes how the candidates will be supported in on-the-job training and career development.

If you can find job postings with these features, you can have a higher degree of confidence that the organization has the capacity to support you in your role. Apply away!

Another consideration when looking for job postings is where the jobs are posted. You can certainly find security jobs on generalist job boards such as Indeed.com or LinkedIn, but for security roles, it is useful to look in places that focus on security organizations. Jobs posted here may be more likely to be real jobs with organizations that understand how to work with security people. Where are those?

- Certification and training companies often include job boards for their members (e.g., ISACA)

- Cybersecurity professional organizations (e.g., ISSA)

- Cybersecurity diversity organizations (e.g., Cyversity or WiCyS)

- For those leaving the military, there are a number of nonprofits and other organizations that specifically find roles suited to ex-military personnel. An internet search for "cybersecurity jobs for veterans" will help you find what you need.

Preparing Your Resume

Once you've identified the job(s) you want to apply for, you must make sure your resume and cover letter are ready. This means tailoring your resume for the specific job you're applying for, and your cover letter for the specific organization you want to work for.

Make sure the following is addressed:

- A short, impactful summary at the top of the resume highlights your *why* for seeking a cyber job and/or the cyber problem you are looking to solve. Include your most applicable experience in this summary and how you can help the organization.

- Job postings typically list required skills and experience in order of importance. Your resume should highlight any matching skills/experience, using the same language.

- Your cover letter provides more detail on your *why*, highlights the most relevant transferable skills, and explains why you want to work for this organization.

- Where possible, include the type of technologies you worked with in each role. Some people prefer to have a "Technologies" section on their resume where they list all the technology they know. We suggest you put the technology into the context of your previous roles as it will allow you to talk about understanding technology without having to be a technology expert, unless you are a technology expert, which should be explicitly called out.

- When listing previous roles, focus on how you helped the organization.

- The more senior you are, the more your resume should call out achievements, not just activities. For example, an IT helpdesk junior person might list the number of tickets worked in an average day. A more experienced helpdesk person might highlight the resulting cost savings for the organization.

- Your achievements should also include any training you've done that supports the role you're seeking. Certifications, bootcamps, competitions, conferences attended are all worth including when you're seeking your first cyber role. Highlight not only what you've done (put that on your resume) but what you learned (if there's not space on your resume, include it in your cover letter).

- Give thought to how your previous work experience has taught you transferable skills. When you are listing previous jobs, call out the cybersecurity skill you learned in each one. Consider the examples in Table 6.1.

Work Experience	Cybersecurity Skill
Retail Customer Service	Dealing with multiple priorities and stakeholders
Legal experience	Understanding governance and compliance security functions
IT Help Desk	Technical experience with authentication/authorization operating systems, etc.
Teacher	Security training/awareness methodologies

Table 6.1 – Transferable skills examples.

Your resume and cover letter should contain enough information for hiring managers to want to know more about you and get you short listed for an interview.

Using Social Media

It's helpful to have an active social media presence when job-seeking. If you don't, start now.

At the time we're writing this book, LinkedIn remains the primary business location for maintaining an online presence. For cybersecurity folks you should start there, but also consider other online locations frequented by cybersecurity people, such as X, BlueSky, Mastodon, Reddit, Medium or any other writing/collaboration sites. As a mid-career job-switcher, it's fine to have a history of non-cybersecurity stuff, but now's the time to start incorporating cyber content into your profile.

Consider:

- Update your LinkedIn profile to highlight the skills and experience you bring to your new role.

- Consider building a personal website that highlights you and your experience, as well as your career aspirations.

- Blogging about your journey of getting a cybersecurity certification.

- Following prominent cybersecurity people and commenting on their posts (ask other cybersecurity people who they follow/admire to get started on this list).

- Show pictures of you competing in cybersecurity competitions or attending cyber meetups or conferences.

- Post questions about the kind of job you're seeking and engage asynchronously with the cybersecurity community. Include hashtags and keywords that will help you be found more easily by other professionals.

The goal here is to use social media so that people can see you in a cybersecurity role. Once your profile is created, you will need to plan for 10 to 15 minutes a day to maintain a minimal presence (if you start blogging, it will take longer!).

Include your social media pages, websites, and handles on your resume.

Smashing the Interview

Congratulations—you've been selected for an interview! Now, you must double down on all the skills and messaging we've discussed in the book's first part. Be ready to talk about why you want to work in security, how your job history has prepared you for this role, what education and training you've done to prepare, and how you'll benefit the company.

Types of Interviews

In your previous job and field, you might have had several interviews. You may find, however, that the interview process in cybersecurity is somewhat different from your prior experiences. Beginning in the 1990's, Microsoft, Amazon, and Google began to evolve their hiring processes. Today, there are a common set of different types of interviews you should expect in your journey to your first cybersecurity job. We will discuss these below. Sometimes, an interview can be a combination of all types of interviews at the same time. Let's review how to understand and prepare for them.

Initial Screening

Recruiters will begin the interview process with a phone call to determine that you're a real human, and that your expectations of the role are close to matching theirs. The interviewer in a screening interview is unlikely to be knowledgeable in cybersecurity topics—their job is to get the right people in front of the hiring manager—so your role here is to make a personal connection with them.

In this interview you should have your "why" statement ready. It is likely they will ask you "why do you want this job?" Now is not the time to mention that you're new to cybersecurity—instead, talk up how you will benefit them. Talk about why you want to work for this particular organization. Ask about their hobbies/background (see the previous section about research).

Here's your chance to find out how this whole process will work (every organization is different). Ask this person the time frame for the hiring process and decisioning. Find out what kinds of interviews you should expect, how many, and with whom. Clarify any questions you have about the job posting.

Depending on the laws in your location, they may also ask you about salary/compensation expectations (in some places they aren't allowed to ask). Be prepared to give a non-specific answer here. It's fine to let them know that you expect a compensation package to match the current market. If there are things you particularly require (health insurance, relocation support, etc.) you can ask about this now, too.

Now's not the time to prepare for in-depth questions about yourself or your background. That comes next.

Technical Interviews

Technical interviews are just as they sound—interviewers will test the candidate's technical competency and working style. They can vary in format from an interviewer (or panel of interviewers) asking questions to doing an online test. Interestingly, you are more likely to be subject to a technical interview for junior roles than senior roles, and some organizations don't do technical interviews at all. The questions can range from the core fundamentals of a role to high-level principles.

Interviewers are seeking to understand your thought process as you problem-solve. They want to know you can problem solve, that your work style will fit with the team, and that you have the potential to learn. Even if you end up with a wrong answer it may not be a strike against you if your thinking process is correct.

Do These Things	Don't Do These Things
• Relax!	• Don't rush. Slow down, take a deep breath, think through your tasks before acting.
• Do an internet search for technical interview questions for the kind of role you're seeking	
• Ask for clarification, and repeat a question back to the interviewer using your own words, to make sure you understand (they may speak in your language, but don't assume you know what they're asking you!)	• Don't be afraid to say "I don't know, but here's how I would find out the answer".
• If you completely mess up a question during the interview, and get a more coherent answer after you're finished, consider noting that when you send your follow up "thank you" message to the interviewer.	
• Be ready to tell a story around how your previous work experience lends itself to this topic	

Table 6.2 – Do and don't do during a technical interview.

Behavioral Interviews

In a behavioral interview you will be asked a bunch of questions so the interviewer can determine how you have thought or acted in order to learn how you will behave in the future. You may not know going into an interview that it will be a behavioral interview—but if they ask you to "tell me about a time when..." they are asking behavioral questions.

Interviewers will ask you to give examples of how you have handled certain scenarios in the past. Typically, the questions aren't technical. Instead, they will ask you about how you have interacted with other people such as difficult customers, or convincing partners/stakeholders of a certain action, or how you have gotten something you needed from a manager.

This is the place where job-switchers can really shine. You have real-world work history that you can draw from, where you can give meaningful examples. Remember to keep your answers as concise as possible—they don't need all the backstory, just the immediate circumstances, the point of conflict/challenge, and how you resolved it. You may not have a direct example, but you might have something that is close to what they're asking for. Feel free to share it. For these answers try to use stories that were from previous jobs, but if you don't have one you can also bring in examples from your personal life. If you have no experience with a certain scenario, it's OK to say that too.

The best way to prepare for these questions is to look at the non-technical job requirements such as teamwork, communication skills, self-driven initiative, attention to detail, etc. Think back to situations in your past where you have demonstrated these skills and write down those examples. You don't have to come across as the perfect human, but you do need to be able to show how your past experience has prepared you for this new role. Pay particular attention to the results of your past actions. It's not enough to say: "I took the initiative to attend a conference where I learned new things." You need to take that example into how it helped the company, so instead: "I took the initiative to attend a conference. I was able to bring what I learned about detection techniques back to my job and start using them immediately."

Prepping for the Interview

Find out anything you can about the people who will be interviewing you. You're trying to understand their perspective, find common ground, and have an opportunity to show that you've made an effort to learn about them. All of this is so you can find a way to connect with the interviewer on a personal level. Learn about:

- Where they have worked before—the kinds of companies and industries
- Where they went to school
- Their age demographic

- Their family situation—married? single? kids?
- Hobbies and volunteering activities

Even if the person you're talking to is a recruiter doing the first interview screen, knowing their personal and professional background can be the difference between getting another interview and getting passed over for a different candidate.

When looking for a cybersecurity job, it's also helpful to know what kind of cybersecurity history the interviewer has:

- What technologies have they worked with? Did they start as a network engineer (infrastructure) or software development (applications)?
- How long have they worked with this security team?
- How long have they worked in security overall?
- Have they posted anything on social media that indicates how they think about cybersecurity (for example, what is their opinion about people needing to be "technical")?
- Do you know anyone in their network? Who do you have in common?

You should also do security homework on the company and the team you'll be a part of. Understand the industry, where the security team sits in the organization (are they part of IT? Legal? Other?). You should know:

- The security threats and vulnerabilities in their industry (reference the most recent Verizon breach report to see the top issues by industry).

- What public security incidents this company has had, and when. Know the technical details of the incident. If there are none, this is worth asking a question about!

- The security regulations the organization is subject to.

This may seem like a lot of research, but if you're selective about the kind of roles you are applying for you will be able to find the right balance. As you do your research, think about the questions you have, and make a list. When the interviewer asks you "do you have any questions" (and they will!), you will have a list ready to choose from.

Lastly, every single interviewer will ask you some variation of "tell me about yourself." Usually this is the first question you will get—so be ready with a concise answer that shows why you want this role, with this company, in this industry, and how your work history has prepared you and made you excited for this role.

When You Get an Offer

Congratulations, you've made it through the interviews and now you have an offer! What do you do next?

First, thank them for their offer, and take some time to reflect on it, even if at first it sounds great! Why? Because there is a lot to an employment agreement and taking the time to get it right is important for your future earnings and job satisfaction.

You have an advantage as a cybersecurity jobseeker: it's hard to find the right talent for the right role. It's even harder to keep someone in a role. So, if a company has decided to offer you a job, they will want to do everything to make this worth your time and effort. Think not only about the salary/bonus, but all the other benefits like time off, travel, tuition, severance packages, stock options, etc. You may need to take a salary dip to move into a new industry (but don't assume that you must!), but you can maximize your offer by including other benefits as well. The hiring manager will want you to have a positive impression as you start in your role—they are highly motivated to respond to a counteroffer.

Please don't think that because this is your first cybersecurity job that you should take the first offer that comes along. There is *always* room for negotiation. So, take it.

Other Things

Using AI To Help Find a Job

Artificial intelligence applications can make job searching and hiring easier and faster. An internet search for "using AI to find a job" will help you use these tools to support your job search activities. AI applications exist to:

- Do a skills gap analysis and learning recommendations
- Draft your resume and cover letters
- Do practice interviews and get feedback
- Research a particular company or industry
- Negotiate a salary

Remember to read anything AI-generated to make sure the output is accurate and matches your style. For letters and email, you can enter in samples of your own writing to help train the application on your "voice," to make it more personalized.

For cybersecurity jobseekers, having experience with AI, even as a typical "end user" and not an administrator/engineer, can boost your value to hiring managers. So don't forget to include this on your resume!

When You Get Stuck

When offers, or even interviews, aren't happening, it's time to reflect and evaluate what might be going wrong. Consider:

- Have you been networking so you can be referred by someone the hirer trusts?

- Have you been active at conferences or industry events, and regularly showing that participation using social media?

- Do your resume and interview answers show how your transferable skills will help you achieve the outcomes the hiring manager is looking for?

- Does this switch to cybersecurity make sense in your overall career plan? In other words, can you articulate your "why"?

If you are applying for jobs without landing an interview, it's time to update your resume and double down on your networking. If you're getting interviews but not landing a job, it could be that your interviewing skills need some work. Take the time to analyze where in the hiring process you're getting stuck and work on that element. And be patient. We promise, the payoff is worth it!

Chapter Summary

- Look for an organization that will continue to invest in your training while you work for them, support work/life balance, be operationally mature, and have a top-down security culture.

- If possible, look for jobs in the organizations and industries you know. Don't try switching to cybersecurity *and* change industries or geographies all at the same time.

- Learn about the other members of the security team. Will they be able to work with you and help you learn on the job?

- The hiring manager can make or break your cybersecurity career. Look for someone who has the time and desire to work with you and develop your skills.

- Prepare for interviews by using networking and informational interviews to find the companies and teams you want to work in.

- Understand what a good job posting looks like and apply to those.

- Prepare your resume and cover letter to tailor it to the role and organization you are applying to.

- Keep an active social media presence that highlights the role you are seeking.

- Understand and prepare appropriately for the different types of interviews you may face.

- Use AI to do research, craft your resume and correspondence, and rehearse interview questions.

- Always negotiate your offer!

- If you get stuck, analyze where and why, and double down on how to address the problem.

Chapter References

Graham, Dawn (2018). *Switchers: How Smart Professionals Change Careers and Seize Success*. Harper Collins.

Chapter 7

Getting the Skills You Need

Getting Started

Very few people who decide mid-career to move into cybersecurity immediately have all the skills and experience they need to land their first cybersecurity job. Welcome to the club!

Reading through this book, you should by now have worked out why you want to do security, the kind of security role you're interested in, and the kind of industry and organization you want to work in. You should also have a feel for what is missing, either skills or experience, that needs to be addressed before or while you look for your first cybersecurity role.

There are many, many options for filling in skills gaps. There are tradeoffs in terms of time, cost, and outcomes that you will need to take into account. Let's discuss them.

Formal Education Options

Degrees

When I (Helen) began my working career, I didn't have a formal degree. Over the course of 13 years, I worked full-time and went to school at night or online. I ultimately ended up with an undergraduate degree in business administration (after cycling through HR management, accounting, MIS, and English majors), then later a Master of Public Policy. When I started my career there was no such thing as a degree in cybersecurity and I wouldn't have thought to pursue it if there was. All my cyber skills were learned on the job, including all my IT skills.

Times have changed, and now you can start learning cybersecurity at any age. There are multiple options for pursuing a formal cybersecurity education. Do you need a formal degree to land a security job? The short answer is "no"—provided you have the "equivalent" work experience to make up for the lack of a degree. Do you need a cybersecurity degree to land a cybersecurity job? The answer is also "no," although a computing degree (computer science, computer engineering, MIS, etc.) is definitely an advantage for a jobseeker.

For the mid-career jobseeker, getting a degree is one way you can help demonstrate that you've acquired some knowledge/skills, you're committed to the career path, and you are capable of learning. All good things to break into the industry. But formal education takes time away from family, away from your day job, and away from friends. It will also take an investment of cash. Make no mistake: a degree is an investment, not just an expense. To make the most of the investment you must choose your mode of education carefully.

If this is the path you want to follow, the question is: what kind of degree? Here's where the trade-offs begin. Table 8.1 lists both benefits and considerations for a variety of degree types.

Degree Type	Benefits	Consideration
2-Year Degree	Suited for entry-level security engineering and incident response roles; Less expensive than other options; Faster to complete if doing full-time; Often linked to industry certifications; Often programs have employer connections that can help with job searching	Less suited for GRC type roles; Curricula can sometimes lag current technologies and cyber techniques
4-Year Degree	Deeper/Broader curricula than 2-year programs; Ability to include cyber-adjacent classes (writing, psychology, ethics, policy); Many programs include internships as part of the program	Longer to complete; In person programs may not be suitable for working adults; More expensive; Curricula can sometimes lag current technologies and cyber techniques
Graduate Degree (e.g. Masters)	Faster than doing another undergraduate degree; Often involves research component	Prerequisite knowledge; More expensive; Unlikely to include internship or other employment links
Professional Certificates	Faster to complete; Often scheduled for working adults;	Assumes undergraduate degree already completed More expensive
Bootcamps	Fastest option; Can be cheaper than a degree, but not always; No previous degree required; More likely to keep up with technology changes; Links to employees	Hard to assess quality of program

Table 7.1 – Benefits and considerations of formal education programs.

In the spirit of "start where you are," if you have no degree at all, any of the undergraduate or bootcamp options above may work for you. If you already have a degree but not in cybersecurity, computer science, or MIS, doing another undergraduate degree is OK, but you may get more value doing a postgraduate degree instead. If you already have an MBA or other postgraduate degree, a professional certificate might be the most effective option.

There is a huge variation in quality for all these options. It's not enough to look for a program name such as "Bachelors of Cybersecurity" or "Cybersecurity Bootcamp." Take the time to look at the individual programs and classes, and the technologies and processes they focus on. Some programs might be more attuned to ethical hacking; others might focus on technology risk management. Find out:

- Do the teaching styles (online, in person, etc.) and schedule (daytime only, nights, a mixture of times) meet your personal and professional needs?

- Is the length of the program aligned to your plans for career transition?

- Does the program offer internships and other practical/hands-on learning experiences, or is it purely theoretical? If your schedule permits, look for programs with a hands-on element.

- Are the technologies covered by the coursework the kinds of technologies you want to learn? For example, do they focus on applications/software, artificial intelligence, infrastructure, or all of the above? We recommend you find programs that include a software/coding component, even if you want to focus on operational technologies (OT) or other devices as your primary technology.

- Do you have time to study cyber-adjacent topics that would be helpful, such as data analytics, ethics, technical writing, and AI? If you do, take advantage of these kinds of classes—they can help differentiate you to hiring managers.

- Are there industry professionals who are actively part of the program? Do those professionals engage in coursework, mentor students, and offer internships and jobs after the program is completed?

- Is this the kind of program that others in the security industry have done? Would this program be recognized by hiring managers and team members?

Choosing the option that works best for where you are now and where you want to go will take time. Leverage your network to find programs that are industry-recognized (in the industries where you want to work). The time you spend up front to find the right program will save you time and money.

Certifications

Certifications are a great place to get book-learning qualifications that go neatly onto a resume and can contribute immediately to your job. Surprisingly, certifications will help you get a job, although you rarely need them to actually *do* a job. Hiring managers will often ask if you have certifications, but they don't think that having a certification indicates skill mastery. Instead, they will use getting a certification as a proxy for knowing that you are interested in the field and have the capacity to learn.

There are two types of certifications: general and specialized.
General certifications such as the CompTIA[36] Security+ certification or ISC2 Certified Information Systems Security Professional (CISSP)[37] give people a broad understanding of cybersecurity concepts and frameworks. These certifications are designed to help you learn as much about the cybersecurity field as possible without going into depth in any specific topic.

Specialist certifications such as Offensive Security Certified Professional (OSCP),[38] GIAC Penetration Tester (GPEN),[39] and others typically assume some level of work or technical experience, and go more deeply into the tools, tactics, and procedures (TTPs) of a given cybersecurity discipline. Some are specific to the software of a particular vendor, such as EnCase forensic software and Splunk for log analysis.

---

[36] CompTIA Security+ Certification, available here:
https://www.comptia.org/.

[37] ISC2 CISSP Certification, available here:
https://www.isc2.org/certifications/cissp.

[38] OffSec. *Information security training and certifications.*
https://www.offsec.com/courses-and-certifications/.

[39] GIAC certifications, available here:
https://www.giac.org/certifications/penetration-tester-gpen/.

Entry-level certifications such as Security+[40] or Certified Ethical Hacker[41] require you to pass an exam. There are no work experience requirements. For a mid-career job-switcher, getting these kinds of certifications will be fastest and cheapest compared with other options. Look for both a general certification as well as a specialist certification in your area of interest.

Mid-career certifications such as CISSP will require you to pass an exam and also show a number of years of work experience covering the professional domains of the certification. You can take and pass the exam, but without the requisite number of years of work experience you cannot get the certification. We suggest it may still be worth it to study and pass the exam and note on your resume that you are pursuing the certification.

Earning and maintaining a certification costs time and money. While it may be faster to get a certification than a degree, there are yearly commitments of membership fees and training costs that you will be assuming if you want to keep an active certification, so choose the certifications you want wisely. Search for the kinds of roles you want in cybersecurity and then focus on the certifications those hiring managers are looking for.

Bootcamps

It has taken educational institutions some time to establish formal cybersecurity degrees. To fill the gap in training, a number of companies have created cybersecurity bootcamps, which often started out as software coding bootcamps. Cybersecurity bootcamps are intensive, short-term training programs that rapidly equip participants with practical, hands-on skills and industry knowledge. Bootcamps can be full-time or part-time, in person, online, or hybrid, and take anywhere from six weeks to a year to complete. Although they can cost hundreds to thousands of dollars,

---

40   CompTIA security certifications, available here:
      https://www.comptia.org/certifications/security

41   EC-Council certifications, available here:
      https://www.eccouncil.org/train-certify/certified-ethical-hacker-ceh/

they are cheaper than an undergraduate or postgraduate degree and require a significant investment of time and money.

It can be challenging for a jobseeker to evaluate the quality of a bootcamp program. There is less oversight of bootcamps than other educational programs, so it is hard to make comparisons between bootcamp programs to find the best one.

If you want to pursue a bootcamp to jumpstart your learning, take the following into account:

- Review the bootcamp content to make sure it aligns to the kind of role you want.

- Look for instructors that work in (or have worked in) cybersecurity functional roles who can bring real world experience to their classes.

- Find bootcamps that partner with employers for career opportunities. Read the fine print of any "job guarantee" options so you know what you must do to meet their requirements.

- If you can, talk to students who have taken the bootcamp and landed a job afterwards. Find out if they would recommend the program.

- Some universities are offering cybersecurity certificates that are run by bootcamp companies. Take time to evaluate the reputation of the bootcamp company, not just the school, to ensure it will give you the outcomes you expect.

Informal Learning Methods

If you don't have the time, money, or inclination to get a formal degree, you can pursue a self-training path. There are plenty of ways to teach yourself cybersecurity concepts and skills. While this is usually a cheaper and time-flexible option, it will take superior self-discipline to pursue this path without getting distracted or lost in the weeds of all the content that is available for you to consume. If you have the organizational skills, though, this might be for you.

Online Learning

Searching for "self-taught cybersecurity training" will reveal a number of resources that you can take advantage of. Look for general cybersecurity courses on online learning platforms like Coursera,[42] LinkedIn Learning,[43] Cybrary,[44] or Udemy.[45] You can also look for cybersecurity classes by technology vendors such as Microsoft,[46] Google,[47] Amazon Web Services,[48] and Cisco.[49]

As before, check out the exact classes included in their series to make sure they line up to the kinds of skills and roles you're interested in. Online classes can cover everything from basic security principles to privacy and governance topics to hacking and research. Start with general theory classes to get introduced to terms and language, then move to more specialized classes.

There is still a fee to join an online learning platform. They're not free, but online courses are significantly cheaper than formal learning methods and allow for a working person to fit in learning where and when they have time.

While you are going through this course work, we suggest you also find a cybersecurity professional who can be a mentor for you, to answer any questions you have and to give you some "real world" perspective on the topics you are learning.

Books, Blogs, and Podcasts

There are a ton of amazing books out there that will introduce you to cybersecurity skills and functions. Reach out to people doing the

[42] Coursera online courses, available here: https://www.coursera.org/.
[43] LinkedIn Learning courses, available here: https://learning.linkedin.com/.
[44] Cybrary courses, available here: https://www.cybrary.it/.
[45] Udemy courses, available here: https://www.udemy.com/.
[46] Microsoft courses, available here: https://learn.microsoft.com/en-us/training/.
[47] Google courses, available here: https://learning.google/.
[48] AWS courses, available here: https://www.aws.training/.
[49] Cisco courses, available here: https://www.netacad.com/cybersecurity.

kinds of jobs you want and ask them for recommendations for your reading and listening lists.

One place to start are books that are study guides for common cybersecurity certifications. Publishers such as Wiley[50] and O'Reilly[51] offer study guides that will give you generalist information.

Look for cybersecurity books at places like Humble Bundle,[52] or on the Amazon[53] best-seller list for "security and encryption." Or you can check out the Cybersecurity Canon[54] for "Cybersecurity Hall of Fame" books covering a variety of topics.

There are plenty of people blogging about cybersecurity. Some favorites of ours include Daniel Miessler's "Unsupervised Learning,"[55] Bruce Schneier's "Schneier on Security,"[56] or Leslie Carhart's "Tisiphone.net."[57] Bloggers typically focus on a specific slice of cybersecurity, so look for people who blog about the type of security you're interested in, or for the "new to cybersecurity" focus.

There are a ton of podcasts that cover cybersecurity. Throw on your headphones while you're cleaning the house or walking the dog and take a listen. Some industry staples include Darknet Diaries,[58] Risky Biz,[59] and the CyberWire.[60] Podcasts are a great way to stay up to date with the latest in cybersecurity without having to spend a lot of time doing your own research.

Don't forget to check out cybersecurity videos on YouTube and cybersecurity threads on Reddit. Sorting through the noise can be

50 Wiley Publications cybersecurity books, available here: https://www.wiley.com/en-us/search?pq=cybersecurity.
51 O'Reilly Publications, available here: https://www.oreilly.com/.
52 Humble Bumble, available here: https://www.humblebundle.com/.
53 Amazon, available here: https://www.amazon.com/.
54 CyberCanon, available here: Cybercanon.org.
55 Miessler, Daniel (2025) https://danielmiessler.com/.
56 Schneier, Bruce (2025) https://www.schneier.com/.
57 Carhart, Leslie (2025) https://tisiphone.net/.
58 Darknet Diaries [Audio Podcast] https://darknetdiaries.com/.
59 Risky.biz [Audio Podcast] https://risky.biz/podcasts/.
60 The Cyberwire [Audio Podcast] https://thecyberwire.com/podcasts.

challenging but you will absorb a lot of unstructured information that can help you round out your more formal learning.

Unlike formal education, bootcamps, and certifications, you are unlikely to list the books and podcasts you've read or listened to on your resume (unless it's a certification/test preparation book). Instead, consider commenting on the things you're reading or hearing on LinkedIn or Reddit or your online platform of choice. Tag the author/host. Find ways to incorporate the things you've read into your interview responses. Use the information you've learned to show that you are interested in the field, and that you've incorporated your learning into how you think about cybersecurity.

Online Practical Learning

After you have learned some theory, it's time to do some training on practical skills. Whether you pursue a degree or a certification, in many cases they have one thing in common—they prove theoretical learning, but don't show hands-on skills attainment. Internships are usually the way to fill the gap between theory and practice, but few mid-career job-switchers have the available time to leave their day job to take on an internship.

How can you get hands-on skills while still earning a living somewhere else? That's where informal learning paths can help.

Start Internal

If you already work for an organization that has an in-house security team, talk to them to see if there are projects you can participate in. This will, of course, take some negotiation with your current manager to give you the time and space to do something like this, so look for things that help your immediate department, for a win-win proposal. It is likely that the internal security team won't have given much thought to what kinds of things you could do for them, where you are—so talk to your mentors and network for ideas, then make a plan. Security teams love people who want to work with them, and will often make time to teach on-the-job, but they usually won't know how your department works. So, take the initiative to propose something (code testing? training and awareness events? compliance assessment?) that you can later put on your resume.

Learning to Code

Not everyone is going to need to learn how to code to do a cybersecurity job. However, learning basic scripting IS a skill used in many jobs, and is a handy general skill to have when you're dealing with a lot of data (which we all do).

Languages like Python, PowerShell, and Ruby are commonly used in the cybersecurity profession. As always, look at the kinds of roles you're interested in, and identify the languages the hiring managers are looking for. Then go learn a little bit about that language. Consider engaging with CodeWars[61] to hone your skills in a simulated environment.

Learning to Hack

The best way to learn to hack is by doing…safely. If you want to be an ethical hacker (researcher, pentester, etc.) this is a required skill, but even if your intended cybersecurity career path is more governance or defensive engineering, knowing how the hacker mindset works is a core skill for any cybersecurity professional, and worth spending some time on.

After you've done some theoretical learning, consider platforms such as HackTheBox,[62] Vulnhub,[63] HackThisSite,[64] and the SANS Holiday Hack Challenge[65] to hone your skills. Other Capture the Flag (CTF) challenges can be found at CTFTime.org. There are online tutorials on YouTube that can help you get started or get unstuck.

---

[61]   Codewars (2025), available here: https://www.codewars.com/.

[62]   HackTheBox (2025), available here: https://www.hackthebox.com/.

[63]   VulnHub (2025), available here: https://www.vulnhub.com/.

[64]   HackThisSite (2025) available here: https://www.hackthissite.org/.

[65]   SANS Holiday Hack Challenge (2025) available here: https://www.sans.org/cyber-ranges/holiday-hack-challenge.

Attend Conferences and Meetups

Hands-on experience is about learning how to apply theoretical concepts in the real world. It's also about understanding the limitations of the theory, and where theory breaks down.

One way to start to learn this is by attending conferences and meetups, where you not only get to listen to great talks, participate in capture the flag and other hands-on competitions, and play with vendor tools, but you get to ask the other attendees for their "war stories."

Every security professional with more than three years on the job has at least one story about something that didn't go as planned—and they want to tell that story. Find a way to ask them:

- What was the most difficult thing you've had to do in your job?
- Have you ever been involved in a security incident/breach? Can you share details about it?
- What was the most challenging security assessment/pentest you ever participated in?
- What do you find most difficult about your role?

Getting people chatting about their security lives will help you build your network, and it will also help you build your hands-on skills. If you participate in conference competitions, make sure to list them on your resume, or mention them in your cover letters or interviews.

Build a Home Lab

If you are interested in cybersecurity jobs that require daily use of hands-on technology skills, one way to prove that you can apply technology theory is to build your own lab. A home lab usually involves having hardware, an operating system (or virtual systems), and applications that you can use to learn and test your skills.

Managing a home lab is a skill that is highly regarded by hiring managers. It doesn't have to be super complicated, but many folks in security will continue to "grow" their labs over time, and as their technical competence grows.

An internet search on how to build a home lab will give you a wide range of resources to choose from—Reddit threads or YouTube videos or blogs.

Consider doing this after you've taken some theory classes on basic networking, operating systems, and scripting. If you have someone in your network who has done this already, ask them for guidance before you start investing money into this effort.

Volunteering

Once you have completed your theoretical learning, consider volunteering your services. It will certainly require you to carve time from your schedule, but it can be worth the effort to ensure you can land that first cybersecurity job. There are a number of ways to volunteer, from short-term projects to ongoing projects; choose what works best for your circumstances.

- You might start with family/friends, helping them learn and install personal security solutions such as backups, password managers, upgrading hardware/software.

- You could consider non-profits and community service organizations in your area who need support doing security assessments, training, or technology upgrades. Work with their IT/Security support companies to learn beside professionals (also a great way to network).

- Participate in Open Source Projects. Check out organizations like the Open Source Security Foundation[66] to find ways to contribute to the security community. This is a great way to learn skills and network.

---

[66] Open Source Security Foundation (2025), available here: https://openssf.org/projects/.

- Volunteer to work at a conference. Great for networking, but you also get to attend the conference free of charge (usually), where you can take advantage of learning labs and other activities. Some conferences also have a security operations center, to monitor the conference network and digital activities, where you can participate in learning SOC work.

And What Else?

Obtaining cyber skills will take time, money, and effort. This is true for any jobseeker and particularly challenging for mid-career seekers who already have time and resource commitments.

If you don't have the resources to do all the things listed above, or even some of them, it doesn't disqualify you from pursuing a cybersecurity career. You likely have other skills that you can emphasize as you job-seek:

- Industry knowledge: for the industries you've already worked in

- Professional skills: understanding how to use skills like empathy, teamwork, and communication to achieve work goals

- Organizational management: knowing how budgets or human resources work, and how that applies to any job role

Hiring managers will not just be evaluating you for your job-related skills, they will also be evaluating you to see if you will be a skill fit for their team. As a mid-career jobseeker, you can provide a lot of experience in areas they may not have—so take advantage of that while you build your cybersecurity skills.

Chapter Summary

- Getting the skills you need will require tradeoffs in time, resources, and outcomes, so plan your approach to skills acquisition carefully.

- Choosing a formal education option has benefits, but can be costly and time consuming, so choose the option that fits with your current education status.

- If you seek a certification, consider getting a generalist certification as well as a specialist certification. The combination can be useful when seeking your first cybersecurity role.

- Bootcamps can be cheaper and faster compared to other education options, but they are difficult to assess for quality. Take time to do your homework on the organizations offering bootcamps.

- Books are a great way to round out your general knowledge. Post your comments about the books you're reading on social media and incorporate the concepts into your interview responses.

- If you are self-training, start by working with your existing organization's security team, if there is one.

- Don't just do online learning for theory, find ways to do "hands on" learning by attending conferences or meetups, or doing online hacking on safe platforms. Consider building a home lab or volunteering your services.

- Volunteering is a great way to get hands-on security experience.

Chapter References

Brooks, A. C. (2022). *From Strength to Strength: Finding Success, Happiness, and Deep Purpose in the Second Half of Life*. Bloomsbury Publishing.

Part 3

Thriving in Cybersecurity: Upskilling and Specialization

Building a Cybersociety:
Upskilling and Identification

192

Chapter 8

Staying Ahead of the Curve

If you've journeyed with us this far, you've already accomplished something significant. You've navigated the complexities of a career transition, assessed your unique strengths, and begun acquiring the foundational knowledge to establish yourself in this dynamic field. You're no longer standing at the cybersecurity starting line; you're on the track, gaining momentum.

The uncomfortable truth about cybersecurity is that today's mastery can quickly become tomorrow's irrelevance. You've secured your role, earned certifications, navigated technical jargon, and proven yourself capable. But being good enough today does not guarantee you'll be valuable next year, let alone five years from now. Cybersecurity is mercilessly dynamic: new threats appear overnight, technology standards change rapidly, and skills once considered cutting-edge become ordinary or, worse, obsolete.

For mid-career professionals like you, staying relevant isn't merely beneficial; it's essential. Consider this realistic scenario: You've spent two years becoming proficient in cloud-based security monitoring. Just when you feel confident, your company merges with a larger competitor that uses an entirely different toolset. Or perhaps a sophisticated breach makes your organization's legacy techniques obsolete overnight, demanding an immediate pivot. Without deliberate, structured efforts to keep pace with change, you risk being sidelined at the exact moment your career should be taking off.

This chapter won't lecture you about change since we have covered that story in depth. Instead, it provides actionable guidance for anticipating and adapting to cybersecurity's relentless evolution. We will explore specific methods for lifelong learning, including effectively utilizing online training platforms, regularly reading industry publications, and following influential thought leaders who offer clear signals about the field's direction. While conferences and professional networking are discussed in depth in Chapter 13, here we emphasize how ongoing engagement through professional organizations such as ISACs, OWASP chapters, or ISSA groups complements your continuous learning strategy and keeps you aligned with industry best practices.

You'll also learn to evaluate and strategically select advanced certifications—beyond your initial foundational credentials—focusing on those tied explicitly to emerging specializations and roles. We provide guidance on determining which certifications deliver genuine career benefits versus those that drain your valuable time and resources.

In addition, we introduce the crucial habit of structured self-directed exploration, going beyond formal training and certification. Practical skills development often requires hands-on experimentation, research, and personal projects. We'll discuss how to build a simple home lab, choose useful open-source tools, and safely experiment to gain practical, real-world cybersecurity skills on your own time and terms.

You'll discover how proactively building expertise beyond your current specialty can open up unforeseen career opportunities, protect you against obsolescence, and reinforce your value as a versatile, forward-looking professional. We'll provide strategies to regularly assess your skill gaps, test your assumptions, and quickly adjust to early signals of stagnation long before minor skill gaps become career-threatening blind spots.

Finally, we'll illustrate these strategies through concrete examples and short vignettes of mid-career professionals who have successfully navigated sudden technological shifts, avoided burnout from continual learning (a key theme addressed thoroughly in Chapter 14), and maintained their marketability in the face of constant change.

Your choice is clear: either commit to staying ahead of the curve or risk being replaced by those who do. This chapter gives you the specific tools, strategies, and mindset you need to ensure your career remains relevant, resilient, and rewarding for years to come. Let's get started.

Developing Intellectual Curiosity, Adaptability, and Proactivity

The single most critical attribute for long-term success in cybersecurity isn't a particular certification or proficiency in a specific tool; it's the mindset of a continuous learner. In a field defined by its relentless pace of change, the commitment to lifelong learning isn't just a good idea, it's a core professional competency.

For many people who transitioned mid-career, previous fields may have had established bodies of knowledge that evolved more slowly. In cybersecurity, the half-life of technical skills can be remarkably short. Security researchers discover new vulnerabilities daily, attackers constantly refine their Tactics, Techniques, and Procedures (TTPs), and new technologies (like AI, quantum computing, and the ever-expanding Internet of Things) continually redraw the security map. Therefore, learning cannot be a phase you complete. Instead, it must become an ongoing professional habit, as fundamental as ethical conduct (Chapter 16) or building your network (Chapter 13). It's the engine that drives relevance and growth.

During your initial transition, your learning was likely focused: "I need to learn X concept to pass Y certification," or "I need Z skill for this job role." This is a necessary and practical approach for breaking in. However, to stay ahead of the curve, this mindset must evolve. The question changes from, "What do I need to get the job?" to "How do I continuously evolve my skillset to excel in my career and anticipate future needs?"

This shift means looking beyond immediate job requirements and thinking strategically about your skill portfolio. It involves understanding trends, such as those we'll cover in Chapter 17, and proactively seeking knowledge and skills that will be valuable not just today, but in one, three, or five years.

Josiah, for instance, earned a bachelor's degree in computer science over two decades ago, well before cloud computing and artificial intelligence became mainstream and before he specialized in cybersecurity. What has proven invaluable throughout his career, however, is the consistent application of core principles: a deep understanding of how computers and networks function, the fundamental constructs of programming languages, and a mindset rooted in adversarial thinking. Not everyone can get or needs a college degree in computer science, but even mid-career professionals may at some point benefit from learning computing basics.

Thriving in cybersecurity requires more than just dutifully completing training courses. It demands genuine intellectual curiosity—a desire to understand how things work, why they break, and how they can be exploited or defended. This curiosity will drive you to explore new topics, ask probing questions, and dig deeper than surface-level explanations. Adaptability is equally crucial; the ability to unlearn old methods and relearn new ones is paramount when cherished tools become obsolete or long-held assumptions are proven wrong. Finally, a proactive stance towards knowledge means not waiting for mandated training but actively seeking out new information, experimenting with new tools, and anticipating future challenges.

Here is an example. Sarah transitioned from a decade in banking to a cybersecurity GRC (Governance, Risk, and Compliance) role. Initially, she focused on mastering frameworks like NIST and ISO 27001. However, noticing the increasing discussions around AI governance, Sarah proactively enrolled in an online course about AI ethics and risk management, even though it wasn't immediately required for her role. This foresight positioned her as a valuable resource when her company began exploring AI adoption, demonstrating the power of a proactive learning stance.

Computer science pioneer David Patterson, reflecting on more than fifty years in research and industry, cautions that "most of us spend too much time on what is urgent and not enough time on what is important."[67] In cybersecurity, where daily fire drills and new threats dominate attention, this insight is especially resonant. The most successful mid-career professionals carve out consistent time for high-impact, non-urgent activities—like building new capabilities, mentoring others, or reflecting on long-term goals. These habits sustain growth, prevent stagnation, and ensure your career evolves on purpose—not just by reaction.

Building Practical Experience through Self-Directed Projects

Theoretical knowledge is important, but practical application solidifies understanding and builds real skills. As a mid-career professional, you've likely already built foundational labs or done basic exercises, perhaps as part of getting the initial skills we previously discussed. Now it's time to go deeper.

Consider tailoring advanced home lab projects to explore specific areas like new attack vectors or defensive technologies. This could involve safely detonating malware in isolated virtual machines, practicing advanced SQL injection techniques, or experimenting with open-source security tools like Security Onion or Wazuh. Cloud security labs, utilizing free tiers from providers like AWS or Azure, allow you to practice configuring Identity and Access Management (IAM) and network security groups.

Participating in more advanced capture the flag (CTF) competitions or cyber ranges, such as those offered by Hack the Box or SANS NetWars, can sharpen skills in reverse engineering, cryptography, or forensics. Contributing to open-source cybersecurity projects is another excellent avenue. This doesn't always mean coding. You can assist with documentation, testing, or rule writing for tools like Suricata or OWASP projects. These

---

[67] David A. Patterson (2025). "Life Lessons from the First Half-Century of My Career." *Commun. ACM* 68, 2 (February 2025), 36–39.

contributions not only enhance your learning but also allow you to give back to the community.

Experience is a great teacher, but only if you actively reflect on it. After completing a significant project or responding to an incident, conduct a personal post-mortem.[68] Using a document like the one shown in Figure 8.1, ask yourself questions such as "What could have gone better?" This structured reflection helps turn experiences, both successful and unsuccessful, into actionable lessons. Develop a simple framework for extracting these lessons learned and actively participate in team-based knowledge sharing and debriefs to amplify learning for everyone.

---

[68] In government and military terminology this is often called an after-action report. While we prefer this forward-looking phrase to the more morbid "post-mortem," the latter is more commonplace in the tech world.

Post-Mortem Review Form

Project/Incident: _____

Date: _____

1. What was supposed to happen?
Describe the intended plan, objective, or outcome.

_____

_____

2. What actually happened?
Summarize the real sequence of events and outcomes, including deviations from the plan.

_____

_____

3. What went well and why?
Identify successes and the factors that contributed to them.

_____

_____

4. What could have gone better?
List challenges, missteps, or inefficiencies.

_____

_____

5. What will I do differently next time?
Turn reflection into action—define specific changes or improvements.

_____

_____

Optional: Key Takeaways to Share with the Team
Use this section to document lessons others could benefit from.

_____

_____

Figure 8.1 – A basic post-mortem report template to reflect on lessons learned from both successful projects and unsuccessful attempts.

Advanced Specialization and Specialized Credentials

Certifications can be valuable, but their pursuit should be strategic, especially post-entry into the field. As we discussed, foundational certifications such as Security+ are often part of the initial skill-building phase. Now, the focus shifts to advanced or specialized credentials that align with your specific career path and goals, not just accumulating acronyms.

One example are GIAC (Global Information Assurance Certification) credentials for specialized technical skills such as GIAC Penetration Tester (GPEN) or GIAC Certified Incident Handler (GCIH) for your respective specialty. There is also OSCP (OffSec Certified Professional) for hands-on offensive security, or CISM (Certified Information Security Manager) if your path is leading towards management or a CISO role. Cloud-specific certifications from AWS, Azure, or Google are crucial if you specialize in cloud security. When evaluating these, consider the cost, industry recognition, relevance to your desired roles, and whether the knowledge gained will tangibly improve your skills and marketability. Talk to peers and mentors in your chosen specialization about which certifications they find most valuable. Ask if your employer will cover courses or exam fees. The same critical evaluation applies to advanced training courses and workshops. Prioritize those that offer deep, hands-on learning from respected instructors and align with the technologies relevant to your specialty.

Avoiding Skill Obsolescence and the Comfort Zone

One of the subtle risks in any established career, and certainly in cybersecurity, is the gradual creep of skill obsolescence. This isn't necessarily due to a lack of effort but can often stem from becoming too comfortable in a role, focusing on familiar tasks, or inadvertently neglecting areas of growth. For mid-career professionals who have successfully transitioned and found their footing, the "comfort zone" can feel like a well-earned reward. However, in the rapidly evolving cybersecurity landscape, what is comfortable today can quickly become outdated tomorrow. Proactively recognizing and addressing this is key to long-term relevance and career vitality, and it directly complements the strategies for navigating the mid-career plateau discussed in Chapter 10.

The first step is awareness. Signs of skill stagnation can include rarely learning anything new on the job, relying on outdated tools or techniques, or finding that newer colleagues seem more knowledgeable about emerging areas. You might feel hesitant to take on projects involving new technologies or consistently find industry buzzwords and new concepts unfamiliar. If the core skills you highlight as your strengths haven't evolved significantly since you entered your current role, it's a red flag.

The antidote to stagnation is intentional discomfort—in a learning sense. Strategically seek out projects, roles, or tasks that push your learning boundaries. Volunteer for challenging assignments, especially those involving unfamiliar technologies or different security domains. Seek cross-functional collaboration; for example, if you're in the SOC, partner with the GRC team on a policy update. Offer to shadow a colleague in a different role or mentor someone in an area where you are strong. Propose improvement projects that require you to research and implement new approaches or technologies. If your organization offers rotational programs, consider them as an excellent way to gain broad experience.

Cybersecurity does not exist in a vacuum. Its effectiveness is deeply intertwined with business context, legal frameworks, data science, and user behavior. Therefore, interdisciplinary learning is crucial. Strive to understand your organization's business goals to better align security efforts. Basic data analysis skills are becoming increasingly important for tasks like threat hunting and security metrics. Stay informed about relevant laws and regulations and gain insights into psychology and user behavior to inform more effective security awareness training. Strong communication and presentation skills are vital for articulating complex technical issues to non-technical audiences.

As explored in Chapter 10, a sense of stagnation is a common experience. The strategies for continuous learning outlined in this chapter are fundamental to maintaining career momentum and engagement. When learning is an ongoing, integral part of your professional life, the risk of hitting a plateau diminishes significantly because you are constantly evolving.

Consider Javier, a network engineer with 15 years of experience who transitioned into network security. He realized he was in a comfort zone, primarily managing firewalls and VPNs, while the company was rapidly moving to cloud infrastructure. Recognizing the signs of stagnation, he proactively took an advanced AWS security course, then volunteered to lead a project migrating a specific application's network security controls to the cloud. This not only updated his skills but also reignited his enthusiasm and made him a key player in the company's cloud strategy.

By actively seeking challenges, embracing interdisciplinary knowledge, and recognizing the early signs of stagnation, you can transform the comfort zone from a potential trap into a secure base from which to launch your next phase of growth and contribution.

Future-Proofing Your Cybersecurity Career

We want to ensure your long-term viability, marketability, and fulfillment in the cybersecurity profession. For mid-career professionals, who have already invested significantly in one or more career paths, the idea of future-proofing is not about predicting the future with certainty but about building resilience and adaptability to thrive no matter how the landscape changes. This final section connects the dots between the continuous learning strategies we've discussed and your enduring career success.

Continuous learning is the bedrock of career resilience. Successful cybersecurity professionals have developed the ability to bounce back from setbacks, adapt to industry shifts, and navigate economic uncertainties. By constantly updating your skills, you become less vulnerable to obsolescence. In a competitive job market, particularly in cybersecurity where current knowledge is paramount, professionals who demonstrate a commitment to ongoing learning are always more attractive. Your proactive learning efforts—new certifications, open-source contributions, advanced lab work—become tangible evidence of your value. Furthermore, continuous learning fuels advancement, whether your goal is leadership (see Chapter 12), subject matter expertise, or specializing in a new area.

As you plan your learning, think about skills in terms of their durability and transferability. Durable skills remain valuable across technological shifts, new attack techniques, and new defenses. These include a deep understanding of foundational concepts like networking protocols (TCP/IP and routing algorithms), operating systems fundamentals, and programming basics (logic, data structures, and algorithms), as well as timeless abilities such as problem-solving, critical thinking, communication, collaboration, and adaptability. Ethical judgment is another constant. Transferable skills, as you've already demonstrated by moving into cybersecurity, can be applied across different roles or specializations. Cultivate broadly applicable skills such as risk management, project management, data analysis, and strategic thinking. While learning specific tools is important, investing in durable and transferable skills provides a more robust foundation for the future. You might even consider going back for a general computer science degree.

Consider Maria, who initially transitioned from human resources to a data privacy specialist role. She diligently mastered the technical implementations for regulations like the California Consumer Privacy Act (CCPA) but realized that privacy landscapes were shifting rapidly. Instead of solely focusing on those current regulations, she proactively studied emerging technologies like differential privacy and homomorphic encryption, anticipating the need for more advanced data protection methods. When her company faced new cross-border data transfer challenges due to changes in international laws, Maria's foresight in studying future-oriented privacy techniques made her an invaluable asset as she could guide the company towards innovative, future-proof solutions.

Future-proofing your career is an active, ongoing process. It's about making deliberate choices in your learning and development that not only address your current needs but also build a versatile and resilient skill set for the years to come. By embracing the mindset and strategies outlined in this chapter, you empower yourself to not just react to the future of cybersecurity, but to actively shape your successful place within it.

Chapter Summary

- Continuous learning is essential for long-term success in cybersecurity, requiring a shift from role-specific training to strategic skill development.

- Practical experience through self-directed projects, like home labs and CTFs, solidifies theoretical knowledge and builds real-world skills.

- Advanced certifications should be chosen strategically to align with specific career paths and emerging specializations, not just accumulated.

- Avoiding skill obsolescence requires proactively seeking challenges, interdisciplinary learning, and stepping out of the comfort zone.

- Future-proofing your career means focusing on durable and transferable skills that remain valuable across technological shifts.

Chapter References

Coursera (n.d.). *Coursera Online Learning* from
https://www.coursera.org

Hack The Box (n.d.). *Hack The Box* from
https://www.hackthebox.com

LinkedIn Learning (n.d.). *LinkedIn Learning Online Courses* from
https://www.linkedinlearning.com/learning

Chapter 9

Mastering Your Craft

You did it! You fought your way through the acronyms, the imposter-syndrome spirals, the résumé rewrites, and the first-day nerves. At some point—maybe yesterday, maybe five years ago—someone handed you a security badge and the phone number for the incident-response rotation. You're no longer "switching to cyber—" you're *here*. The urgent question now is: What kind of cybersecurity professional will you become?

Plenty of people stop at competence. They learn the playbooks, close the tickets, and keep the lights on. In a field as persistent as ours, that alone can sustain a solid career. But it won't satisfy the deeper urge that brought most mid-career changers to cybersecurity in the first place—the drive to solve thorny problems, to safeguard people and systems that matter, to leave the digital world a little safer than we found it. Competence keeps you employed. *Mastery* lets you change the game.

Mastery is not a job title, a salary band, or a single certification.[69] It is a craftsperson's mindset: an unblinking commitment to sharpen skills, deepen judgment, and multiply the impact of everyone around you. It means learning to see patterns others miss, to spot weak signals before they become breach headlines, and to translate technical nuance into decisions executives can act on. It means refusing to let yesterday's win become tomorrow's complacency.

---

[69] Some organizations have adopted an apprenticeship model (apprentice, journeyman, master) to refer to the progression of skill and experience, such as for red team operators. These levels are one indicator of mastery but are neither widespread nor the end of a lifelong learning journey.

This chapter is your roadmap from functional to exceptional. We will look at what true experts actually do—the daily habits, feedback loops, and deliberate practices that separate top performers from competent colleagues. You'll learn how to carve out time for deep work in a world of never-ending alerts, choose the domains worth mastering, and transform hard-won experience into force-multiplying tools and guidance for your team. We'll talk candidly about the pitfalls too: burnout disguised as hustle, over-specialization that strangles curiosity, and the arrogance that can blind even seasoned pros to new threats.

By the end of this chapter, you'll have the basics for a concrete plan to keep your edge sharp and your purpose clear, whether you're reverse-engineering malware, architecting cloud defenses, or leading a national SOC. Mastery is a journey with no finish line, and we cannot cover the nuance of mastery in every role in cybersecurity. But every mile traveled makes you more valuable to your organization, your peers, and the people who rely on the systems you protect. Ready to level up? Let's begin.

What Mastery Looks Like in Cybersecurity

In Chapter 2 we discussed identifying your transferable skills. Now it's time to deliberately leverage those skills toward mastery. Your prior experiences are not merely historical baggage; they are raw material for sharper judgment and deeper insight.

Competent cybersecurity professionals meet objectives reliably; masters advance the discipline. Where the competent complete tasks, the master evaluates underlying risk, anticipates emergent threats, and improves the systems and people around them. Competence is largely transactional—swap a drive, block an IP, tick a compliance box. Mastery is relational and systemic. It begins the moment you stop asking, "How do I clear my queue?" and start wondering, "How do we make this class of problems vanish?" Table 9.1 illustrates these distinctions and sets the benchmark for the development that follows.

Dimension	Competent Practitioner	Master of the Craft
Pattern Recognition	Spots known IoCs and follows playbooks.	Detects weak signals such as latent mis-configs, user-behavior anomalies, precursor events and ties them to emerging threat narratives.
Judgment Under Fog	Escalates or defers to policy when data are incomplete.	Weighs risk, business context, and adversary intent in real time, then revisits choices to refine intuition.
Depth & Breadth	Knows tool UIs and key commands.	Understands protocols, data flows, and failure modes; sees how one change ripples through the stack.
Communication	Explains findings to technical peers.	Shapes the story for developers, executives, orboard directors and converts technuance into business impact.
Proactive Improvement	Flags issues as they arise.	Automates pain points, writes docs, mentors newcomers, and seeds cultural shifts that outlast individual effort.

Table 9.1 – Comparison between competent cybersecurity practitioners and masters.

Think back to Chapter 2 where we catalogued transferable skills. That inventory was a mirror; mastery is a lens, revealing where to focus those skills for greatest leverage. The project manager who once juggled timelines now orchestrates cross-functional remediation. The classroom teacher who translated calculus into everyday language now distills adversary tradecraft for overwhelmed executives. Masters see their earlier experience not as pre-cyber baggage but as raw material for sharper judgment.

Judgment deepens fastest when you treat every incident, audit finding, or architecture review as a live-fire exercise in pattern recognition. Finish the work, then pull the thread: What surprised me? Why did it surprise me? How would I respond differently next time? Capture the answers in a running log—nothing fancy, a

Notes file will do—then circle back once a month to hunt for recurring blind spots. Over time you will notice that "What surprised me?" becomes a shorter list while "What I'd do differently" grows increasingly nuanced. That is the feedback flywheel in motion—deliberate practice informed by honest retrospection, the same loop you will use in Chapter 10 to break a mid-career plateau.

Masters also make space for deep work. Deep work can look like uninterrupted stretches when you reverse-engineer a malicious macro or redesign a privilege model. Cal Newport popularized the idea, but cybersecurity gives it a unique urgency: shallow attention begets shallow detection.[70] You will never spot the one-packet aberration in a PCAP if Slack notifications fire every thirty seconds. Reserve blocks on your calendar, close the SOC dashboard, and burrow into the hard thing until mental exhaustion nudges you to stand up and refill a water bottle. That rhythm, more than raw IQ, breeds intuition.

A useful self-check is to notice when colleagues start asking for your opinion before they take action. It is flattering, but it is also data: your judgment has become a trusted proxy for the organization's risk appetite. Equally revealing is the moment someone else onboards a new analyst with a runbook you wrote six months ago. Tools and documents that survive your absence are evidence that you are operating as a force multiplier rather than a lone hero.

Mastery has hazards, of course. Burnout can masquerade as dedication; over-specialization can calcify curiosity; early success can inflate ego and dull the urge to learn. We will tackle those pitfalls later in the chapter. For now, remember that mastery is less a destination than a direction—one hash mark on the compass labelled "ever better." Keep walking toward it and the field, your team, and the people who depend on both will be safer for the effort.

---

[70] Newport, C. (2016). *Deep Work: Rules for Focused Success in a Distracted World.* Hachette UK.

The Habits of Expert Performers

Technical skill is necessary for mastery, but it is a sustained, disciplined habit that differentiates high performers from capable colleagues. Three practices recur in the careers of the most effective professionals and can be adopted by anyone, regardless of specialty or seniority.

1. Structured, Continuous Learning

The best practitioners formalize their development. They maintain a short, written plan that identifies one knowledge gap to close each quarter—perhaps a cloud-logging nuance or a new adversary technique—and reserve scheduled time to study or experiment. Certifications may appear on that plan, but they are never the only objective; reading source code, reproducing conference talks, or building a small proof-of-concept often provide greater insight. Just as important is a steady information diet: a chapter each month from the Cyber Canon,[71] a weekly listen to podcasts such as Risky Business[72] or the CISO Series,[73] and a quick scan of curated threat-intel newsletters to stay grounded in history and trend lines. Progress is reviewed at regular intervals, echoing the personal skill inventory introduced in Chapter 2, and preventing drift into unfocused curiosity.

2. Deliberate Reflection and Documentation

Incidents, audits, and architecture reviews each generate lessons that can either vanish in chat threads or become institutional memory. High performers capture the context, decision points, and resulting adjustments within twenty-four hours, when details remain clear. A concise post-mortem turns experience into reference material that others can trust. Over time, this habit reduces repeated errors and accelerates onboarding, amplifying the author's impact far beyond individual output. It also feeds the

---

[71] https://cybercanon.org/.
[72] https://risky.biz/.
[73] https://cisoseries.com/podcast/.

monthly self-review process described earlier in the chapter, ensuring incremental refinement of judgment.

3. Intentional Knowledge Transfer

Masters regard teaching as a responsibility, not an optional extra. A newly-written detection rule is released with a one-page rationale; a junior analyst receives a live, camera-on walkthrough instead of a link to the wiki. Beyond the team, seasoned practitioners join industry working groups, contribute to open-source tooling, or publish concise blog posts so the wider community benefits from lessons learned. Inside the organization they run brown-bag sessions, invite reverse mentoring from newer staff, and pair senior engineers with mentees on defined, six-month goals. Sharing expertise clarifies assumptions, exposes blind spots, and steadily builds the credibility and trust required for cross-functional influence (see Chapter 12). Over a career, this cycle of giving and receiving knowledge weaves a lattice of relationships that accelerates problem-solving both within the company and across the industry.

These habits reinforce one another. Planned learning creates material worth documenting; documentation becomes the basis for teaching; teaching refines understanding and informs the next learning cycle. Practiced consistently, they move the practitioner along every dimension in Table 9.1, turning competence into mastery.

The Role of Judgement and Experience

Automation has displaced much of the routine pattern matching that once defined entry-level security work, but no tool can yet replicate sound professional judgment. Selecting an appropriate containment action in a partially understood incident, calibrating the acceptable risk in an architectural exception, or deciding whether to disclose a breach before the root cause is confirmed— each demand more than a decision tree. It requires a practitioner who can weigh incomplete evidence against business priorities and adversary intent, then articulate the rationale clearly to stakeholders.

Judgment grows out of experience, but it requires active cultivation. Two analysts may handle the same number of incidents, but the one who pauses afterward to ask, "Why did this succeed, what did I miss, and what would I change next time?" builds a far richer internal model of cause and effect. In the next chapter we will recommend a structured personal after-action review for overcoming career plateaus; here, the same discipline accelerates the conversion of raw experience into tacit knowledge. Over time, the practitioner develops an intuition for weak signals—a brief spike in outbound DNS, a developer question on an internal forum—that often precede a documented compromise.

Diverse exposure also sharpens judgment. Mid-career professionals bring perspectives from healthcare scheduling, military mission planning, or retail inventory controls that let them recognize patterns invisible to colleagues who have lived their entire working lives inside a SOC. When that variety is reinforced through deliberate job rotation, cross-team shadowing, or participation in industry sharing groups such as the ISACs (see Chapter 13), the practitioner learns to test assumptions under multiple operating conditions, a core element of the Cynefin sense-making framework introduced earlier in the book.

Finally, judgment matures fastest when it is made transparent. Writing a brief decision memo—three sentences on context, options considered and chosen action—subjects reasoning to peer scrutiny and forces the author to surface implicit assumptions. Where policy allows, practitioners should also publish sanitized lessons learned through personal blogs, conference talks, or posts on professional social platforms such as LinkedIn. Redacting confidential details while preserving the decision logic both protects the organization and enriches the wider security community. Our mistakes become collective learning rather than private embarrassment, and good calls can be traced and repeated under pressure. Over months, this habit not only refines individual judgment; it elevates the decision quality of the entire team, fulfilling the master's mandate to act as a force multiplier rather than a lone expert.

By cultivating reflective practice, seeking varied engagements, and exposing reasoning to constructive critique, a cybersecurity professional converts scattered experiences into reliable judgment. That capability, more than any certification or tool proficiency, distinguishes those who merely close tickets from those entrusted with shaping an organization's risk posture.

Becoming a Force Multiplier

Mastery reaches its full value when it raises others' performance. The best practitioners treat every script, workflow, and debrief as an opportunity to eliminate friction for the team. They automate repetitive checks so junior analysts can focus on analysis, publish concise primers so architects avoid common design errors, and maintain reference playbooks that new hires can trust on day one. Doing this well demands more than deep functional expertise; it requires broad systems thinking—an understanding of how processes, people, and technologies interlock so that an improvement in one area does not create risk in another. Their influence is visible in metrics like faster triage or lower rework, but also in quieter signals: colleagues quoting their guidance in architecture reviews; managers reallocating headcount because entire classes of incidents have disappeared.

This leverage is rooted in generosity rather than heroics. A master analyst who silently resolves incidents may appear productive, but the organization remains vulnerable when that person is away. By contrast, the analyst who invests an extra hour to script indicator extraction or clarify an escalation path turns individual insight into collective capability. Over months, these small acts compound and shift the culture from dependency on a few experts to a system that continuously improves itself.

That kind of influence doesn't happen in a vacuum. Successful professionals don't just build technical credibility—they invest early in building intentional, often informal, networks across their organization. As one article in the *Harvard Business Review* observed, "transition success depends on creating connections to and goodwill with not only key stakeholders and formal leaders, but also people who might not necessarily be viewed as important."[74] Deputies to senior leaders, peers in operational roles, and support colleagues all carry unique insights into workflows, priorities, and blind spots.

For mid-career professionals entering cybersecurity, proactively forming relationships with these overlooked insiders can dramatically accelerate your impact. These early allies help you avoid missteps, understand organizational dynamics, and connect your contributions to strategic goals. Mastery isn't just about tools and techniques—it's about navigating the human infrastructure that shapes decisions and defines success.

Pitfalls on the Path to Mastery

Pursuing excellence carries risks. The most common is burnout disguised as commitment. Long hours feel justified when the work is engaging and outcomes matter, yet cognitive fatigue erodes judgment. That is the very faculty mastery depends on. Setting boundaries, using leave, and rotating duties preserve the mental bandwidth required for deep analysis.

A second hazard is over-specialization. Deep focus is essential for expertise, but when it calcifies into territorialism the practitioner loses adaptability. Paradoxically, extreme adaptability can create a different problem: the "indispensable" expert who becomes a single point of failure because knowledge is hoarded rather than shared. Continuous documentation and deliberate cross-training keep expertise distributed and the team resilient.

A third danger is complacency born of early success. Positive feedback can harden into certainty, dulling curiosity and discouraging peer critique. Encourage reverse-mentoring. Invite new team members to question assumptions and walk the "master" through fresh eyes to surface blind spots that senior staff may overlook. Regular participation in external forums, candid

---

[74] Cross, R., Pryor, G. and Sylvester, D. (2021). "How to succeed quickly in a new role." *Harvard Business Review, 99*(6), 60-69.

post-mortems, and intentional exposure to unfamiliar domains counteracts the echo chamber and keeps assumptions testable.

Mastery is less a destination than a professional posture. It begins with disciplined habit, matures through reflective judgment, and achieves reach when it amplifies the effectiveness of others. The practitioner who internalizes these principles remains relevant no matter how tools evolve or adversaries adapt.

Chapter Summary

- Mastery extends beyond technical competence to a disciplined, craft-focused mindset that sharpens judgment, anticipates risk, and elevates colleagues.

- Deliberate habits—structured quarterly learning plans, rapid post-incident reflection, and routine knowledge-sharing—turn everyday work into continuous skill development.

- Sound professional judgment grows from active experience-logging, transparent decision memos, and exposure to diverse environments; it is the differentiator no automation can replace.

- Force multipliers transform personal insight into collective capability through automation, clear documentation, and mentor-driven culture change.

- Common pitfalls including burnout, over-specialization, and complacency can be mitigated with work-life boundaries, periodic breadth projects, and external peer feedback.

- Mastery is an ongoing commitment: by adopting disciplined habits and investing in others, practitioners secure both sustained personal growth and enduring organizational impact.

Chapter References

Ericsson, K. Anders and Robert Pool (2016). *Peak: Secrets from the New Science of Expertise*. Houghton Mifflin Harcourt.

Part 4

Career Advancement

Chapter 10

Navigating the Mid-Career Plateau

You made the leap. You overcame the doubts, learned new skills, landed the cybersecurity role, and maybe even surprised yourself with how quickly you adapted. For a while, everything felt new and energizing. There was momentum, growth, purpose.

And then… it leveled out.

If you're reading this chapter, you may have hit that strange middle ground where you're no longer the new person, but you don't feel like you're progressing, either. You're competent—maybe even well-respected—but some days, it feels like you're just showing up. The adrenaline of the transition has faded, and in its place, you're left with a quiet question: *Is this all there is?*

That feeling is what we call the mid-career plateau, and it's not a sign that you've failed or chosen the wrong path. It's a natural and well-documented stage in most professional journeys. In fact, the very skills that made you successful in your career pivot—your discipline, stability, and willingness to master new systems—can sometimes lead to this sense of stagnation once the learning curve flattens out. This can be particularly disorienting for mid-career professionals who have already made one major leap and expected that shift to reignite momentum.

In cybersecurity, this plateau can feel particularly unsettling. The field is dynamic, constantly shifting, always innovating. Yet paradoxically, many roles—especially in large organizations—can feel repetitive, narrowly scoped, or siloed. It's easy to assume that if you're not constantly leveling up, you're falling behind. But that's not true. What's true is that the plateau is an invitation, not a verdict. It's a signal that something needs to shift—not necessarily your job, but your mindset, your direction, or the way you're engaging with the work.

This chapter is here to help you make sense of that shift. We'll walk through how to recognize when you're in a plateau, explore strategies to move through it, and offer ways to reconnect with the deeper motivations that brought you to cybersecurity in the first place. The goal isn't to escape the plateau overnight but to learn how to use it as a platform for the next stage of your growth.

Signs You Have Hit a Plateau

The mid-career plateau doesn't always arrive with a dramatic crash. More often, it drifts in quietly. You might not even notice it at first. Things are fine. You're not failing, not burned out, not even unhappy—just… a little flat. But if you're honest, the spark that once energized you to tackle challenges, learn new tools, or stay up late reading threat intel blogs has dimmed. You're still doing good work, but you're not growing.

One of the clearest signs of a plateau is a creeping sense of disengagement. You might find yourself going through the motions, completing tasks efficiently but without much curiosity or drive. Projects that once felt exciting now feel routine. You're not learning much, or you don't feel the urgency to. Perhaps you've even stopped setting goals, or if you do, they don't motivate you the way they used to.

Another signal is internal doubt, not about your competence but about your direction. You may find yourself wondering if this is what you really signed up for, or if you're truly using your potential. You might question whether you want to specialize, change teams, or even start over again, but without a clear next step, those thoughts just hover in the background, unresolved.

It's also common to feel underutilized or overlooked. Even if you're technically succeeding in your role, you may sense that your broader experience—especially the skills and insight you brought from your previous career—aren't being tapped. You're contributing, but not in the ways you imagined when you first made the leap into cybersecurity.

These feelings don't mean something is wrong with you—or with your career. They're signals, not alarms. Recognizing them is the first step to regaining agency and moving forward with intention. In the next sections, we'll explore how to turn this period of uncertainty into a productive, energizing inflection point in your professional journey.

Reconnecting to Your Why

When you first transitioned into cybersecurity, your motivation was probably crystal clear. But over time, even the most powerful motivations can lose definition. Once the urgency of the career change fades, and the new role becomes the new normal, it is easy to forget what brought you here in the first place. And without that anchor, it's easy to drift.

Reconnecting with your "why" is one of the most powerful tools for navigating a plateau. It helps you evaluate whether the job you're in now still aligns with the deeper reasons you made the switch and whether you need to adjust your direction, your mindset, or both. This doesn't mean your original motivation was wrong. More often, it just means that it needs to evolve. A goal that once centered on proving yourself might now shift toward influence or impact. A desire for security might give way to a hunger for mastery. That shift is not failure, it's growth.

To reconnect, reflect on these questions: *What did I hope this role would provide? What did I envision myself doing or feeling by now? What has changed?* This reflection can reignite your internal dialogue. You may find your "why" is still valid but neglected, or that your priorities have shifted and your role hasn't adapted.

Taking the time to reconnect with your purpose doesn't just help you move through the plateau. It helps you do it on your terms, guided not by urgency or burnout, but by clarity. In the next section, we'll look at practical strategies to regain momentum without needing to start over or chase promotions, evolve within your current role, and rediscover a sense of progress.

Strategies to Break Through (Without Jumping Ship)

When you're feeling stuck, it's tempting to assume the only solution is to leave. A new company, a new title, a clean slate—it's easy to believe that change alone will bring progress. And sometimes it does. But jumping ship too quickly can lead to a cycle of short-term relief followed by the same long-term uncertainty. Before you polish your resume, it's worth exploring how to reignite momentum where you are.

One of the most underused tools for breaking through a plateau is lateral exploration. That doesn't mean changing careers again—it means shifting your angle of approach. Cybersecurity is broad, and many professionals underestimate how much range exists within it. If you've been working in vulnerability management, perhaps dabbling in threat intelligence or governance gives you a new lens. If you're steeped in compliance, taking on a temporary project related to incident response or cloud security might reveal a new area of passion. These lateral moves keep you learning without requiring a leap.

Another powerful tactic is to look for stretch projects, initiatives that push you beyond your comfort zone, even if they fall slightly outside your formal role. Propose a new process. Volunteer to lead a post-incident review. Create a knowledge-sharing session on AI. These kinds of efforts often go unnoticed on org charts but can reinvigorate your sense of ownership and purpose. They also signal to your colleagues and your manager that you're still growing, even if you're not climbing a title ladder.

You can also find new energy by collaborating across functions. If your current team feels stale or siloed, look outward. Can you partner with product managers, engineers, legal, or training teams? Cross-functional work is especially well-suited to mid-career professionals who already know how to navigate complex teams. It gives you a chance to apply your communication skills, see new perspectives, and make your work feel more connected to the broader mission.

And finally, be strategic with your learning. Upskilling for its own sake can feel performative but upskilling with a purpose is transformational. Choose a certification, course, or technical skill that solves a real problem you're facing or opens a door to something you're genuinely curious about. Use it as a chance not just to add a credential, but to reframe how you think about your role and what's possible next.

You don't need to switch companies or start over to grow. Sometimes, the breakthrough happens not when you change everything, but when you change how you engage with where you already are.

Reigniting Purpose Through Volunteer Service

One of the most overlooked ways to reignite your energy and direction in cybersecurity is to contribute your time and skills outside of your job. Volunteer service doesn't just help others—it often restores a sense of purpose, community, and agency that can get lost during a career plateau. It's also a way to explore new directions without making a formal career move.

Cybersecurity offers no shortage of meaningful volunteer opportunities, especially for mid-career professionals. You could help organize a local security meetup or chapter of an organization like ISSA, WiCyS, or OWASP—groups that rely on volunteers to run events, manage logistics, or coordinate speakers. These roles often allow you to practice leadership, event planning, and public speaking in low-risk, high-reward ways. If you've been craving more visibility or cross-disciplinary collaboration at work, organizing community events can scratch that itch.

You might also consider mentoring newer professionals. Programs like NPower, Year Up, or CyberUp connect experienced security professionals with people just starting out—often from underrepresented or nontraditional backgrounds. Mid-career professionals are uniquely positioned to help because you've been both the outsider and the insider. Guiding someone else can sharpen your own thinking, expand your empathy, and remind you of how far you've come.

If you're more technically inclined, contributing to an open-source security project can push your skills forward in unexpected ways. You might help maintain documentation, test detection rules, assist with QA, or even contribute code. Many projects welcome contributors of all skill levels and contributing to something public gives you tangible work to show for your time.

In the United States, some states such as Ohio and Michigan have volunteer cyber reserve organizations where trained civilian professionals offer their technical expertise to assist during critical cyber incidents, bolstering state-level cyber resilience through rapid response and mutual aid.

For those drawn to public service, nonprofits, schools, and community organizations often need cybersecurity help but lack in-house expertise. You could advise a local nonprofit on their security practices, offer a "Cyber Safety 101" workshop at a public library, or help a food bank secure their donor database. These efforts don't just make you feel useful—they give you hands-on experience with real-world problems.

The common thread is this: volunteering lets you step into new roles, apply your skills differently, and reconnect with the bigger picture of why cybersecurity matters. And in doing so, it often gives you back the momentum you didn't realize you'd lost.

When It's Time to Consider a Bigger Challenge

Sometimes, despite your best efforts, the plateau isn't just a phase—it's a signal. Not every period of stagnation can (or should) be solved by tweaking your current role, picking up a new project, or waiting patiently for things to shift. In some cases, the most honest and empowering thing you can do is acknowledge that what you need next might not be possible where you are.

This doesn't mean you failed. It means you have grown.

One of the hardest parts of mid-career navigation is discerning the difference between a temporary lull and a deeper misalignment. Maybe your organization doesn't offer a path toward the kind of work you want to do. Maybe your values have evolved, and what once felt like a great fit now feels restrictive. Maybe you've realized that you're not just bored—you're underused or stuck in a role that was never designed to accommodate your full range of experience and ambition. These realizations can feel disappointing, even disloyal. But they're also signs of clarity, and clarity is momentum.

If you're considering a bigger change, start with honest questions: Have I outgrown this role, or am I still learning from it? Do I respect the leadership around me? Am I energized by the work—or just enduring it? Can I see myself here in two years? If the answers point consistently toward dissatisfaction, it may be time to look beyond your current team, company, or even specialty. You don't need to rush, but you do need to act with intention. Talk to peers. Research roles that align with your new goals. Reconnect with what drew you to cybersecurity in the first place and use that as a guide for where you might go next.

Leaving a job—especially one you fought hard to earn—can be emotional. But it can also be the most honest and strategic move you make. Not every role is meant to carry you forever. Some are steppingstones. Some are proving grounds. Some are places you outgrow, and that's a sign of progress, not failure.

The Plateau as a Pathway

Plateaus aren't the end of the road. They're invitations to re-evaluate, reimagine, and reengage. If you're feeling stalled in your cybersecurity career—even after making the bold leap into the field—you're not broken, and you haven't made a mistake. You're simply in the quiet, often uncomfortable space between one chapter of growth and the next.

What matters most now isn't speed or title, it's direction. This moment is your chance to reconnect with why you came here in the first place, to look honestly at what's changed, and to explore new ways of applying your strengths. Whether that means deepening your expertise, shifting into a new domain, mentoring others, or even beginning to look beyond your current role, you have options. And more importantly, you have experience. You've already reinvented yourself once. You can do it again—this time with even more clarity, confidence, and purpose.

The plateau is neither a flaw nor a setback, but an intrinsic phase of transformation within your career. Embrace this pause, maintain your momentum by continuously expanding your knowledge, and remain actively committed to both the ongoing development of your professional self and the evolving vision of your professional future.

Chapter Summary

- The mid-career plateau in cybersecurity is a common phase, not a failure, and often signals a need to shift perspective or engagement.

- Recognizing signs like disengagement, doubt, and feeling underutilized is key to addressing a plateau proactively.

- Reconnecting with your "why" helps realign your current role with your initial motivations and allows for necessary evolution.

- Lateral exploration, stretch projects, cross-functional collaboration, and strategic learning can reignite momentum without requiring a job change.

- Sometimes a plateau indicates a need for a bigger challenge, and acknowledging this growth can lead to a more fulfilling path forward.

Chapter References

Nagoski, E. and Nagoski, A. (2019). *Burnout: The Secret to Unlocking the Stress Cycle.* Ballantine Books.

Sinek, S. (2009). *Start with Why: How Great Leaders Inspire Everyone to Take Action.* Portfolio/Penguin.

Chapter 11

Negotiating Salary, Benefits, and Promotions

Most of us cannot afford to work for free, even if we love our jobs. Fortunately, cybersecurity has enjoyed the luxury of commanding good salaries and benefits. Knowing how to get them and grow them is an art that we explore in this chapter. We will discuss strategies for advocating for your worth and securing the compensation and recognition you deserve.

If you are coming from another sector such as retail, hospitality, military, or a unionized workforce, be prepared for a different negotiation experience. This chapter will reveal tips for you. Cybersecurity roles often come with perks that are negotiable on top of salary, including remote work, training budgets, and conference attendance.

Many organizations are increasingly transparent about cybersecurity salaries. As of March 2025, several U.S. states including California and New York have enacted pay transparency laws requiring employers to disclose salary ranges in job postings or upon request. Private sector roles, in particular, can have negotiation flexibility.

Cybersecurity professionals often have leverage in negotiations due to the high demand for talent. Many of these negotiable perks can make a significant difference in job satisfaction, career growth, and work-life balance. Government jobs have historically had little room to negotiate but private-sector cybersecurity roles often allow more flexibility in structuring a total compensation package.

Your Market Value

A common question for those starting in cybersecurity is, "What am I worth?"

Market value is one of the most powerful negotiation tools for mid-career cybersecurity professionals, whether they're negotiating an initial job offer or advocating for a promotion. Unlike some industries with rigid pay structures, cybersecurity salaries fluctuate based on demand, specialization, and regional factors. Professionals with in-demand skills—such as cloud security, threat intelligence, or penetration testing—often find themselves in a seller's market, where companies are willing to pay a premium to secure top talent. Before negotiating, it's crucial to research salary benchmarks from sources like industry salary reports, job postings, and networking discussions with peers. For instance, the ISC2 Cybersecurity Workforce Study presents salary trends, skills demand, and workforce gaps. Another resource is Levels.fyi which focuses on tech companies and provides detailed salary breakdowns, including base salary, bonuses, and stock options.

When negotiating an initial job offer, market value helps ensure that professionals don't undervalue themselves. Employers may attempt to anchor an offer based on internal budgets or a candidate's previous salary, but informed professionals can counter with data-driven expectations. For example, if industry reports show that a cybersecurity analyst with five years of experience earns $120,000 on average, but a company offers $100,000, the candidate can leverage market data to negotiate a better deal.

Market value is equally important but often overlooked for promotions. Many companies attempt to promote from within without adjusting salaries to match external market rates. A mid-career cybersecurity professional moving from an analyst role to a senior engineer or security manager should compare their new responsibilities with market salaries for similar roles at other companies. If an external hire would be paid significantly more for the same position, that information can be used to negotiate a fair compensation adjustment. In some cases, cybersecurity professionals secure better raises by exploring external offers and using them as leverage to negotiate within their current company. Understanding market value ensures that professionals don't accept pay stagnation simply because they've been internally promoted rather than hired from the outside.

Developing a Personal Value Proposition

As a mid-career professional transitioning into cybersecurity, you bring unique experiences and perspectives that can be incredibly valuable. However, effectively communicating this value to potential employers requires a strategic approach. Your personal value proposition must bridge your past achievements with the cybersecurity skills and mindset employers seek.

Quantifying Achievements

Cybersecurity is fundamentally about managing risk, improving efficiency, and solving complex problems. Regardless of your previous field, you've likely developed skills and achieved results that demonstrate these capabilities. The key is translating these accomplishments into language that resonates with security hiring managers.

Consider these examples of quantified achievements from different backgrounds:

- Project Management: "Managed cross-functional teams that consistently delivered projects 15% under budget and ahead of schedule, demonstrating my ability to coordinate complex technical initiatives while maintaining security and compliance requirements."

- Healthcare Administration: "Implemented new patient data handling procedures that reduced privacy incidents by 40% over 18 months and ensured 100% compliance with HIPAA regulations."

- Retail Management: "Identified and resolved inventory shrinkage patterns that saved $250,000 annually by implementing new physical security protocols and training staff on loss prevention."

- Military Service: "Led a team of 12 personnel responsible for maintaining communication systems with 99.8% uptime in high-stress environments, ensuring operational security for sensitive information."

- Finance: "Detected and investigated irregular transaction patterns that prevented approximately $175,000 in potential fraud losses over a two-year period."

Notice how each example focuses on measurable results (percentages, dollar amounts, time saved) while highlighting security-adjacent skills like risk assessment, compliance, investigation, and process improvement.

For your own achievements, ask yourself:

- What problems did I solve?
- How much time/money did I save?
- What risks did I identify or mitigate?
- What processes did I improve or streamline?
- How did I ensure compliance or accuracy?

Storytelling: Making Your Background an Asset

Cybersecurity needs diverse perspectives to identify and address the full spectrum of threats. Your unique career path isn't a liability—it's potentially your greatest strength. Effective storytelling helps employers see this value.

Maria's Story

Maria spent 12 years as a criminal investigator before transitioning to cyber-security. Rather than downplaying her law enforcement background, she emphasized in her job interview how it prepared her for threat hunting.

"As a criminal investigator, I developed a methodology for tracking patterns and anomalies that others missed. In one case, I noticed subtle inconsistencies in witness testimonies that ultimately led to solving a complex fraud case affecting over 200 victims. This experience trained me to think like an adversary and anticipate their moves—skills directly applicable to identifying potential security breaches. While I'm new to certain technical aspects of cybersecurity, my investigative mindset has already helped me excel in threat hunting exercises during my security training, where I was able to identify attack patterns that more technically experienced classmates missed."

Jason's Story

Jason was a high school teacher for 15 years before transitioning to cyberse-curity awareness and training. Here is how he tells his story:

"In my years teaching advanced mathematics, I developed techniques to make complex concepts accessible to students with diverse learning styles. My teaching methods improved test scores by an average of 22% compared to departmental averages. In cybersecurity, this translates to my ability to communicate sophisticated security concepts to non-technical stakeholders. During my security certification training, I created analogy-based learning tools that helped my study group improve their practice test scores by 17%. My background in education isn't just relevant to security awareness roles—it's a competitive advantage in an industry where the ability to effectively communicate risk is just as important as identifying it."

Keys to Effective Storytelling:

- Identify the parallels between your previous role and cybersecurity challenges.
- Highlight transferable skills like critical thinking, pattern recognition, communication, or crisis management.
- Use specific examples that demonstrate these skills in action.

- Connect past achievements to specific cybersecurity functions.
- Address potential concerns about your transition proactively.
- Show enthusiasm for continuous learning and growth.

Remember that your non-traditional background gives you perspectives that lifelong security professionals may lack. A former healthcare worker understands HIPAA compliance from the ground up. A retail manager knows how security controls affect customer experience. A teacher understands how to communicate complex concepts effectively.

When crafting your personal value proposition, don't just list skills and experiences—weave them into a compelling narrative that shows employers how your unique journey has prepared you to address cybersecurity challenges in ways others cannot.

One powerful tool for cybersecurity career changers is the ability to practice job interviews with large language models (LLM) like Claude or ChatGPT. These AI assistants can simulate realistic interview scenarios, helping you refine your responses before facing actual hiring managers. The real advantage is getting immediate, constructive feedback on how effectively you're communicating your transferable skills and addressing potential concerns about your background. Unlike practicing with friends who might not understand cybersecurity hiring needs, you can ask LLMs industry-specific questions and evaluate your answers against current expectations. To try this yourself, copy this prompt into Claude or ChatGPT:

> "I'd like to practice for a cybersecurity job interview. I'm transitioning from [your current/previous field] to a [specific cybersecurity role] position. Please act as a hiring manager conducting an interview. Ask me challenging questions about my background transition, technical knowledge, and how my previous experience applies to cybersecurity. After each of my responses, provide brief constructive feedback on the

strength of my answer, areas I could improve, and how I might better highlight my transferable skills. Start with an introduction and your first question."

Preparing for the Offer Negotiation Process

In cybersecurity, most companies expect that you will negotiate the salary and benefits, and it is wise to be prepared to do so. Your market research will help in this process. Salary is most negotiable as is a starting or hiring bonus. Most companies will not negotiate benefits, but if you don't need all the benefits, sometimes companies will provide a salary increase in lieu of some of the benefits. For example, if a company offers a $2,000 relocation stipend, but you don't need to move or will be working remotely, you can ask for that as part of a bonus to start or in salary since they will not have to move you. If you have health coverage through your veteran status or through a partner, that saves an employer a tremendous amount of money that they may apply to increasing your salary.

Don't fall for the trap when an employer asks what you expect in a salary. Your best move is to ask the company to make the first offer. Don't be afraid to ask for more, this is expected. Many people have gotten more money simply by asking if their offer was the best they could do, and it was not!

A note for those transitioning to industry from government and military: you only get to do this transition once where you can hand-wave some of the details of your experience due to classification. Government has traditionally had a great reputation among tech companies. Don't underestimate your value and use this to your advantage.

Category	Negotiable Terms
Bonuses and Financial Incentives	• Sign-on bonus • Performance bonuses • Equity/stock options • Retention/longevity bonus
Career Growth and Education Support	• Certification reimbursement (CISSP, OSCP, CISM) • Conference attendance (Black Hat, DEF CON, RSAC) • Tuition reimbursement for degrees or courses • Conference travel assistance
Work-Life Balance and Remote Work	• Remote or hybrid work options • Flexible work hours or four-day workweeks • Extra PTO or holidays • Enhanced parental leave
Job Role and Responsibilities	• Defined career path and promotion structure • Specialization in a preferred security domain • Negotiation of job title
Equipment and Resources	• Home office stipend (desk, chair, monitor) • Access to cybersecurity labs or training platforms • Company-paid phone or internet
Relocation Assistance	• Coverage for moving costs • Temporary housing support • Commuter benefits (parking, transit reimbursement)
Job Security & Contract Terms	• Severance package in case of layoffs • Review or adjustment of non-compete agreements • Additional pay for on-call duties

Table 11.1 – Potentially negotiable items.

When negotiating cybersecurity job offers, you'll likely encounter these common objections:

- "This is our standard package."
- "We can't exceed our budget."
- "You lack direct cybersecurity experience."
- "This is already our top range."

Your success in pushing back on these objections depends on prepared responses that highlight your unique value.

- For experience objections, emphasize transferable skills: "While I'm new to cybersecurity, my experience managing complex healthcare data systems taught me to identify vulnerabilities and ensure compliance with strict privacy regulations."

- For budget constraints, suggest alternatives: "I understand budget limitations. Could we discuss a performance review in six months, additional certification funding, or flexible working arrangements?"

Remember that effective negotiation focuses on mutual benefit, not winning.

- Always frame requests in terms of the value you'll bring to their security program.

- Support your position with specific market data.

- Suggest creative alternatives when direct salary increases aren't possible.

- Acknowledge constraints while offering solutions.

- Maintain a collaborative tone rather than an adversarial one.

- Be prepared to explain why investing more in you specifically addresses their security challenges.

- If they won't budge on salary, consider negotiating for performance bonuses, additional training budget, conference attendance, or flexible work arrangements.

Promotions in Cybersecurity

In the dynamic landscape of cybersecurity careers, promotion timelines typically range from one to three years, though advancement paths vary significantly across organizations and specialties. While larger corporations offer structured progression with formalized benchmarks, smaller companies and startups may provide accelerated advancement opportunities despite less defined career ladders. Industry sector plays a crucial role, with financial services and government contractors generally adhering to more rigid promotion schedules compared to technology firms. Practitioners specializing in high-demand areas such as cloud security, security architecture, or penetration testing often experience faster career progression, particularly when complemented by relevant certifications.

For aspiring cybersecurity professionals transitioning from non-technical fields, understanding the industry's unique job mobility dynamics is essential. Unlike traditional career paths where company loyalty often yields steady advancement, cybersecurity careers frequently accelerate through strategic employer changes. This "hop and level-up" approach has become normalized in the industry, and professionals may achieve a salary increase and title promotion with each well-timed move. Many cyber professionals find themselves plateauing at an organization after two to three years, having absorbed available knowledge and reached compensation ceilings. The market values fresh perspectives and diverse exposure to different security environments, making someone who has implemented security measures across multiple organizations often more attractive than a candidate with equivalent years at a single company. For career-changers, this means building foundational skills at an initial position with reasonable expectations, then leveraging that experience to make calculated jumps that rapidly advance both responsibility and compensation.

In cybersecurity, the value you bring to an organization often outweighs your job title. Unlike traditional corporate structures where promotions are tied to tenure or managerial responsibilities, cybersecurity professionals can command higher salaries and influence based on their ability to mitigate risk, improve security posture, and respond to emerging threats. A skilled penetration tester, security engineer, or incident responder may have more strategic impact on a company's bottom line than a director with a broader but less technical focus. This means that negotiating for a raise or career advancement should focus on the tangible impact of your work—reducing breach risks, ensuring regulatory compliance, preventing financial losses, or securing critical infrastructure—rather than simply pushing for a higher title. Many cybersecurity professionals advance their careers by proving their expertise through certifications, project successes, and measurable security improvements, rather than following a rigid corporate ladder. When negotiating, it's often more effective to demonstrate the business value of your contributions rather than relying solely on job seniority as leverage.

Negotiating a promotion may involve making a business case that focuses on risk reduction, compliance, or cost savings—more than just proving leadership skills.

Chapter Summary

- Thoroughly research cybersecurity salary benchmarks from industry reports, job postings, and networking to understand your worth in the current market.

- Present your mid-career transition as an asset, emphasizing how your previous industry experience provides valuable perspective for cybersecurity challenges.

- Consider the full compensation package including bonuses, equity, certification reimbursement, conference attendance, and flexible working arrangements.

- Recognize that cybersecurity compensation structures vary significantly across sectors, with private industry often offering more flexibility than government roles.

- Remember that in cybersecurity, significant advancement often comes through strategic employer changes, with 15-30% increases common when moving companies.

- Frame your value in terms of risk reduction, compliance improvements, and cost savings rather than just technical skills or experience.

- Track and present your contributions with specific metrics to strengthen your position during promotion and raise discussions.

Chapter References

Bazerman, Max H (2025). *Negotiation: The Game Has Changed.* Princeton University Press.

Levels FYI, https://www.levels.fyi/.

Voss, Chris, and Tahl Raz (2016). *Never Split the Difference: Negotiating as if Your Life Depended on It.* Random House.

Chapter 12

Leading in Cybersecurity

Becoming a Cybersecurity Leader

The word *leader* gets used a lot in cybersecurity, sometimes to describe those with formal authority and other times to refer to individuals with influence, expertise, or a strong voice in the community. Both types of leadership matter. This chapter, however, focuses on those who hold formal management roles: professionals responsible for leading cybersecurity teams, running programs, and aligning security efforts with organizational priorities.

Cybersecurity has room for many kinds of leadership. Some of the most respected figures in the field are individual contributors—technical experts whose thought leadership shapes the direction of the industry. But there is also a more traditional leadership path: from practitioner to team lead to functional manager to CISO. In this chapter, we'll explore what it means to lead from one of these formal roles, and how effective cybersecurity managers show up for their teams, their organizations, and the profession.

As a mid-career jobseeker, it's possible you may move directly into a cybersecurity organizational leadership role, or you may move into an individual contributor role and maybe later move into cybersecurity team leadership. As someone new to the profession, it may take you some time to build up the technical experience to be that kind of leader.

Regardless, it is important to understand what cybersecurity leaders do differently than other leaders and to be prepared to lean into these areas.

Cybersecurity Leadership Elements

A cybersecurity leader shares many traits with any other kind of leader: having business acumen; partnerships; communications; strategic planning. Cybersecurity leaders must lean into some areas more than other leaders, and in some cases has unique skills requirements due to the nature of cybersecurity.

Table 12.1 lists some of the most important goals of a leader, why they matter specifically in cybersecurity, and what leaders must do to achieve the goals.

Leadership Goal	Importance in Cybersecurity	Leadership Actions
Investing in Training and Networking	Not only must cyber teams keep up with changes in the technology, they must keep up with the threat actors and threat vectors as well. This means security teams spend a larger portion of their budget on training conferences. Some companies like to invest in online, generic training tools but security people need to get hands-on, in person training. Security teams that fail to do this will have higher turnover of staff.	Leaders must make the case that their budget for training and travel is greater than other technology functions, and must use this to attract and retain talent.
Advanced skills in enrolling support and buy-in from non-security leadership	Security leaders must know how to engage stakeholders — particularly organizational leaders and get buy-in for the security program. Without this skill, security programs are underfunded and under-prioritized. While this is true of non-security functions, most other functions can make direct correlation to revenue eneration, whereas cybersecurity usually cannot.	Leaders must have advanced communication (verbal and written) skills, empathy and partnership skills, and influencing capabilities, so that they can "sell" their security ideas.

Table 12.1– Leadership goals, importance in cybersecurity, and actions.

Leadership Goal	Importance in Cybersecurity	Leadership Actions
Ingesting new information quickly	Unlike any other non-military function, security leaders must understand and adapt to constantly changing adversary tactics and techniques.	Cybersecurity leaders must ensure their teams are designed to absorb new information, have the skills and bandwidth to respond to externally-driven changes, and maintain an external awareness to learn of and understand changes.
Measuring a negative success metric	When security is done well, it can be invisible to organizational leaders. When it's done poorly, the impact is highly visible. This is opposite other business functions.	Security leaders need to understand how to measure the success of programs and educate other leaders on what cybersecurity success metrics mean.
Monitor the regulatory environment	Every business function has some regulatory or legal mandate; cybersecurity has more than any of them, and these laws and regulations are constantly changing. Failure to pay attention to local, state, federal and international mandates will harm the organization.	Security leaders should ensure they have access to legal and policy specialists who can monitor and advise on the cybersecurity legal and regulatory environment.

Table 12.1 – Leadership goals, importance in cybersecurity, and actions
(continued).

Leadership Goal	Importance in Cybersecurity	Leadership Actions
Enhanced industry networking	Security is a young profession, and there aren't common ways of doing things. There are no guidebooks. Understanding what problems exist, and how to address them, requires an external network of informed sources. To understand how to build and maintain a security program, a leader needs constant feedback from the professional community outside their immediate organization.	Security teams should ensure a significant portion of their time is allocated to external engagements, and not just with vendors. They should set this expectation with their leadership also.
Deep end-to-end process understanding	In order to understand potential threat vectors that require protection, the security team must understand organizational processes end-to-end, and not just their own piece of that process. This means partnering with the business operations as well as other technology groups, to fully understand workflows.	Security leaders should have access to business analysts and process engineers who can help map complex business processes. Recognizing poorly designed processes is a leadership skill to develop.
Foster a security culture	Organizations are inherently insecure in the technologies they use and the processes they follow. Security leaders must focus on improving the organizational culture to pay attention to and value appropriate security activities.	Security leaders must recognize that organizational change takes time and effort. Having the tenacity to continue to push for cultural change over months and years takes a lot of mental stamina that a security leader must cultivate.

Table 12.1 – Leadership goals, importance in cybersecurity, and actions (continued).

Balancing the Strategic with the Tactical

Of all the elements cybersecurity leadership must consider, the most impactful factor to the way people lead cybersecurity programs is that leaders must be prepared to defend against external attackers. No other non-military leader needs to factor this into their leadership planning.

Why does this matter? Most C-suite executives are expected to be primarily strategic in their thinking and in the way they design and run their areas. For cybersecurity, leaders must leave space to be reactive and tactical depending on the current cybersecurity threat/attack landscape. This is a difficult and sometimes career-limiting problem for cybersecurity leaders to address.

The first thing a new leader must do in practice is to ensure that incident response processes are in place and effective, in case some significant cyber event happens when the new leader is still getting acclimated to the organization. It means the cybersecurity leader must continue to pay attention to industry current events—news cycles, emerging threat awareness, national security events, and even international conflicts. It means staying in touch with all aspects of business and technology across the company so there are no security surprises when the organization installs new tech, completes a merger, or contracts with a vendor, any of which may change the risk surface of the organization.

How can a leader make this balance work?

Counterintuitively, we suggest making sure you do indeed have a strategic plan which describes new security and business outcomes. This isn't just a consideration of what tools you want to buy next, but a roadmap for maturing the security program over the next one to three years. It should be high-level enough that even in the face of tactical events (a breach of your organization, a general industry event, a change in regulations, etc.) you can keep working towards that strategic vision.

Concurrently, make sure you have structured your security team so they can make progress towards the strategic vision and also have the bandwidth to monitor and respond to external events. Don't make the mistake of expecting them to do industry monitoring and response *on top of* their formal responsibilities. That will lead to burnout. These must be incorporated into the expectations of their role.

Every security person on your team, for example, may have a work-breakdown that includes:

- **"Keep The Lights On" (KTLO) Work.** Day-to-day operational tasks, the main reason they were hired.

- **Project Work.** The things they do to move towards the strategic vision, improve processes, or otherwise make changes to your operating environment.

- **Training and Development.** Monitoring of industry events, general awareness of trends and issues, and expanding technical skills.

- **Incident Response.** Not every security role will directly include incident response, but you might consider how non-incident responders can help pick up any slack when incident responders are actively engaged in an incident.

The more junior the employee, the larger percentage of time is spent on KTLO activities. More senior resources spend more time on project-related work. A security leader's KTLO work is the work of directing the team, partnerships with stakeholders, and so forth.

Everyone on the security team needs to make sure their roles include these elements in their planned working day. Otherwise, the inevitable fire-drills from external events will consume everyone's time (detecting, responding, reacting, recovering), and your partners will consider the security leader to be "too tactical."

The Power of Decision-Making Frameworks

For the uninitiated, cybersecurity seems like a constant swirl of new things requiring new techniques. A cybersecurity leader will be unsuccessful if they continue to treat threats and technology changes like a brand-new problem to solve. Mature cyber leaders have preferred decision-making frameworks to help manage their environments. A good framework will be complex enough to create insight, but simple enough to allow for execution—a difficult combination to achieve. Table 12.2 lists some frameworks that are commonly applied in cybersecurity decision making.

Regardless of the models chosen, a leader must share their frameworks with their team and partners and make sure there is alignment and understanding amongst everyone involved.

Framework	When To Use It
Capability Maturity Models	Found in most security frameworks (e.g. NIST), a maturity model allows leaders to assess their organization against a process or standard, then show improvement over time. Often described in five levels—initial to optimized—a leader can decide what level of maturity aligns to an organization's risk appetite.
Cynefin Framework	When confronted with a new problem or technology, the Cynefin Framework enables a leader to make sense of complex situations based on what is known or unknown. It gives guidance on how to respond.
OODA Loop (Observe, Orient, Decide, Act)	Useful to iterate quickly in a changing environment. A tactical model when fast responses are required.
Pareto Principle (80/20 Rule)	Recognizing that focusing on a subset of issues/controls/efforts might be more efficient than spreading resources thinly, a security leader can follow this model to focus the efforts of their team.

Table 12.2 – Example operating models and when to use them.[75][76][77]

Branching Out: Becoming a Systems Thinker[78]

The growth of an individual through a cybersecurity career, whether as a team leader or an individual contributor, will follow a predictable path. In the first decade or so of their career, new cybersecurity professionals will focus on one or two functional areas and become highly competent in those areas. We often call this person a subject matter expert. As they mature, cybersecurity professionals' technical focus will shift from being deep to being

[75] See https://nvlpubs.nist.gov/nistpubs/CSWP/NIST.CSWP.29.pdf#page=29.11.
[76] See https://thecynefin.co/about-us/about-cynefin-framework/.
[77] See https://thedecisionlab.com/reference-guide/computer-science/the-ooda-loop.
[78] For more, see https://www.simplypsychology.org/pareto-principle.html.

wide—taking a systems-management approach to their knowledge, working environment, and influence.

People looking to move into a leadership role should therefore understand that to truly lead they need to understand more than their own function, team, or company. They must find network partners and work experiences that cut across multiple functions, departments, and organizations.

This is typically the point in someone's career where they realize they must focus not only on the technical issues, but also on the people and process issues that accompany their cybersecurity goals. Here are a few of the actions we see in successful leaders:

- Cybersecurity leaders should look for network contacts and mentors that help them reach widely across different parts of the security function, and beyond. Consider joining cybersecurity advisory boards, non-profit leadership boards, or even public boards.

- Within an organization, seek to engage in projects and initiatives that cross multiple departments and functions, not just IT or security functions.

- Read/watch/listen widely. Understand the history of the profession, paying attention to trends that extend across decades, not just current affairs.

- Pay attention to the security vendor community. Understand what drives that market, what functional areas are receiving investment dollars from venture capitalist, and where the market is headed.

- Understand regulatory and policy trends not just for cybersecurity, but also for general IT, artificial intelligence, privacy, and data management.

As a cybersecurity leader, your role isn't just to help your organization operate efficiently and effectively, it is also to help the organization prepare for changes in the way it operates and the environment in which it operates. The only way to do this is to deliberately spend a portion of your working life thinking beyond your immediate team, organization, region, and industry.

Changing Leadership Roles

There is much debate in the industry about the future of cybersecurity leadership. What will a leader be responsible for? Who will they report to? What personal liability will a leader assume when taking a security leadership role in an organization? How much will they need to leverage technical skills versus organizational skills? Will security leaders need to be licensed?

For now, the job description of a security leader is set by the organization hiring the leader, at least until the security leader defines the role for themselves. This means that a new leader often has the flexibility to define the type of security leader they want to be. Table 12.3 lists some typical security leadership roles.

Security Leader Type	Description
Technical / Operational	Has a deep technical background; can lead an organization who needs to strengthen their security controls; often used for young/start-up organizations, or to lead smaller security teams.
Risk-Focused	Usually found in highly regulated industries; leads boards and C-suites to manage cyber risk, with a heavy emphasis on regulations and security frameworks.
Business-Aligned	Works closely with front-line and C-suite stakeholders to design a security program that supports business objectives. The role is often customer-facing; common in organizations where security is a big part of the customer experience.
Post-Incident / Crisis Manager	CISOs with deep experience responding to and recovering from breaches, these CISOs are brought in to turn around organizations that have suffered from a major security incident.
Virtual / Fractional CISO	Contracts to organizations, usually on a short-term or part-time basis, to create and oversee a security program. May work independently or as part of a services company.

Table 12.3 – Various types of security leader roles and responsibilities.

Within each of these security leader types, a person can decide if they want to be transformational (building/growing a team/function) or steady state (if it works, don't fix it). Many people are a hybrid of all of the above roles depending on the needs of the organization.

As the technology environments of organizations become more distributed amongst their supply chains, as the types of threats and attacks against organizations gain in scope and scale, and as the regulatory environment becomes more complicated, it's nearly impossible for one person to be all of the security leader types. When looking for a cybersecurity leadership role, jobseekers should be clear on the type of leader they want to be, and the type of leader the organization needs. Look for commonality between the leadership style and the organization's expectations to avoid failing in the leadership role.

Chapter Summary

- Being a cybersecurity leader involves understanding and focusing on security-specific leadership elements which differentiate cybersecurity from other technical functions.

- Ensure that you have a security strategic plan to give longer-term guidance on the right work to do, and to continue to mature the security function.

- Operationally, build time for cybersecurity incident response into the work schedule of every security team member, including the security leader.

- Mature cybersecurity leaders use mental models to organize, sense, and respond to their environments so that they lead strategically, not reactively.

- Leaders think and act broadly. They consider people and processes, not just technology, and their influence extends to entire systems, not just individual functions.

- There are many types of security leaders; make sure you know what kind of leader you are (or want to be) and look for organizations that suit your leadership style.

Chapter References

Bonney, B., Hayslip, G., and Stamper, M. (2023). *CISO Desk Reference Guide: A Practical Guide for CISOs (Volume 1, 3rd ed.)*. CISO DRG Publishing.

Dykstra, J. A. and Orr, S. R. (2016, October). *Acting in the Unknown: The Cynefin Framework for Managing Cybersecurity Risk in Dynamic Decision Making*. In 2016 International Conference on Cyber Conflict (CyCon US) (pp. 1-6). IEEE.

Howard, Rick (2023). *Cybersecurity First Principles: A Reboot of Strategy and Tactics*. Wiley.

Chapter 13

Building Your Network

The Importance of Networking

Throughout this book, we have emphasized the importance of building and maintaining a professional network. This network helps you in a variety of ways:

- Finding your first cybersecurity job and finding future jobs as you move through your career;

- Providing resources to help you stay in touch with emerging technologies, security techniques, and practices;

- Offering emotional and mental health support, providing people who will support you on your professional journey; and

- Creating a place to build your brand and give back to the cybersecurity community.

Managing our network is an important business skill, doubly important for an unstructured and constantly changing industry like cybersecurity. While letting our network grow organically can be useful, if you are a mid-career professional looking to move into cybersecurity for the first time, it is important to be focused and deliberate in building your network.

In this chapter, we will explore how to network intentionally and efficiently so you can make the most of your time and talents and maximize the benefits of being part of the cybersecurity community.

Who Do You Need?

When thinking about a network, certain people will be helpful to you as you move into the cybersecurity profession. At this stage, these people will help you identify your skills gaps, connect to potential job opportunities, and support you as you evaluate job options and emerging issues.

By now, you should have contemplated why you want to work in cybersecurity, the "problem" you wish to solve, and the kind of role you are looking for. With this information in hand, you can start adding people to your network who focus more on the kind of work roles you want. Author and career coach Pete Schramm refers to these people as your personal "Board of Advisors." [79] What kind of people might you need?

- A Functional Mentor: This person is experienced in the cybersecurity industry and can provide guidance and knowledge. These people can take two forms:
    - An industry expert with many years of experience who can provide "big picture" advice, or
    - A functional leader who is two to four years ahead of you in your chosen career and who can offer tactical guidance.

- A Supportive Peer: People on the same journey as you, roughly at the same point in their career, perhaps with the same characteristics as you (e.g., gender, age, race). They can be sounding boards and provide useful feedback and collaboration. They can also be someone at your existing organization that works in cybersecurity.

- Your Immediate Supervisor: They can provide useful feedback on your transferable work skills, and they can help you navigate your organization if you are looking to move laterally into a security role at your existing company.

---

[79] Schramm, Pete (2023). *Pathfinders: Navigating Your Career Map With a Personal Board of Advisors.* Latitude, Inc.

- A Coach: A person who can help you hone your skills in a specific functional area. This may be a security-focused skill like red-teaming or governance or a professional skill like technical writing or public speaking.

- A Sponsor: Someone who will connect you to opportunities and advocate for you. This person may be in your company (a member of the cybersecurity team?), but perhaps they are outside your company in the cybersecurity industry.

Your professional network will include more than just people in these roles; however, these are the people you will invest time in to build an ongoing, mutually beneficial relationship. They will help you move forward in an organized way and help you stay focused on the things that are important to you.

If you already have all these people, great! If not, or if some of them need to be "refreshed" to focus on cybersecurity, consider what is most important now and in what order you'll add to your board of advisors. Don't assume these people have to be personal friends (although some of them inevitably will be). Consider these transactional relationships and establish clear boundaries and goals for what you want to achieve.

Continue to evaluate these relationships over time. Some will become more important, and others will lose their value to you. It's OK to decide to leave an advisor relationship when it is no longer serving your (or their) purpose and to replace it with someone else.

How Do You Start?

You already have a network. That is, you have people you know and have a relationship with already. Family, friends, co-workers, neighbors, and others are already available to you. Can any of them fill the advisor roles you need? Can any of them get you information about working in cybersecurity?

Chances are, they probably can't. Not everyone works in cybersecurity after all. But those people might know someone who does. Their second-level contacts can be very useful to you. Your first-level contacts may work for companies with security teams—can they make an introduction? In her book, *Switchers,*[80] Dawn Graham suggests that you engage the relationships you already have to get to those second-level contacts at the companies you're targeting for your first cybersecurity job. Ask your primary network to introduce you to those secondary contacts (a warm introduction is much better than a cold outreach). If your immediate network doesn't know anyone at those target companies, reach out on social media or attend meetups where those people will be and introduce yourself.

It sounds easy, doesn't it, to just say "introduce yourself?" For some people, it is easy, and for others it's a fate worse than death. You might be surprised at how often people reply to a cold connection. Josiah once emailed a Nobel Prize winner, never expecting a response, but was thrilled to receive a reply!

If you are making a cold connection on social media, try to find something the person has done that you can comment on, such as:

- *"I really appreciated your perspective in your blog about [x] and would love to discuss this further. Would you have time to connect?"*

- *"I see you are involved with the [industry organization]. Can we connect to discuss what they are doing?"*

- *"Regarding your question about [x] that you posted this week, I saw this article that may be interesting to you."*

- *"I saw you speak at [conference] and was interested in your [security topic]. Would you have time to meet with me to discuss further?"*

The purpose of the cold introduction is to try to build connections with the person, so using something they're already interested in is a great way to start. But be patient: this is a long game, not a sprint. If they don't respond immediately, don't badger them. Give them

---

[80] Graham, Dawn (2018). *Switchers: How Smart Professionals Change Careers and Seize Success.* Harper Collins.

a month and try again. If you try three times with no response, leave it. Building your network is a numbers game. You will need to reach out to many people in order to build the network you need. Don't expect everyone to respond, and don't pin your hopes on connecting with just a few people. Widen your search for contacts and be open to meeting with people whenever the opportunity comes up. Not only might they be a useful connection (now or in the future), but they may have connections of their own who could be useful to you, too.

When you're showing up in person at an event, the idea is to have a conversation with people to build your network. If it helps you to bring a friend to a meetup, do that. Make a point to introduce yourself to any of the speakers and thank them for their comments. If you don't know anyone there, find the other people standing around solo and introduce yourself to them. Always talk to vendors at booths. You will learn about their products, but they are also likely to have their own networks that might be useful for you.

Whether you are getting a virtual meeting with a new person or meeting someone during a happy hour, approach the interaction with curiosity. Ask them:

- What do you do?
- What do you like/not like about what you do?
- What is new/different about your role now compared to [x] years ago?
- I recently saw [something newsworthy] in the news—how does it impact you?

At the beginning of a relationship, don't give them your elevator pitch, and don't ask them for anything. Just learn about them. If you decide this person is someone you want to maintain a relationship with, we suggest you stay in touch by following up online or in person. If, during your conversation, the other person suggests something that you act on, follow up with the person to let them know what happened and to thank them again for the suggestion. Conversely, if there is someone you know who would be helpful to the person you are talking to, offer to make an introduction (it's what super connectors do!) or share their contact information (with permission from the third person).

All this network building takes time. For people trying to break into the cybersecurity industry, we believe that building your network is as important as learning cybersecurity skills so allocate your time accordingly. Invest in your network to find the people who can best advise, coach, and mentor you. In the beginning, this may take you a lot of time (exactly how much time will depend on your personal circumstances). Expect to spend time on this daily until you have the people you need. After that, maintaining your important connections can take a few hours a week.

Networks are only as useful as the effort you put into them. As you move into cybersecurity, then progress through the industry, plan to continue the habit of maintaining and building your network as part of your weekly activities. Without networking, you won't be able to get into cybersecurity and grow once you're there. Networking is a skill you must learn!

Where Do You Start?

These days, not everything must happen in person. There are multiple places where you can apply your networking skills to build relationships and find people who will help you develop your cybersecurity career.

- Networking events: For cybersecurity, this usually means conferences and meetups. If you can't travel, look for things happening locally.

- Leverage social media: Successful use of social media can begin by following cybersecurity people (particularly those who work at your target companies) and commenting on their posts.

- Joining professional organizations: Organizations like ISSA, ISC2, and others often have local chapters. Attend their events (even better, find a way to volunteer or speak) and get to know their leaders.

- Join online communities: Participating in online spaces where learning/work happens can be a wonderful way to network while adding skills to your resume.

If you have the time to engage in all these methods, do it. If you must choose, choose those interactions that create connection—in person is best, but virtual is OK. Don't be passive, reach out and talk to people.

Maintaining Your Network

Once you have made contact with people who will be useful to your career aspirations, you must build those relationships and maintain them over time. How can you do this?

In his 2005 book, *Never Eat Alone,* Keith Ferrazzi emphasizes the need to give to your network before asking anything of it. He notes that for most people, the things that drive them boil down to "health, wealth, and children." Think about your network and the people in it. What do they want? Can you help them with these things? If so, don't wait to ask. Reach out and offer assistance. When someone mentions a problem, see if you have a way to offer a solution.

Find ways to stay in constant contact with the people in the inner circle of your network.

- Getting together for meals or meetings is great, but don't forget more quick-touch things like remembering birthdays, offering a quick link to an interesting article, or even commenting on social media posts with a personal message.

- Stay constant and stay relevant. There are applications to help you keep in contact with your network, remember key dates, and keep track of your communications and meetings. Use them as needed.

- Don't hesitate to bring multiple networking contacts into the same space. Invite more than one person to meet for a beverage or meal at the same time. They may enjoy meeting new people too!

Every so often, review your network. It is OK to remove people who aren't adding value to you, and you may need to add in new people depending on your career or personal needs. Be intentional about who is on your advisor list, who is helpful for referrals and coaching, and who is useful for general information.

Is Your Network Working for You?

If you're going to spend a lot of time networking, and you should, you need to know if the effort you're putting into the network is worth it. As in any cybersecurity job, measuring the outcome of your effort is important, and will help keep you on track. What should you keep an eye on?

- Basic numbers: How many people are in your network? How many are core Advisors, versus loose connections, versus social media follows/followers? Are these good numbers for your career objectives?

- Connection: How often are you meeting with your key network contacts? Based on the kind of thing you need from them, are you meeting often enough? Do you (or they) keep rescheduling meetings, or fail to connect?

- Diversity: Are there people in your network that will help you understand the different parts of cybersecurity? You may be focused on a certain kind of cybersecurity job and will need people in your network who can help you understand that function—but you will also need to know other security functions as well. Alternatively, you may have people in your network who are in your target industry, but you may need people doing the same security function in other industries, to get a well-rounded view of the function.

- Quality: When you meet with your advisors, are they helping you in the way you need? Are conversations meaningful for both of you? Are you continuing to learn from them? Do they reach out to you too, or are all the interactions initiated by you?

- Career goals: Is your network helping you achieve your goals? Are they making introductions/referrals for you? Helping you learn more about cybersecurity? Assisting in getting job interviews?

- Celebrate successes: Recognize when something good happens because of your network. Make sure your network contacts know this too. Get an interview? Celebrate. Make a valuable new connection? Celebrate. Learn something new through a network contact? Celebrate.

The value of your network is not its size; the value is in how it can help you with your goals. Make sure the people in your network understand how much they mean to you, and make sure you stay connected.

Chapter Summary

- Job-switchers should be deliberate about building and growing their networks to reap network benefits quickly and efficiently.

- Expect to spend significant time building your network, and regular time afterwards maintaining your network.

- Focus on creating a personal "Board of Advisors" to help you land your first cybersecurity role, then grow from there. Evaluate the effectiveness of your board over time and make changes when necessary.

- Use your immediate network to get introduced to Advisors and extend your network to focus on your cybersecurity needs.

- Where possible, finding common interests between you and the person you're trying to connect with is a good way to introduce yourself and get a meeting.

- Add value before you ask for anything yourself.

- Stay in regular contact with key members of your network.

- Regularly assess the value of your network and adjust accordingly.

Chapter References

Ferrazzi, Keith (2005). *Never Eat Alone.* Crown Publishing

Graham, Dawn (2018). *Switchers: How Smart Professionals Change Careers and Seize Success.* Harper Collins

Schramm, Pete (2023). *Pathfinders: Navigating Your Career Map With A Personal Board of Advisors.* Lattitude, Inc.

Part 5

Additional Guidance and Considerations

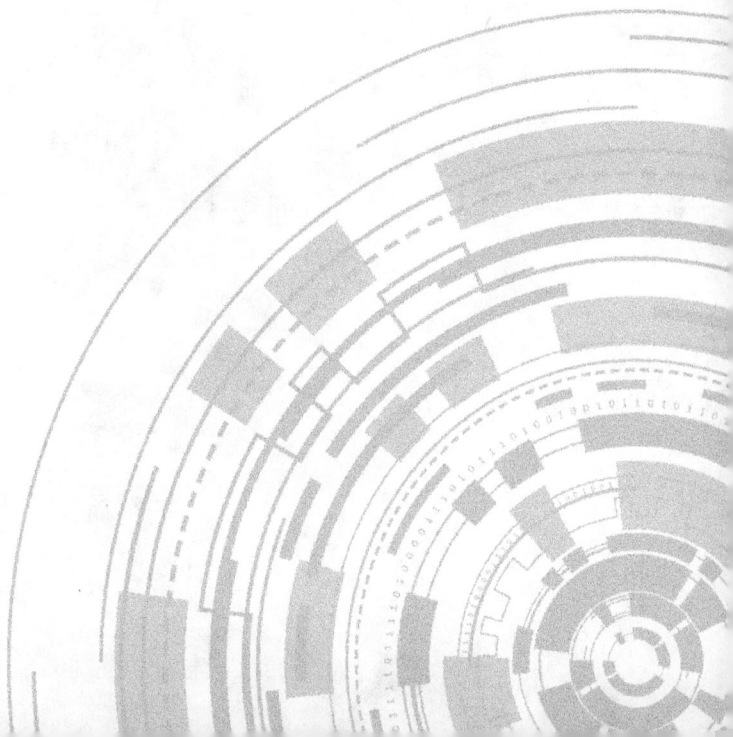

Chapter 14

Maintaining Work-Life Balance

Early in his career Josiah worked as a tactical cyber operator for seven years. This was high-risk, high-value, complex work. Like a fighter pilot, performance was highly correlated with speed and precision. He sometimes worked night shifts. His role expanded over time to include training and mentoring junior peers and leading special projects. In all, this work started to take a toll.

The job was eye-opening. It was fun, exciting, and rewarding, even though it was difficult and occasionally exhausting. Wanting to understand and draw attention to the human aspects of cybersecurity, Josiah moved into a research-focused role and proceeded to collaborate on studies for the next 10 years to understand fatigue, frustration, and burnout.[81] In interviewing others who had worked in and left similar roles, some described their attraction to the work as "addicting."[82] The research revealed that the longer the operations, the greater the risk to the task *and* the human operator.

What role does work play in your life? Is it core to your identity or a means to an end? Does it give you self-confidence and self-worth, a sense of purpose and meaning? Our work is a part of us, but not our whole self.

---

[81] Paul, C. L. and Dykstra, J. (2017). "Understanding operator fatigue, frustration, and cognitive workload in tactical cybersecurity operations." *Journal of Information Warfare*, 16(2), 1-11.

[82] Rangarajan, A., Nobles, C., Dykstra, J., Cunningham, M., Robinson, N., Hollis, T., Paul, C.L., and Gulotta, C. (2025). "A Roadmap to Address Burnout in the Cybersecurity Profession: Outcomes from a Multifaceted Workshop," *HCI International 2025*.

Coming into cybersecurity as a mid-career professional brings some risk to work-life balance. The fresh start is bound to be good for you, as we have discussed, but that comes with the risk of tipping the balance. This new pursuit may be so refreshing and engaging that it leads to an imbalance towards work, driven by the adrenalin and desire to succeed.

In this chapter, we will talk about balance and considerations for balancing cybersecurity work with the non-work parts of ourselves.

Evaluating Priorities and Values

A theme throughout this book has been that mid-career professionals have priorities that have changed from our early career. Having the *right* job is more important than having *any* job. This is especially salient when considering work-life balance. Table 14.1 shows some lifestyle considerations you may be faced with.

Value	Opportunities for Protecting this Value	Trade Offs for Keeping this Value
Managing people	Management roles	Spending less time doing technical work; more likely in-office work
Highly technical roles	Senior technical roles such as architects, senior engineers, etc.	Harder to find senior technical roles that don't also come with a management component
Physical time with family	Remote-only jobs	Increased travel, turning down jobs that require relocation
Geographic stability (Living/Basing in a certain location)	Remote-only jobs, local employers	Increased travel to work and for work, potential career stagnation
Flexible schedule	Individual contributor, work from home, flexible deadlines	No jobs with shift work, mandatory work schedules, on-call responsibilities
Predictability and routine	Compliance roles with regularly scheduled audits and periodic reporting	Less variety, more rigid processes, limited flexibility, reduced high-stakes challenges
Job stability and long-term security	Jobs in government and mature, established companies	Few jobs at startups, less highly-innovative, high-risk work
Professional growth and development	Certifications, mentorship, ongoing training, industry events	Time investment; slower transition to leadership roles
Compensation and benefits	Competitive salary, bonuses, robust healthcare, retirement plans	Initial cybersecurity pay may be modest
Company culture and values	Companies with stated mission, vision, and values; policies and initiatives	Evolving cultures, potential misrepresentation, longer search process
Autonomy and decision-making authority	Empowered roles; independent decisions; project flexibility	Newcomers may face limited authority; structured oversight

Table 14.1 – Opportunities and tradeoffs for various personal values and priorities.

When Helen's child was school age, she agreed with her husband that they wouldn't move away from Columbus, Ohio. Family first! This meant that she either needed to find jobs that were based in Ohio or find remote roles that usually involved a lot of travel. Traveling worked well for a while, but even that became difficult when family circumstances required her to be at home more often. Helen had to navigate this with her employer, turning down opportunities to travel internationally for a while, and ultimately leaving the company for an Ohio-based position. These kinds of tradeoffs don't usually apply to your entire career—kids grow up, partners change, pandemics happen—so consider some of these tradeoffs to be seasonal, not permanent.

Imagine that you and your partner live in Kansas City. You own a house you love. Your partner has a stable and desirable job. Your values include:

Stability and Security: You want to provide a comfortable and secure life for yourself and your loved ones. You may prioritize financial planning, job security, and building a strong foundation for your future.

Exploration and Adventure: You love to travel and value exploration and adventure, seeking new experiences and opportunities to broaden your horizons. You believe that traveling and trying new things is essential to personal growth and happiness and may prioritize saving money and taking time off to pursue these interests.

Balance and Quality of Life: As someone who is established in their career and personal life, you value balance and quality of life, seeking to strike a healthy equilibrium between work, relationships, and personal pursuits. You prioritize spending time with loved ones, pursuing hobbies and interests, and maintaining a sense of well-being and fulfillment, recognizing that life is not just about achieving professional success, but also about enjoying the journey and nurturing physical, emotional, and mental health.

Clearly, we had priorities earlier in our careers, but these may have changed. Early on, we may have prioritized income for entertainment over income for retirement. Beyond the obvious, what do these things mean for work-life balance in a cybersecurity career?

As you are looking at jobs, ask questions such as:

- How predictable is the schedule? Are there on-call requirements? Will I be expected to be available and responsive to messages around the clock?

- What percentage of my time can I dedicate to staying current with industry changes, the latest threats, and emerging technologies?
- I enjoy a week-long family trip every Summer. How well does that fit the schedule and culture of the organization?

What We Control

Imagine that you take a cybersecurity job that is highly structured, like incident response. Every incident might be slightly different, but all in all, the last one resembled the one before. Microsoft was interested in this kind of burnout. Among 35 people, more than half (19) experienced burnout. These professionals shared a high workload (more than 40 hours per week), limited control over their work, unusually poor teamwork, inadequate recognition, and after-hours work demands.[83]

As you seek and select a job in cybersecurity, it is critically important to consider the organizational factors of a potential employer. Interestingly, a high workload and a lack of control over your situation are more likely to lead to burnout than personal characteristics.

Author Matthew Kelly suggests something interesting. Satisfaction, he says in his book, *Off Balance*, is a better goal. Your purpose and priorities can help guide your choices. "Excellence in any field requires that we miss out on other things." This is partially due to the fact that we cannot control everything.

Boredom and Habituation

We commonly think about burnout from long hours, working hard, and lack of rest and recovery. We want to also acknowledge and discuss the opposite end of the spectrum: boredom.

---

[83] Nepal, S., Hernandez, J., Lewis, R., Chaudhry, A., Houck, B., Knudsen, E., ... and Czerwinski, M. (2024). "Burnout in Cybersecurity Incident Responders: Exploring the Factors that Light the Fire." Proceedings of the ACM on Human-Computer Interaction, 8(CSCW1), 1-35.

Wait a second, you might be asking, *didn't you say cybersecurity was fast paced, demanding, and always changing?* We did and that is very often the case. But as with every profession, there is repetitive work. Analyzing malware, performing digital forensics, responding to incidents… each of these can start to feel monotonous the more we repeat the tasks. Moreover, even in ever-changing jobs, we can start to habituate and tune out the novelty.

You may have experienced this in a previous job or another part of your life. Humans can become accustomed to all sorts of things, good and bad, from blissful marriage to misinformation. What makes cybersecurity work susceptible to habituation is that the field requires constant vigilance, attention to detail, and a proactive mindset—traits that can wane when the work starts to feel routine or predictable.

Boredom and habituation in cybersecurity can have real consequences. When tasks feel repetitive, professionals may begin to operate on autopilot, leading to oversights or missed details that could signal a critical threat. For example, reviewing logs or triaging alerts might become so routine that subtle signs of a sophisticated attack are overlooked. This isn't just about individual performance—it can affect the broader security posture of the organization. Recognizing the potential for boredom and actively managing it is essential for sustaining engagement and effectiveness in this high-stakes field.

So how can mid-career professionals entering cybersecurity maintain their sharpness and avoid habituation? One approach is to build variety into your work whenever possible. Seek out opportunities to learn new tools, take on diverse tasks, or cross-train in areas outside your immediate role. Another strategy is to regularly revisit the "why" behind your work, reminding yourself that every log analyzed, or process audited contributes to protecting people and organizations. Finally, cultivating mindfulness and taking regular breaks can help reset your focus and keep your attention fresh. Addressing boredom proactively ensures that you remain both motivated and vigilant, even when the work becomes familiar.

Time Management

Time management is a critical skill for cybersecurity professionals, but its application in this field presents unique challenges that set it apart from other industries. Cybersecurity roles often involve unpredictable workloads due to the 24/7 nature of incidents. Professionals must be ready to address urgent threats or breaches at any time, which can disrupt planned schedules. To mitigate this, it is important to build resilience into time management strategies, such as scheduling flexible buffer periods for unforeseen tasks and prioritizing recovery time after intense work demands.

Another unique aspect of time management in cybersecurity is the constant need for learning. The rapidly evolving threat landscape requires professionals to stay up to date with the latest tools, threats, and regulations. Unlike in other fields, this isn't just a periodic requirement but an ongoing part of the job. Allocating time for professional development, whether through structured courses or microlearning, ensures that professionals remain effective while balancing other responsibilities.

Cybersecurity also demands a high tolerance for multitasking and strict prioritization. Professionals frequently juggle responsibilities like system monitoring, user support, and strategic planning, all under high-pressure deadlines. Effective time management here involves using frameworks like Eisenhower's Matrix to prioritize urgent tasks, leveraging automated tools to handle repetitive processes, and reserving distraction-free time for deep work on critical initiatives.

For remote or hybrid cybersecurity roles, managing work-life boundaries is another challenge. The always-on nature of cybersecurity can make it difficult to log off, so setting clear work hours and creating physical or digital boundaries to signal the end of the workday is essential. Collaborative tools, such as shared task boards, can also streamline team coordination, ensuring tasks are evenly distributed and time is used efficiently.

Finally, cybersecurity professionals can enhance their time management by incorporating field-specific practices, such as maintaining incident response playbooks and using monitoring tools to filter out non-critical alerts. These approaches save time in high-stakes situations and allow professionals to focus on strategic efforts. By recognizing and addressing the unique time management demands of cybersecurity, mid-career professionals can better navigate the field while maintaining a healthy work-life balance.

Taking Breaks to Rejuvenate

When books or mentors tell us to take breaks, it's commonly about daily habits. Getting up and taking a walk or perhaps even a vacation is good advice. That said, we want to open the aperture even further to include other kinds of breaks.

It is commonplace in academia for faculty to get a sabbatical. These are extended breaks, sometimes three months to a year, that allow employees to focus on professional development, pursue new interests, or rejuvenate. This exact benefit is unfortunately uncommon elsewhere. But what if you could mimic the benefits of a sabbatical using options that are available to you?

One way to get a break from your job is a temporary assignment on another task or with another team. Focusing on something else for a few days or a few weeks helps our brains recharge and helps us appreciate our regular work when we return to it.

Leaving the office and attending a conference or workshop can be refreshing. Several long-running cybersecurity conferences are held each summer in Las Vegas, including Black Hat, DEF CON, BSides, and The Diana Initiative. These have come to be called Hacker Summer Camp. A change of pace might also include self-improvement, a proven way to feel a new sense of accomplishment. If your job is reviewing software for vulnerabilities, consider experimenting with machine learning and cybersecurity data science.

Reevaluate Once in a While

The fact that you're considering a career change to cybersecurity is evidence that you have at least one experience in reevaluating your work situation. Remember this experience. Even more importantly, remember to keep checking in with yourself once in a while to ensure you are still on the path you want to be on.

In economics, opportunity cost is the concept of what we give up when making one choice over another. Staying in one job means necessarily giving up other jobs. When you land in cybersecurity, we hope you thrive and stay. Even in a job we think we love, we owe it to ourselves to take a thoughtful and deliberate look at our situations. The answer might be an affirmative, "Yes, this is the place for me, given my options." It won't help anyone to jump jobs too soon or too often since that looks like a lack of commitment, but a once-a-year reevaluation is healthy.

Resilience for Work-Life Balance

An important concept in cybersecurity is resilience. Often, we mean this in a technical sense: the property of a system to withstand attacks and bounce back to normal. Resilience is also important as a human attribute.

Resilience as a cybersecurity professional requires proactive strategies to handle the inevitable demands of the field without burning out. Resilience isn't a fixed trait; it's a skill we refine over time by balancing preparation, recovery, and adaptability.

Resilience means knowing when to escalate. Cybersecurity professionals often take pride in solving complex problems independently, but resilience requires recognizing when collaboration is more effective. Build a habit of regularly communicating with peers, even when things are running smoothly. This creates a foundation of trust and support that you can rely on when crises arise. Treat these relationships as part of your professional infrastructure—just as a resilient system requires robust external connections, so does a resilient professional.

Finally, invest in "adaptive recovery." Unlike basic rest, adaptive recovery involves actively learning from stressors and fine-tuning your responses. After an intense workweek, reflect on what triggered the most stress and identify one small, actionable change for the next week. For instance, if late-night alerts are a recurring issue, explore how your team might streamline escalation policies or implement better alert management tools. Resilience isn't about avoiding every difficulty; it's about continuously improving your ability to face them without sacrificing your well-being or long-term effectiveness.

Chapter Summary

- Own Your Workload: Recognize the toll of high-stakes work and set boundaries appropriately.

- Be Human-Centric: Acknowledge and address fatigue, burnout, and frustration that may wear you down.

- Balance Work and You: Keep your career from overshadowing the other parts of your values and identity.

- Fight the Boredom: Break the routine to stay sharp and engaged. Be aware that habituation can mask good and bad.

- Master Your Minutes: Use prioritization and flexibility to handle the unpredictable demands of cybersecurity work.

- Take Real Breaks: Step away with the purpose to recharge and refresh, such as conferences, workshops, and temporary assignments.

- Check Your Compass: Reevaluate your career path annually to stay aligned with your goals.

- Build Resilience Daily: Adapt, recover, and collaborate to thrive under pressure.

- Choose the Right Employer: Look for organizations that value balance and teamwork.

Chapter References

Kelly, M. (2011). *Off Balance: Getting Beyond the Work-Life Balance Myth to Personal and Professional Satisfaction*. Penguin.

Sharot, T. and Sunstein, C. R. (2025). *Look Again: The Power of Noticing What Was Always There*. Simon and Schuster.

Chapter 15

For the Underrepresented

The State of the Industry

If you have never attended a cybersecurity conference or meetup, let us paint you a picture of the people in attendance. There are more men than women, only a few people of color, and a preponderance of people older than forty. And those are just the things you can easily observe. Other factors, such as neurodiversity, accessibility requirements, or economic status, are also unbalanced in the cybersecurity industry.

The security industry's demographics reflect various systemic influences that create challenges to entry and promotion for people in the non-dominant culture. There are many annual workforce study reports, and they generally show that:

- Women make up 25% of the entire cybersecurity workforce and less than 20% of security leadership;[84]
- Non-white people make up 34% of the U.S. security analyst workforce;[85]
- The industry trends are older… between 30 and 54 years for the average worker. This age bracket may change as more traditional students pursue cybersecurity careers.

Why is this important to consider? The function of cybersecurity is to ensure our IT systems are reliable and trustworthy. This means the cybersecurity function supports and influences every part of our organization and society. It follows that cybersecurity needs to be

---

[84] GCF and Boston Consulting Group (2024). "Cybersecurity Workforce Report": https://api.gcforum.org/api/files/public/upload/8eaba644-0889-49b4-8c7d-8de3840decac_one-Cybersecurity-Workforce-Report-(002).pdf.

[85] https://www.zippia.com/cyber-security-analyst-jobs/demographics/.

responsive to the entire business community. A homogenous workforce means that the needs of others may be overlooked.

Additionally, we need more people working in cybersecurity. If we cannot attract them because our workforce has too many barriers to entry or promotion, we will not succeed in our purpose. In short, a homogenous cybersecurity workforce leads to a less secure organization and society.

For the mid-career jobseeker, being aware of these factors can help you be better prepared to find roles in the industry and manage the inevitable challenges that occur once you're in. It doesn't matter whether or not you identify as someone in an underrepresented group. Everyone in cybersecurity must be aware of the reality, impacts, and available resources. This chapter will explore ways for people to find support and resources to help them succeed.

Industry Groups for the Underrepresented

Cybersecurity exists within a larger culture, and the challenge of being part of a non-dominant group in the workplace isn't unique to cybersecurity. An internet search for "[non-dominant group description] in the workforce" will reveal lots of resources and writings to advise you on this topic (and we've listed some in the chapter resources).

There are organizations that have been created to try to assist people in our industry with their specific concerns, provide resources to hiring managers, and create cultures that welcome and support non-dominant groups.

- **Cyversity,** whose mission is to achieve the consistent representation of women, underrepresented communities, and all veterans in the cybersecurity industry through programs designed to diversify, educate, and empower. (https://www.cyversity.org/)

- **Women in Cybersecurity (WiCys)**, whose mission is to "Recruit, retain and advance women in cybersecurity to build a robust cybersecurity workforce." (https://www.wicys.org/)

- **The Women's Society of Cyberjutsu (WSC)** is dedicated to raising awareness of cybersecurity career opportunities and advancement for women in the field, closing the gender gap and the overall workforce gap in information security roles. (https://womenscyberjutsu.org/)

- **Executive Women's Forum (EWF)**, whose core mission is to engage, develop, and advance all women in the Information Security, IT Risk Management, and Privacy industries through education, leadership development, and the creation of trusted relationships. (https://www.ewf-usa.com/)

- **Women in Cybersecurity and Privacy (WISP)**, advances women and underrepresented communities to lead the future of privacy and security. (https://www.wisporg.com/)

- **Hackers in Heels:** For every woman to have the knowledge, confidence, and supportive community in cybersecurity. (https://www.hackerinheels.com/)

- **Black Girls Hack** is a training-focused nonprofit organization that was created to help increase diversity in cybersecurity by helping to bridge the gap between what is taught in educational institutions and what is necessary for careers in cybersecurity. (https://www.blackgirlshack.org/)

- **National Society of Black Engineers (NSBE):** Supporting Black Engineers in advocacy, education and career advancement.
  (https://nsbe.org/)

- **Blacks in Cybersecurity** is a meetup group and conference series to help highlight and elevate the Black community in cybersecurity.
  (https://www.blacksincyberconf.com/)

- **Minorities in Cybersecurity (MiC)** developed out of a unique passion to help fill the gap in the support and development of women and minority leaders in the cybersecurity field.
  (https://www.mincybsec.org/)

- **Neurodiverse Hackers** empowers and supports neurodiverse individuals in the cybersecurity field while creating a community of inclusivity.
  (https://neurodiversehackers.com/)

- **Neurocyber** is driven to improve career outcomes for neurodivergent colleagues, to enrich the sector, and thereby positively impact the cyber skills gap in the UK.
  (https://www.neurocyber.uk/)

New groups are being added regularly. Use these groups to build your network for learning, job references, and support.

Finding a Job for the Underrepresented

To succeed in cybersecurity, looking for a manager, team, and organization that will help you succeed is useful. In previous chapters, we've discussed this from the perspective of training and general career development. For a person in an underrepresented group, there are additional considerations.

Jobseekers in any industry are challenged to show up authentically for interviews without creating barriers that stop them from getting a job offer. As a mid-career jobseeker, you've likely experienced this tension already. Applying for cybersecurity jobs is no different than any other profession. Before beginning the interview process, take some time to note what you're willing to accept, your specific needs, and how you want to show up in the hiring process.

For example, some people conceal as much as possible during the hiring process, only asking for accommodations, if needed, once on the job. Others choose to include their membership in minority groups on their resumes, even if they are concerned this will eliminate them as candidates ("If they don't want me for this, then I don't want to work there"). Still, others will specifically ask about job accommodations during the interview process.

Regardless of how obvious you want to be, during the interview process evaluate the company to see if they can support your needs. Consider:

- What is the makeup of the team, the leadership team, and the people interviewing you? Will you be unique, part of a small minority, or fully-represented?

- Does the company offer employee resource groups for minority groups, where you can go for support?

- Will the company fund your attendance at networking events and conferences where you can find industry support groups?

- How does the hiring manager communicate? Will they support your communication needs?

- What is the leave policy at the organization? Will it support your needs for childcare, health appointments, or other personal needs?

- What is included in benefits packages? Will things like maternity/paternity leave be covered, or mental health support or other benefits specific to your needs?

It is unlikely you will find an organization, team, or manager who has everything you need. Go back to your original list of the things you must have, the things you can compromise on, and the things you can ignore. If you decide to take the job despite missing pieces, you are at least prepared to manage your expectations and look for needed support elsewhere.

Getting Help If You Are Underrepresented

When looking for a job or once on the job, it is helpful to have support from people who have walked in your shoes. The resource groups mentioned above can be one place to look, but there are others.

- Mentors: Finding people who can help you navigate the job market and workplace, even if they are not part of your minority group, can be useful. Look for people a couple of years ahead of you career-wise. Your meetings with these people will be ad hoc—dealing with situations as they arise—but having their perspective and guidance can be invaluable. Look for these folks in your existing company or while attending meetups or conferences.

- Online Forums: If you can find a safe group on Reddit, Slack, or your social media platform of choice, this can be a wonderful place to raise questions or concerns to help you navigate your personal situation.

- Allies: Whether they identify as you do or not, some people are willing to help you be successful in cybersecurity. Ask around; you'll find people willing to coach, mentor, and be a sounding board for your concerns. These people are found in training classes, conferences, and online forums.

When Things Get Tough

We hope that you're never in a situation where you feel that your position is compromised because of your minority status, but it does happen occasionally. How can you manage this situation?

- **Network:** One reason to network before, during, and after you land a job is to give yourself options away from your day job. In other words, if you have a network of cybersecurity professionals outside your company, you can turn to them for advice or even new job opportunities if the situation requires it. Give yourself options and agency and foster your network all the time.

- **Determine how widespread the problem is:** Sometimes, a challenging work situation is due to the manager/employee relationship alone. In this case, do you have the option to stay with the company but move to a different manager or team? Consider this before moving completely or staying too long in a toxic environment.

- **Consider how long you have been in the role:** If you have just joined a company or team and alarm bells are going off, leaving and looking for another role might be feasible without damaging your future job prospects. If, however, you've been there at least six months and the situation allows it, you should persevere for a year before moving so you can look for new roles without damaging your credibility with future hiring managers.

- **Know your options:** Sometimes, it can be helpful to get legal advice to know the best way to deal with a work situation. Although you can talk to an internal HR or legal person, understand that they exist to, first and foremost, protect the company, not you. When in doubt, seek external guidance that works for you.

- **Put yourself first:** Consider what *you* need. Suppose you are learning a particular skill or getting experience in a particularly useful function. In that case, hanging in there may be in your self-interest until you've completed that thing, even if the work environment is less than optimal. In this case, start networking now to have the next role lined up as soon as you can step away from your current role.

Suppose you decide to stay at a company that doesn't support your needs; gather support around you. Join networking groups and get a mentor. Document your experiences. You'll need this documentation if you ever need to make a formal complaint. Be intentional about why you're staying and for how long. Set boundaries to know when it's time to leave.

If you decide to leave a cybersecurity job because the work environment is not supporting you, exit gracefully. The cybersecurity profession is relatively small and well-connected. Burning bridges at one company may accidentally result in you burning bridges at multiple companies, which will not help you in the long term. Do your best to leave on good terms.

Chapter Summary

- The security industry struggles to hire inclusively.

- There are organizations dedicated to helping minorities in cybersecurity succeed. Seek them out.

- When job-searching, evaluate the potential company based on how much support you will want or need. Be selective.

- Seek out allies, coaches, and mentors to help you on your journey.

- If your work environment doesn't support your needs, understand your options and exercise them.

Chapter References

Brooks, A. C. (2022). *From Strength to Strength: Finding Success, Happiness, and Deep Purpose in the Second Half of Life.* Bloomsbury Publishing.

Washington, Ella F. (2024). *Unspoken: A Guide to Cracking the Hidden Corporate Code.* Forbes Publishing.

Chapter 16

Ethics in Cybersecurity

No discussion about working in cybersecurity would be complete without talking about ethics—how the profession thinks about the topic, what kinds of ethical dilemmas a person might face in this industry, and where to look for guidance on how to behave ethically.

A dictionary definition of ethics is:[86]

> *the principles of conduct governing an individual or a group.*

How cybersecurity professionals conduct themselves has an enormous impact on the success of a security program and related organizational outcomes. Cybersecurity is concerned with maintaining trust in our IT systems—and if the security team is untrustworthy, so too are the organizations that rely on them.

Ethics play a crucial role in cybersecurity that you may not have encountered before. Unlike many professional domains where ethical questions revolve around passive risks or foreseeable process failures, cybersecurity operates in an environment of active, adaptive adversaries and borderless digital impact. Security teams must decide in real time how much customer data to inspect to detect fraud without violating privacy, whether to deploy intrusive monitoring that may undermine employee trust, or how to share vulnerability intelligence that could as easily arm attackers as protect defenders. The dual-use nature of most security tools, the speed at which a misstep can propagate globally, and the clash of overlapping legal jurisdictions make cybersecurity ethics more dynamic—and more public—than the static codes governing

---
[86] https://www.merriam-webster.com/dictionary/ethics.

finance, medicine, or engineering. Each incident merges technical urgency with profound questions about autonomy, transparency, and collective safety, demanding a blend of rapid decision-making and principled restraint rarely encountered in non-cyber domains.

In this chapter, we will explore the topic of ethics in cybersecurity so that you can have a frame of reference to navigate the murky waters of ethical behavior.

Values and Ethics

In everyday language the terms values and ethics blur together, yet security decisions become clearer when we separate them. *Values* describe what we prize—privacy, availability, transparency, equity, profit, safety. They can exist at several levels: your personal convictions, your organization's published culture statements, and the national or industry frameworks that shape regulatory priorities. *Ethics* describe how we act when those values collide in a real situation. They provide the reasoning that translates a principle into an admissible, defensible decision. For instance, if an organization values transparency and national law mandates breach disclosure, the ethical question is not "do we disclose?" but "how quickly and to whom?" Clear terminology keeps debate focused on the real point of tension—often a clash between two worthy values rather than ignorance of right and wrong.

Cybersecurity professionals operate at the intersection of individual conscience, corporate policy, and diverse cultural norms. Your own sense of fairness might compel you to notify an affected user immediately, while corporate lawyers insist on a short delay to verify facts, and a host-country's privacy law sets a strict deadline. Global teams face further nuance: data localization rules in France, public-interest exceptions in the United States, or collectivist expectations in Japan can alter what "responsible" looks like. Mastery of cybersecurity ethics therefore requires fluency in three arenas: (1) your personal red lines, (2) your organization's code of conduct and risk appetite, and (3) the external legal and cultural constraints that govern stakeholders. The frameworks that follow will help you reconcile these layers when seconds matter and scrutiny is guaranteed.

Triads: Core Values of Cybersecurity

Throughout the career of a security professional, decisions are made where the answer isn't immediately obvious and sometimes can be a choice between less-desirable outcomes. In these circumstances, a professional must rely on core values to guide their decision-making.

Much of the work we do in cybersecurity is based on the values outlined by a long-standardized and widely-known framework, the CIA triad: confidentiality, integrity, and availability. This triumvirate of values forms the basis for many cybersecurity frameworks and regulations. Our systems and data should be reliably **confidential** (access is limited to people with a business need to know), **available** (when and where it is required based on organizational objectives), and have **integrity** (maintained in the state that is expected, avoiding unauthorized changes).

More recently, in the face of new technologies and threats, the CIA triad has been updated to become the DIE triad—distributed, immutable, and ephemeral.[87] In this triad, systems become resilient when they are distributed (so there are no single points of failure), immutable (so changes are easier to see and reverse), and ephemeral (to make it harder for attackers to persist in an environment).

The CIA and DIE triads form a values-based lens through which a security professional performs their role, and which becomes the touchstone whenever decisions need to be made.

Consent and Privacy – Respecting the Person

Introducing cybersecurity tools and techniques to an environment always results in contradictory values. To monitor an environment for threats, the security professional may see data or activities that

---

[87] https://www.slideshare.net/slideshow/distributed-immutable-ephemeral-new-paradigms-for-the-next-era-of-security/140096422#1.

someone else would want private including conversations and personal data. The very act of monitoring—even if the security professional cannot see the detail of the data—can feel intrusive to some people and seem to impinge on confidentiality values.

Employee privacy rights vary by country and even by sector. In some regions, employers may monitor corporate devices and networks with relatively few restrictions; elsewhere, data-protection laws and labor agreements grant workers explicit rights to personal privacy, even on company systems or when accessing organizational resources from personal devices. Before implementing any monitoring, security leaders should balance the security benefit against potential erosion of employee trust, verify compliance with applicable laws and collective-bargaining agreements, and communicate clearly (preferably in writing) what data are collected, how they are used, and how long they are retained. Monitoring should always be proportionate to identified risks and aligned with the stated values and legal obligations of the organization and the jurisdictions in which it operates.

Security professionals are often subject to non-disclosure and confidentiality agreements from their employers or business partners because in their work they see sensitive events involving employees or customers, or organizational secrets. Ethically, security professionals must take these agreements seriously and will often assume confidentiality even if no legal agreement exists.

Security activities must also be considered against the values of trust and transparency. For example, it is common practice for security teams to phish their own employees. The stated purpose is to train employees to be wary of and identify potential malicious emails, texts, or messages. In practice, many employees feel tricked or entrapped, which generates ill-will toward the organization or the security team and results in less-secure behavior by employees. Again, a security professional must weigh the potential benefits of this training activity against the potential lack of trust that results.

Responsible Disclosure

"Responsible disclosure" (also called coordinated vulnerability disclosure) is a fundamental concept in cybersecurity of reporting a newly discovered security weakness to the people who can fix it—and eventually to those who may be affected—without giving attackers an advantage. Imagine finding an unlocked back door in a hotel: you could keep quiet, exploit it, or alert management so they can secure it before publicly warning guests. In the digital world that "back door" might be a software bug, a misconfigured cloud bucket, or an audit finding that exposes customer data. The discoverer must decide when, how, and to whom to disclose the flaw so that (1) the organization can patch or mitigate the risk, (2) customers and partners are informed in time to protect themselves, and (3) the information released cannot be weaponized by attackers before a fix is available. Balancing those goals involves technical, legal, and ethical judgement, and the security community continues to debate where the ideal disclosure timeline lies.

Questions arise, such as:

- Are we legally required to disclose this? (Often regulations leave a lot of room for interpretation, or are completely silent on the issue.)

- Who is harmed if we disclose it? Or if we don't?

- How impactful is the issue?

- If the organization decides not to disclose, but the security professional disagrees with that decision, should they escalate or be a whistleblower?

- Should we fix the underlying problem before disclosing there is issue to partners and customers?

For most of these questions the answer is unclear… "it depends." These murky decisions could arise in almost any cybersecurity role, and professionals should be prepared to consider these questions to understand their personal boundaries on these issues.

Dual-Use Misconduct

With great power comes great responsibility… and so it is for cybersecurity professionals. We have privileged access to people's computers and communications, we have access to organizational databases, we can surveil people in the name of protection, we can test the effectiveness of security controls.

With this technological power we can theoretically spy on people's computers and communications without having a security purpose, we can peruse organizational systems just to satisfy our curiosity, we can watch people move around our buildings, we can hack a system just because we can. None of these things are ethical.

Adding another security tool to an environment or hiring another cybersecurity researcher adds to the attack surface of the organization. The benefits may outweigh the harm, but sometimes they don't. Security professionals should take care to make sure that organizations are aware of and consent to that risk, and that security programs take steps to monitor their own behaviors and use of security technologies.

The ethical principle here is "beneficence," also known as "do no harm."

Codes of Ethics

To try to ensure that cybersecurity is practiced in an ethical manner, several professional organizations have created codes of conduct and require members to agree to abide by these codes. A reading of these codes shows that there are many items in common—act professionally, respect confidentiality, obey laws, etc. But there are some variations depending on the purpose of the organization.

The following section details some common codes of conduct. Even if you don't belong to these organizations, it is helpful to see the conduct that they believe deserves ethical considerations.

Organization: ISC2

Code of Conduct: "Code of Ethics" [88]

- Protect society, the common good, necessary public trust and confidence, and the infrastructure.

- Act honorably, honestly, justly, responsibly, and legally.

- Provide diligent and competent service to principals.

- Advance and protect the profession.

Organization: ISACA

Code of Conduct: "Code of Professional Ethics" [89]

- Support the implementation of, and encourage compliance with, appropriate standards and procedures for the effective governance and management of enterprise information systems and technology, including: audit, control, security, and risk management.

- Perform their duties with objectivity, due diligence, and professional care, in accordance with professional standards.

- Serve the interests of stakeholders in a lawful manner, while maintaining high standards of conduct and character, and not discrediting their profession or the Association.

- Maintain the privacy and confidentiality of information obtained in the course of their activities unless disclosure is required by legal authority. Such information shall not be used for personal benefit or released to inappropriate parties.

- Maintain competency in their respective fields and agree to undertake only those activities they can reasonably expect

---

[88] https://www.isc2.org/ethics.
[89] https://www.isaca.org/code-of-professional-ethics.

to complete with the necessary skills, knowledge, and competence.

- Inform appropriate parties of the results of work performed including the disclosure of all significant facts known to them that, if not disclosed, may distort the reporting of the results.

- Support the professional education of stakeholders in enhancing their understanding of the governance and management of enterprise information systems and technology, including: audit, control, security, and risk management.

Organization: ISSA

Code of Conduct: "Code of Ethics" [90]

As an ISSA member, guest, and/or applicant for membership, I have in the past and will in the future:

- Perform all professional activities and duties in accordance with all applicable laws and the highest ethical principles;

- Promote generally accepted information security current best practices and standards;

- Maintain appropriate confidentiality of proprietary or otherwise sensitive information encountered in the course of professional activities;

- Discharge professional responsibilities with diligence and honesty;

- Refrain from any activities which might constitute a conflict of interest or otherwise damage the reputation of or is detrimental to employers, the information security profession, or the Association; and

---

[90] https://issa.org/code-of-ethics/.

- Not intentionally injure or impugn the professional reputation or practice of colleagues, clients, or employers.

Organization: The CISO Association

Code of Conduct: "Code of Professional Conduct" [91]

- Members shall strive to conduct all their relations with honesty and integrity.

- A Member shall strive to conduct themselves with professional courtesy and to treat all persons with dignity, respect, fairness and without discrimination.

- A Member shall ensure that they have the appropriate education and experience to ensure the skills and knowledge for the tasks required for their role, such as laid out by the PAC or other entities as applicable to the Member's role as a cybersecurity professional.

- Members shall consistently, visibly and transparently disclose, to an organization's stakeholders, the organization's current cybersecurity risks, threats, and the adequacy of controls for the organization's stated risk tolerance.

- A Member must not disclose to another party any Confidential Information unless explicitly authorized or required by applicable law or legal obligations.

- Members shall take appropriate steps to ensure that their cybersecurity communications, whether written, electronic, or oral, are clear and appropriate to the circumstances and its intended audience and shall work to ensure that these communications include all relevant and pertinent information.

---

[91] https://theciso.org/wp-content/uploads/2024/11/CodeofProfessionalConduct.pdf.

- Members shall avoid the use of communications containing a material misrepresentation of fact, omitting a material fact, or otherwise commenting on a subject without firm evidence.

- A Member shall ensure their interests and relationships, including personal or financial, do not have the appearance or potential to interfere with the Member's ability to make impartial decisions in their professional role (a Conflict of Interest), and when such potential exists, it is appropriately disclosed to affected parties.

- Members shall not solicit or accept direct or indirect compensation from more than one party, unless the circumstances are fully disclosed and agreed to by all interested parties.

- Members shall be transparent in their actions including the disclosure of activities that may be perceived as exposing the Member to undue or external influence over their decisions or actions, including through the receipt or exchange of Gifts, Meals, Entertainment, Travel, or Future Compensation ("GMETFC").

- A Member who believes that they are being asked or required to act in violation of the Code shall confirm and clarify the ask, explain why they believe the ask conflicts with the Code and work to ensure an outcome that is consistent with this Code. If such a discussion is not possible or not successful, the Member may seek an opinion from the Committee of Professional Conduct.

- A Member with knowledge of an apparent, unresolved, meaningful violation of the Code, shall attempt to resolve the apparent violation through discussion and clarification. If such a discussion is not attempted or is not successful, the member shall disclose the violation to the appropriate counseling of the Association, except where the disclosure would be contrary to law, would divulge Confidential Information.

- Members shall respond promptly, truthfully, and fully to request for information by, and cooperate fully with, an appropriate counseling and disciplinary body of the Association in connection with any disciplinary, counselling, or other proceeding of the Association relating to the Code subject to applicable laws and legal obligations.

- Members shall be open and cooperative with authorized external parties as part of an investigation into potential violations of regulations, this Code, or the Law.

Organization: ACM

Code of Conduct: "Code of Ethics and Professional Conduct"[92]

1. GENERAL ETHICAL PRINCIPLES.
   1.1 Contribute to society and to human well-being, acknowledging that all people are stakeholders in computing.
   1.2 Avoid harm.
   1.3 Be honest and trustworthy.
   1.4 Be fair and take action not to discriminate.
   1.5 Respect the work required to produce new ideas, inventions, creative works, and computing artifacts.
   1.6 Respect privacy.
   1.7 Honor confidentiality.

2. PROFESSIONAL RESPONSIBILITIES.
   2.1 Strive to achieve high quality in both the processes and products of professional work.
   2.2 Maintain high standards of professional competence, conduct, and ethical practice.
   2.3 Know and respect existing rules pertaining to professional work.
   2.4 Accept and provide appropriate professional review.
   2.5 Give comprehensive and thorough evaluations of computer systems and their impacts, including analysis of possible risks.

---

[92] https://www.acm.org/code-of-ethics.

2.6 Perform work only in areas of competence.

2.7 Foster public awareness and understanding of computing, related technologies, and their consequences.

2.8 Access computing and communication resources only when authorized or when compelled by the public good.

2.9 Design and implement systems that are robustly and usably secure.

3. PROFESSIONAL LEADERSHIP PRINCIPLES.

3.1 Ensure that the public good is the central concern during all professional computing work.

3.2 Articulate, encourage acceptance of, and evaluate fulfillment of social responsibilities by members of the organization or group.

3.3 Manage personnel and resources to enhance the quality of working life.

3.4 Articulate, apply, and support policies and processes that reflect the principles of the Code.

3.5 Create opportunities for members of the organization or group to grow as professionals.

3.6 Use care when modifying or retiring systems.

3.7 Recognize and take special care of systems that become integrated into the infrastructure of society.

4. COMPLIANCE WITH THE CODE.

4.1 Uphold, promote, and respect the principles of the Code.

4.2 Treat violations of the Code as inconsistent with membership in the ACM.

The industry does not yet have a formal licensing mechanism, or any licensure-enforced codes of conduct. Yet, jobseekers should know what is included in these professional organization codes so they can perform their security jobs according to current behavioral and ethical standards.

Putting These into Practice

Professional associations hope to facilitate professional, competent, trustworthy and transparent behavior. As aspirations, these are worthy goals. In the day-to-day of a cybersecurity job, there are two main elements to consider:

- Loyalty to an organization/management versus responsibility to all stakeholders/community. This means balancing what is good for the immediate organization in terms of reputation or market value, and what is necessary to protect the entire community and supply chain.

- Professional courage. When faced with ethical dilemmas, having the ability to act according to personal and professional codes of conduct, even in the face of opposition from other stakeholders.

Professionals will be confronted with situations where the right answer will be determined by adhering to their own personal and professional values, but the obvious or easy answer may not be clear cut.

To prepare for this, security practitioners should:

- Network with other professionals and learn from their experiences.

- Participate in exercises, either alone or in groups, where consideration is given to hypothetical (or not) ethical dilemmas, examining the nuances of those use cases in a non-threatening environment. Putting ethical dilemma scenarios into existing table-top exercises can be a great way to make this happen.

- Pay attention to industry reporting and conversations around newsworthy ethical situations and learn from those case studies.

Chapter Summary

- Ethical behavior by security professionals is a requirement for trustworthy computing.

- The CIA and DIE triads form the professional core values upon which security programs are based.

- There is a balance between imposing security tools and processes on people and giving them the ability to consent to those activities.

- All security professionals will at some point be asked to make choices about how and when to disclose security weaknesses to an organization and its community—be prepared.

- Security tools and activities have a lot of power and can be used for good or bad.

- Professional organizations have tried to enforce ethical behavior using codes of conduct that are a condition of membership.

- Practice dealing with these situations before you must deal with them on the job.

Chapter References

Bursell, Mike (2022). *Trust in Computer Systems and the Cloud.* Wiley.

Maurer, Paul and Skoudis, Ed (2024). *The Code of Honor: Embracing Ethics in Cybersecurity.* Wiley.

Chapter 17

The Future of Cybersecurity

Here is a list of cybersecurity predictions from a popular vendor. This kind of list is released by various authors annually. What year do you think this list was published?

- Cyberextortion will be the most rapidly growing new threat family.
- Cyberattackers will target a wider range of data and assets.
- Email-borne threats will become more social and lead to more data breaches.
- Social media will be fertile ground for cybercriminals.
- Social media will fall subject to aggressive regulation.

Predictions for something as dynamic as the use and misuse of technology is prone to two extremes: generic truisms and wild speculation. We guarantee that you will see people trying to predict the top cyber threats. Our advice is to take such predictions with a grain of salt. Some forecasts align well with actual threats, while others misjudge the scale or form of future risks due to rapid technological change, adversarial behavior, and unforeseen threat vectors.

This chapter is not about predicting the biggest cyber threats next year. Instead, we will look at trends that have already emerged and could realistically impose an impact on the field of cybersecurity and your work in it.

We are going to focus on the five-year horizon because there is so much uncertainty farther out. Cybersecurity professionals were tracking AI for many years before ChatGPT came out in 2022, but that dramatically changed the landscape of AI. Things can and do take dramatic twists.

However, sudden technological advances are the exception, not the norm. Many advances in technology, threats, and cybersecurity evolve over time and remain persistent. The list of predictions at the beginning of this chapter was released in 2014.[93] With very little rewriting they all still apply more than a decade later. These remain difficult and unsolved problems and, we imagine, will still be on the list for the next five years unless an unexpected solution or forcing function emerges.

As you step into a cybersecurity career, this chapter provides a glimpse into areas that you will need to know about and how they are likely to impact your new career.

Trend #1: Artificial Intelligence Shapes Cybersecurity

Artificial intelligence (AI) is poised to become one of the most consequential forces shaping the future of cybersecurity. Over the next five years, AI will play a dual role as a powerful tool in the hands of defenders and as an equally potent weapon for attackers. Understanding this dynamic is essential for anyone entering the field.

AI as a Threat Amplifier

Cybercriminals are beginning to leverage AI in ways that significantly enhance the scale, speed, and sophistication of attacks. In particular, AI enables automation and personalization at levels that were previously impossible.

Phishing, long the most common and effective form of social engineering, has evolved through the use of natural language generation tools. Attackers can now generate highly convincing, personalized phishing messages in seconds, eliminating grammatical red flags and mimicking tone and writing style with alarming accuracy. These messages may incorporate publicly

---

[93] https://www.proofpoint.com/us/threat-insight/post/Cybersecurity-Predictions-2015.

available information from social media or scraped business websites to appear contextually appropriate and trustworthy.

We are starting to see more and more use of deepfake technology to impersonate voices and faces in real-time communication. While once limited to high-profile scams, the technology is becoming increasingly accessible and may soon be used in targeted attacks against employees, executives, or even entire organizations. One specific concern is for helpdesks trying to validate users who are doing emergency password resets.

AI also plays a role in malware development. Adversarial machine learning techniques allow malicious software to adapt to security environments in real time, avoiding detection by modifying its behavior dynamically. This type of "smart" malware represents a significant shift in the nature of cyber threats.

AI as a Force Multiplier for Defense

At the same time, AI is revolutionizing the way security teams detect, analyze, and respond to threats. Security platforms now routinely incorporate machine learning to monitor network activity, flag anomalies, and automate incident response.

One of the most impactful uses of AI is in the area of threat detection and correlation. Rather than relying on signature-based detection alone, modern platforms analyze behavioral patterns and historical data to identify suspicious activity, even when it doesn't match a known threat. This capability allows for earlier detection of attacks and reduces reliance on constant manual oversight.

AI also supports automation in triaging alerts and prioritizing incidents based on risk, helping reduce the burden on overworked security teams. Automated threat intelligence feeds can correlate data across systems and recommend or even execute responses without human intervention. As AI tools become more sophisticated, the role of the human analyst shifts—from directly performing routine tasks to overseeing and validating the actions of intelligent systems.

Implications for Mid-Career Professionals

For professionals entering the field, the increasing integration of AI into security operations represents both a challenge and an opportunity. Technical roles involving AI-specific tools and platforms will become more prominent, but there will also be a growing need for professionals who can manage the strategic, ethical, and operational implications of these systems.

Mid-career professionals bring strengths that are increasingly valuable in this context. Skills in decision-making, critical thinking, and communication are essential as organizations adopt AI tools that require oversight, policy development, and risk evaluation. Furthermore, professionals who can bridge the gap between technical experts and business leaders will play a central role in guiding responsible AI adoption in security programs.

It is not necessary to become a machine learning expert to thrive in this space. However, developing a foundational understanding of how AI is used in cybersecurity—and the limitations and risks it presents—will position professionals to lead, advise, or support AI-enabled teams effectively.

Practical Considerations

There are several ways mid-career professionals can begin to engage with AI in the context of cybersecurity:

- **Familiarize yourself with core AI concepts.** Introductory courses in AI and machine learning, particularly those aimed at business professionals, can provide valuable context. Resources from Coursera, edX, or vendor-specific training platforms can offer accessible entry points.
- **Explore security tools that incorporate AI.** Many enterprise security products now include AI-driven capabilities. Gaining hands-on experience with tools such as endpoint detection and response (EDR) platforms, extended detection and response (XDR) systems, and

modern SIEM solutions will help build practical familiarity.

- **Engage with ethical and policy conversations.** As AI becomes more embedded in decision-making processes, organizations will need professionals who can navigate the ethical and compliance challenges that follow. This includes questions of bias, transparency, and accountability.

In the years ahead, AI will be neither a silver bullet nor an existential threat, but it will be a transformative force. Those entering cybersecurity today are well-positioned to shape how it is used, implemented, and governed. Building awareness now will pay dividends in the years to come.

Trend #2: Privacy and Regulation Influence Cybersecurity

In the next five years, privacy will become a defining issue in cybersecurity and a key driver of new career opportunities. As governments around the world introduce new regulations to protect individuals' personal information, organizations of all sizes will be under increasing pressure to demonstrate compliance, manage risk, and build trust with customers and patients. For professionals transitioning into cybersecurity from healthcare, finance, law, education, or other industries, this trend presents a strategic entry point.

The Expanding Regulatory Landscape

The regulatory environment is becoming more complex and globally interconnected. The European Union's General Data Protection Regulation (GDPR), which took effect in 2018, set a precedent for privacy legislation that has since inspired similar frameworks elsewhere. In the United States, the California Consumer Privacy Act (CCPA) and its successor, the California Privacy Rights Act (CPRA), reflect a growing state-level effort to give individuals more control over their data. Other states are following suit, and federal privacy legislation is under active debate.

Outside the U.S., countries in Asia, Latin America, and Africa are also introducing or strengthening privacy laws. This global shift means that even small or regional organizations may find themselves subject to international privacy obligations—particularly if they serve clients, users, or patients across borders.

In this environment, cybersecurity professionals are increasingly expected to understand the regulatory context in which they operate. Compliance is no longer the exclusive domain of legal departments; it now requires close collaboration between technical and non-technical teams.

Privacy as a Security Priority

The line between privacy and cybersecurity continues to blur. Protecting sensitive data from unauthorized access, disclosure, or alteration is a core objective of both domains. However, privacy introduces additional concerns: ensuring that data is collected only when necessary, retained only for appropriate periods, and used only for agreed-upon purposes.

This broader perspective is changing the way organizations approach data security. For example, data minimization—a principle rooted in privacy law—requires organizations to collect only the data they need. From a security standpoint, this reduces the attack surface. Similarly, data subject access requests (DSARs) and the "right to be forgotten" require organizations to track and manage data throughout its lifecycle, increasing the need for secure data inventories, access controls, and deletion workflows.

Cybersecurity teams are now tasked not just with defending against intrusions, but also with implementing the technical safeguards necessary for privacy compliance. This creates new intersections between legal, operational, and technical roles and opens doors for professionals with experience navigating complex regulations.

Implications for Mid-Career Professionals

For individuals coming from regulated industries—such as healthcare, insurance, finance, education, or law—privacy and compliance represent one of the most natural bridges into cybersecurity. Many mid-career professionals already have experience managing protected information, adhering to strict data handling procedures, or interpreting compliance frameworks. These are precisely the skills organizations need to build effective cybersecurity programs in a privacy-focused world.

In particular, the following roles are expected to grow over the next five years:

- **Privacy Engineers and Analysts**, who work at the intersection of IT, legal, and compliance to ensure privacy principles are translated into technical controls.

- **Governance, Risk, and Compliance (GRC) Specialists**, who manage policies, frameworks, and audits across security and privacy domains.

- **Data Protection Officers (DPOs)**, a role required under GDPR and increasingly adopted elsewhere, responsible for overseeing compliance with privacy laws and practices.

- **Vendor Risk Managers**, who assess the security and privacy posture of third-party providers handling sensitive data.

These roles are not limited to individuals with deep technical skills. In many cases, organizations seek professionals who can understand regulatory language, communicate risk to leadership, and coordinate across departments.

Practical Considerations

Mid-career professionals interested in privacy and compliance should consider the following actions:

- **Leverage your existing industry knowledge.** Experience with HIPAA (healthcare), FERPA (education), SOX (finance), PCI-DSS (retail), or similar regulations can translate directly into cybersecurity-related roles focused on privacy and data protection.

- **Pursue relevant certifications.** Credentials such as the Certified Information Privacy Professional (CIPP), Certified Information Privacy Manager (CIPM), and Certified in Risk and Information Systems Control (CRISC) are increasingly valued by employers and can help formalize your expertise.

- **Stay current with emerging legislation.** Privacy law is evolving rapidly. Following updates from regulatory bodies, industry associations, and legal analysts will help you remain informed and position yourself as a knowledgeable candidate.

- **Develop cross-functional communication skills.** Privacy work often requires translating between legal, technical, and executive stakeholders. Professionals who can navigate these conversations will be indispensable.

As cybersecurity continues to expand beyond firewalls and incident response, privacy and regulatory compliance will offer some of the most stable and rewarding paths into the field. For mid-career professionals with an eye toward long-term impact, these areas represent not only accessible entry points but also opportunities for leadership and influence.

Trend #3: Persistent Workforce Shifts and Shortages

For years, the cybersecurity industry has experienced ongoing workforce challenges, with demand for qualified professionals consistently outpacing supply. This talent gap is expected to continue in the coming years as organizations face evolving threats and expanding digital footprints. The need is particularly pronounced in specialized areas such as cloud security, incident response, governance, and compliance. While the exact scale of this shortage is debated among industry experts, the consensus remains that developing and retaining cybersecurity talent will be a critical priority for organizations across sectors.

While the numbers tell one story, the underlying shift is more complex. Cybersecurity is not just growing in size; it is growing in scope. As digital risks expand across industries and into new domains, the definition of "cybersecurity work" is broadening. Security now intersects with legal compliance, business continuity, public safety, software development, education, and even ethics. This means that roles once limited to highly technical professionals are now open to those with diverse experience and skill sets.

What This Means for You

For those entering the field today, this trend offers both opportunity and responsibility. The shortage of qualified professionals has made employers more open to hiring candidates from non-traditional backgrounds, but it also means you must be ready to demonstrate how your skills apply to real-world security challenges.

Mid-career professionals bring strengths that are often in short supply: clear communication, cross-functional collaboration, strategic thinking, and domain knowledge from regulated industries. These are precisely the qualities needed in areas like risk management, policy development, security awareness training, and incident response coordination.

In other words, the field doesn't just need more people... it needs people like you.

Practical Advice

- **Focus on credibility, not perfection.** Employers aren't looking for experts in everything. They're looking for professionals who understand the fundamentals, communicate well, and keep learning. Build a strong foundation and grow from there.

- **Be ready to explain your value.** Learn to articulate how your background enhances your cybersecurity potential. Whether it's managing operations, interpreting regulations, or leading teams, your experience matters.

- **Start small but stay focused.** Consider contract roles, analyst positions, or hybrid responsibilities within your current organization. These can be excellent steppingstones into more specialized roles.

The cybersecurity field is not just looking for people who can write code or analyze malware. It is looking for leaders, translators, collaborators, and lifelong learners. If you bring that mindset and a willingness to grow, there is space for you in this field.

Emerging Trends and Wildcards

While many of the trends shaping cybersecurity over the next five years can be forecast with reasonable certainty, others remain difficult to predict but too important to ignore. These emerging developments and "wildcards" may not yet dominate job descriptions or strategy documents, but they are already influencing how the field evolves. For mid-career professionals, staying informed and being open to evolving with the field is one of the most effective ways to maintain a resilient, adaptable career.

Quantum Computing and Cryptography

Quantum computing has long been the subject of speculation in security circles, but it is gradually becoming a real—and urgent—concern. When scalable quantum computers become viable, they will have the potential to break many of the encryption methods currently used to secure everything from financial transactions to patient records.

Although practical quantum attacks remain years away, governments and industry leaders are already preparing for a post-quantum future. The U.S. National Institute of Standards and Technology (NIST), for example, is leading efforts to standardize quantum-resistant encryption algorithms. These efforts are expected to lead to widespread cryptographic updates (sometimes referred to as "crypto agility") in both public and private sectors.

While deep expertise in quantum computing is not required for most cybersecurity roles, professionals should be aware of the long-term impact. Understanding the basics of cryptography, key management, and upcoming standards will be valuable, especially for those working in infrastructure, compliance, or risk management.

Supply Chain Security

Cyberattacks targeting the software supply chain have surged in recent years, with high-profile incidents such as SolarWinds and Log4Shell demonstrating the ripple effects of a single compromised component. As organizations rely on increasingly complex ecosystems of third-party vendors, open-source libraries, and managed services, securing the supply chain has become a strategic imperative.

This trend is accelerating as regulators begin to require organizations to demonstrate due diligence in vendor security. In the United States, executive orders and federal mandates are already placing new compliance burdens on critical infrastructure and government contractors.

Supply chain risk management is creating demand for roles that focus on vendor assessments, software bill of materials (SBOM) management, and third-party compliance audits. Professionals with experience in procurement, legal review, or project management may find opportunities here even without a deep technical background.

Security for IoT and Operational Technology (OT)

The growing use of Internet of Things (IoT) devices in homes, businesses, and industrial environments is creating new attack surfaces that traditional security tools are not designed to address. From smart sensors in hospitals to control systems in energy plants, these devices often lack basic security controls and are difficult to patch or monitor.

Operational technology (OT) environments—particularly in manufacturing, transportation, and utilities—face unique challenges due to their reliance on legacy systems and the potential for physical harm in the event of a cyberattack. As IoT and OT systems become more integrated with enterprise networks, the risks become more significant and more urgent.

IoT and OT security are emerging niches with growing importance. Professionals with experience in healthcare, logistics, engineering, or facilities management may be well-positioned to contribute. While technical upskilling is required, domain knowledge in these environments is a valuable asset.

AI Ethics and Algorithmic Risk

As artificial intelligence becomes more embedded in security operations and business decision-making, new questions are emerging about bias, fairness, accountability, and transparency. AI systems can perpetuate existing inequalities or produce unintended outcomes if not carefully designed and governed.

Cybersecurity professionals are increasingly involved in evaluating the risks associated with AI deployments—not only in defending against AI-powered attacks, but in assessing whether their own tools are operating responsibly. This overlap between cybersecurity, ethics, and governance is likely to become a specialized field in its own right.

Mid-career professionals with backgrounds in compliance, policy, data governance, or ethics may find opportunities to help organizations establish frameworks for AI oversight. This is an area where communication skills, critical thinking, and multidisciplinary collaboration are particularly valuable.

Action Steps and Your Next Five Years

The future of cybersecurity is dynamic, complex, and full of opportunity. As the field evolves in response to new technologies, regulatory shifts, and emerging threats, professionals entering from other industries have a critical role to play. The next five years will demand not only technical capability, but also adaptability, sound judgment, and the ability to connect security goals to broader business and societal priorities.

For mid-career professionals, this moment presents a unique window. The workforce shortage is real, the diversity of cybersecurity roles is expanding, and the field is increasingly welcoming professionals who bring experience from outside traditional technical pipelines. The challenge is not simply to learn a new skill set but to recognize how your existing strengths can be applied in new ways.

Action Steps to Take Now

The following steps can help guide your transition into cybersecurity and position you to thrive in the years ahead:

1. Build foundational knowledge.

Begin with an introductory certification or course that covers the basics of cybersecurity principles, terminology, and best practices. Options like CompTIA Security+, ISC2's Certified in Cybersecurity (CC), or free online resources from CISA or Coursera are excellent starting points.

2. Map your transferable skills.

Identify how your current experience—in project management, compliance, education, healthcare, finance, or another domain—aligns with cybersecurity roles. Employers often value communication, risk assessment, leadership, and operational expertise just as much as technical knowledge.

3. Choose one emerging area to follow closely.

Whether it's AI, privacy, cloud security, or governance, pick a focus area that aligns with your interests and background. Staying current on developments in one specialized area will help you build credibility and confidence.

4. Engage with the community.

Join cybersecurity organizations, attend webinars or local meetups, and connect with practitioners online. The field is filled with professionals who made a mid-career shift—many are eager to share insights and help others get started.

5. Pursue continuous education.

Cybersecurity changes quickly. Seek out ongoing learning through certifications, workshops, podcasts, reading lists, and real-world experience. Commit to regularly listening to one podcast, reading one newsletter, and regularly checking one website.[94] Make learning part of your professional identity.

6. Explore roles beyond the obvious.

Not every cybersecurity career is focused on threat hunting or penetration testing. Investigate job titles like security analyst, compliance manager, privacy consultant, risk advisor, security awareness trainer, and incident response coordinator. These roles often align closely with the strengths of career changers.

Looking Ahead

You don't need to predict the future of cybersecurity to prepare for it. By taking deliberate, informed steps now, you can position yourself not only to enter the field, but to contribute meaningfully

---

[94] We have mentioned them throughout the book already, but as a reminder some include the Risky Business podcast, TL;DR Sec newsletter, and the Hacker News website.

as it evolves. The coming years will require professionals who can think critically, communicate clearly, and act decisively under uncertainty.

Cybersecurity is not just about technology: it is about people, systems, decisions, and trust. For mid-career professionals ready to bring their skills into a new domain, the future is full of possibility.

Action Steps and Your Next Five Years

- AI in cybersecurity presents a dual challenge: it empowers both attackers (through enhanced phishing, deepfakes, and adaptive malware) and defenders (through automated threat detection and incident response).

- Privacy regulations are increasingly driving cybersecurity priorities, creating career opportunities for professionals with backgrounds in regulated industries.

- The cybersecurity field is expanding beyond traditional technical roles to include specialized positions in areas like compliance, supply chain security, and AI ethics.

- Emerging trends like quantum computing, IoT/OT security, and supply chain risk management will reshape cybersecurity priorities in the next five years.

- Mid-career professionals can successfully transition into cybersecurity by leveraging transferable skills, pursuing targeted education, and focusing on emerging niches aligned with their backgrounds.

- Despite rapid technological changes, many cybersecurity challenges remain persistent.

- The future of cybersecurity requires professionals who can balance technical skills with business context, policy awareness, and strategic thinking.

Chapter References

Hoofnagle, C. J. and Richard III, G. G. (2024). *Cybersecurity in Context: Technology, Policy, and Law.* Wiley.

Russell, S. and Norvig, P. (2022). *Artificial Intelligence: A Modern Approach, 4th ed.* https://aima.cs.berkeley.edu/.

Goodman, D., Phillips, J. and Stamper, M. (2022). *Data Privacy Program Guide: How to Build a Privacy Program that Inspires Trust.* CISO DRG Publishing.

Chapter 18

Guidance for Hiring Managers

So far in this book we have covered extensively how cybersecurity is evolving rapidly as is the talent needed to meet its increasingly complex challenges. In this final chapter, we shift our focus to those who may be reading this book from the perspective of attracting and recruiting mid-career professionals.

Traditionally, hiring managers have turned to candidates with proven technical cybersecurity backgrounds, frequently overlooking a deep and rich talent pool: mid-career professionals transitioning from other fields. Yet, by widening your scope beyond traditional candidates, your organization gains immediate access to maturity, diverse expertise, and unique perspectives—qualities that are often difficult to find in early-career hires.

Mid-career professionals bring not just skills, but wisdom gained through experience lacking in entry-level candidates. Mid-career candidates have already successfully navigated complex problems, learned from their mistakes, managed risk, and developed strong interpersonal and leadership capabilities. Many are actively looking for a meaningful career shift—one that allows them to leverage their existing strengths while learning new skills and making a significant impact. Organizations that understand how to effectively attract and retain these candidates will reap considerable rewards in the form of fresh ideas, diverse insights, and accelerated growth.

Yet many hiring managers unintentionally exclude these talented individuals through overly rigid job descriptions, outdated interview techniques, or assumptions about what cybersecurity talent "should" look like. This approach, while conventional, creates unnecessary barriers to entry and significantly limits your candidate pool.

To succeed, hiring managers must rethink traditional strategies. This chapter provides practical guidance to help you attract, interview, onboard, and retain mid-career cybersecurity talent effectively. You will be able to adjust your job descriptions and interviewing practices to attract high-quality mid-career talent.

Rethinking the Hiring Strategy

Consider this common scenario: A hiring manager posts a cybersecurity analyst position, carefully listing the technical certifications, degrees, and cybersecurity-specific experience required. Yet after weeks or even months, the position remains open, causing frustration and workload pressure on the existing team. Meanwhile, talented mid-career candidates with years of practical experience managing compliance programs, directing complex projects, or solving nuanced problems in law, finance, healthcare, or operations never apply. They see overly prescriptive criteria and conclude the job isn't a good match. Both sides lose.

To effectively capture this overlooked talent, hiring managers must reconsider what makes an ideal cybersecurity professional. Unlike entry-level hires who often possess fresh technical training but limited experience navigating complex organizational environments, mid-career candidates typically come with seasoned problem-solving abilities, professional maturity, and the kind of judgment that only years of real-world experience can provide.

These professionals are not seeking entry-level pay or minimal responsibility. They often approach cybersecurity as a deliberate, thoughtful career transition motivated by purpose, intellectual curiosity, and a desire to have a measurable impact. Hiring managers who recognize and respect this motivation can tap into a powerful source of mature, highly driven talent—one that entry-level recruiting rarely uncovers.

A critical starting point is reconsidering your job descriptions. Traditional cybersecurity job postings frequently focus on stringent technical qualifications and required certifications, inadvertently filtering out experienced career-switchers who could quickly acquire cybersecurity-specific skills. Instead, craft job descriptions around essential competencies and responsibilities—clearly communicating that your organization values adaptability, mature judgment, professional experience, and a demonstrated ability to rapidly learn new skills. Frame these postings to openly welcome candidates from diverse backgrounds, highlighting that professional maturity and relevant transferable experience are as critical as technical proficiency.

The interview process itself must also adapt. Rather than emphasizing specific cybersecurity trivia or deeply technical assessments, consider evaluating candidates through scenario-based and behavior-focused questions. Ask experienced candidates to share past professional challenges, describe how they adapted to new environments, and explain their approaches to complex organizational problems. For instance, a candidate who previously managed compliance in healthcare may lack direct cybersecurity credentials but can demonstrate an extraordinary ability to interpret regulatory requirements, navigate complicated situations, and communicate clearly across teams—exactly the skills most cybersecurity positions urgently require.

Furthermore, competing for mid-career professionals requires more than just adjusting job descriptions and interview methods. Established professionals are evaluating your organization just as carefully as you're evaluating them. They often have mortgages, families, community ties, and clear expectations for career growth and job stability. To attract and retain them effectively, your organization must thoughtfully communicate about compensation, work-life balance, professional development opportunities, and job stability. Be transparent about career trajectories and highlight specific stories of other mid-career hires who have successfully transitioned and thrived in cybersecurity roles within your team.

For example, imagine a former finance director with significant experience in risk management who decided cybersecurity was her next step. What made her choose your organization might not have been the job description alone, but rather your clear commitment to professional development, flexible working arrangements, or compelling real-world examples of others who successfully made similar transitions. Communicating these factors openly and explicitly is essential in drawing experienced professionals away from competitors and from other career paths altogether.

Ultimately, the strategic shift required by hiring managers today is more than procedural; it's cultural. It involves embracing the idea that cybersecurity teams benefit deeply from diverse career experiences, transferable skill sets, and professional maturity. By proactively adapting your approach, from job descriptions and interviewing to onboarding and professional development, you're not merely filling positions; you're strategically building teams that can meet the evolving demands of cybersecurity's complex future.

Who Mid-Career Candidates Really Are

You may think you know all the obvious and necessary characteristics of mid-career jobseekers. In reality, there is even more variety and diversity among this group.

As we have explored throughout this book, mid-career cybersecurity candidates represent a diverse group of professionals who come into cybersecurity after years—even decades—in other professional fields. At this stage of their careers, they're not fresh graduates or early-career individuals still learning workplace fundamentals. Instead, they bring rich and varied experiences accumulated in professions such as healthcare, finance, law, education, operations, and management. Each candidate's unique journey adds a layer of insight and maturity that traditional hiring practices often overlook.

While their professional backgrounds differ greatly, mid-career candidates share several defining traits. Most notably, they possess strong foundational skills that naturally translate to cybersecurity roles. They've navigated complex organizational structures, managed budgets and deadlines, developed policies, handled crises, and collaborated across departments and levels of seniority. They have learned, through years of trial, error, and success, how to communicate clearly, solve problems effectively, and think strategically—qualities that often take years to develop from scratch.

In addition, mid-career candidates are often highly motivated by a genuine sense of purpose. Unlike individuals who may be entering cybersecurity solely for salary or prestige, these candidates typically seek meaningful work and intellectual stimulation. They understand cybersecurity's importance to society, are drawn to the profession's mission-driven aspects, and recognize that their skills can immediately contribute to meaningful outcomes. Many come from industries where compliance, regulation, ethics, and risk management were daily concerns, making them uniquely suited to understand and address similar challenges in cybersecurity.

Importantly, mid-career professionals typically have clear, realistic expectations about the kind of support and training they need to make their transition successful. They recognize that learning cybersecurity-specific technical skills and terminology may require deliberate effort and patience. Yet, they are quick learners, often leveraging their well-developed professional skills to accelerate their integration. Moreover, they're proactive about pursuing certifications, training programs, and mentoring opportunities. They understand how to learn and adapt because they have done it many times before.

Yet their mid-career status also brings considerations hiring managers must carefully acknowledge. Unlike early-career candidates, these professionals frequently have significant personal and family commitments. Many have established homes, children in local schools, spouses with stable careers, and deep ties to their communities. Relocation may not be straightforward or even desirable for many of them. Thus, flexibility, stability, and work-life balance often become deciding factors in their decision to accept or decline job offers.

From your perspective as a hiring manager, it's crucial to view these qualities not as constraints, but as indicators of professional maturity and clarity of purpose. Offering flexibility such as remote or hybrid work, predictable schedules, or family-friendly policies can become a powerful competitive advantage. Similarly, clearly communicating your organization's long-term stability and opportunities for ongoing learning will resonate deeply with this candidate group.

You may recall examples earlier in this book highlighting mid-career professionals who successfully transitioned into cybersecurity roles. These stories reveal a consistent theme: hiring managers who clearly understood and appreciated the strengths and circumstances of these candidates succeeded in recruiting exceptional talent. Those who overlooked these nuances or stuck rigidly to traditional expectations missed out on potentially transformative hires.

In short, recognizing who mid-career cybersecurity candidates really are and understanding their unique value positions you to not only attract exceptional individuals but also build robust teams capable of meeting the dynamic cybersecurity challenges your organization faces.

Crafting Job Descriptions That Attract Mid-Career Talent

When you imagine writing a cybersecurity job description, you likely envision listing required certifications, specific technical skills, and a certain number of years in cybersecurity. While this approach may seem straightforward, it often unintentionally excludes exceptional mid-career candidates who have substantial professional experience but may lack direct cybersecurity credentials. To effectively attract these high-value candidates, hiring managers must rethink how job descriptions are crafted, shifting their approach toward highlighting competencies, responsibilities, and opportunities rather than rigid technical requirements.

Instead, consider writing job descriptions that clearly communicate openness to candidates from non-traditional backgrounds. Acknowledge directly that relevant professional maturity and adaptability are as critical to success as technical proficiency. Frame your postings around core competencies and outcomes rather than specific cybersecurity credentials. For instance, a statement such as "We seek experienced professionals who excel in critical thinking, managing risk, interpreting complex regulatory frameworks, and rapidly acquiring new technical skills" sends a powerful message that you genuinely welcome and value mid-career candidates.

Furthermore, it can be helpful to explicitly state your organization's commitment to onboarding and professional development. Experienced candidates are deeply aware they'll need targeted training and support to transition successfully. Including language such as "We provide structured professional development and mentorship programs to rapidly integrate your existing expertise into cybersecurity" clearly demonstrates that you understand their concerns and have concrete plans to support them.

Crafting your job descriptions thoughtfully, with a clear emphasis on transferable skills, organizational support, and authentic storytelling, positions your organization as uniquely appealing to mid-career professionals. Rather than limiting your candidate pool, you significantly expand it, attracting experienced, mature professionals whose presence can substantially enhance your cybersecurity team.

Sample Job Description

Job Title: Intrusion Analyst
Location: Remote or Hybrid (U.S. Based)
Employment Type: Full-Time

We're looking for an Intrusion Analyst to join our growing cybersecurity team and help protect our organization from evolving threats. This role is ideal for professionals who thrive in fast-paced environments, are naturally curious, and are ready to apply their existing expertise in a new and meaningful way.

We welcome candidates transitioning into cybersecurity from other industries. You may have previously worked in healthcare, finance, law, education, compliance, or operations—and developed strong analytical, decision-making, and communication skills. If you're excited to bring that experience into the cybersecurity world, we want to hear from you.

Responsibilities:

- Monitor, analyze, and investigate suspicious network activity using SIEM tools and threat intelligence platforms.
- Document and communicate findings clearly to technical and non-technical stakeholders.
- Collaborate with internal teams to improve detection capabilities and response strategies.
- Contribute to the development of playbooks and workflows for incident response.
- Stay current on emerging threats, attack patterns, and industry trends.

Qualifications:

- Strong critical thinking, communication, and problem-solving skills.
- Experience working in regulated, high-stakes, or fast-moving environments.
- Demonstrated ability to learn new systems, tools, or processes quickly.
- Familiarity with cybersecurity concepts, or completion of foundational training (e.g., online courses, bootcamps, or certifications such as Security+).
- Prior experience with cybersecurity tools is a plus but not required we will train the right candidate.

We offer structured onboarding, mentorship, and professional development. You'll be part of a collaborative team that values your perspective, respects your experience, and supports your growth from day one.

If you're eager to contribute, ready to learn, and excited to build a new chapter in your career, we encourage you to apply even if your background doesn't match every bullet point.

Effective Interviewing—Evaluating for Potential

Interviewing mid-career professionals making their first move into cybersecurity requires a shift in both mindset and method. Traditional interviews in this field often emphasize technical minutiae or focus on candidates with direct cybersecurity experience. But for career-changers, this approach risks missing their most valuable qualities: adaptability, sound judgment, communication skills, and the ability to learn quickly under pressure.

Effective interviews with mid-career candidates are not about testing what they already know about firewalls or SIEMs—they're about exploring how they think, how they problem-solve, and how they've navigated high-stakes situations in other industries. The best interviews create space for candidates to reflect on how their past experiences have prepared them for this transition, and for you as the hiring manager to assess whether their mindset, temperament, and skillset align with your team's needs.

Rather than viewing the interview as a checkpoint for existing technical proficiency, approach it as an opportunity to discover potential. Scenario-based questions, behavioral prompts, and open-ended reflections reveal far more about a candidate's readiness than memorized terminology ever could. When done well, this kind of interviewing not only surfaces great talent—it shows candidates that your organization is genuinely invested in helping people grow into cybersecurity, not just screen them out.

Interview Question Bank: Evaluating Mid-Career Cybersecurity Candidates

When interviewing mid-career professionals who may have little direct cybersecurity experience, traditional technical questions often miss key insights into their true potential. Instead, use the following sample questions to evaluate critical transferable skills, professional maturity, learning agility, adaptability, and their capacity for growth.

Category 1: Assessing Transferable Skills and Professional Maturity

- "Describe a challenging professional situation in your previous career. How did you approach the issue, and what did you learn?"

  (Evaluates: problem-solving, critical thinking, maturity, and adaptability.)

- "Tell me about a time you had to quickly become proficient in something completely new to you. What was your approach?"

  (Evaluates: learning agility, adaptability, resourcefulness.)

- "Give an example of how you managed risk or compliance in your previous role. What steps did you take, and what were the results?"

  (Evaluates: experience handling regulated environments, risk management skills, methodical thinking.)

Category 2: Evaluating Motivation and Alignment

- "Why have you decided to move into cybersecurity at this stage of your career? What aspects of this field appeal most to you?"

  (Evaluates: genuine motivation, awareness of the cybersecurity field, clarity of purpose.)

- "Given your experience and skillset, how do you see yourself contributing most effectively in a cybersecurity role?"

  (Evaluates: self-awareness, ability to align past skills to future role.)

- "Describe the kind of organizational culture or environment where you believe you would thrive most as you transition into cybersecurity."

  (Evaluates: cultural fit, maturity, and alignment of expectations.)

Category 3: Assessing Communication and Collaboration

- "Tell me about a time you had to explain a complex or technical concept to a non-technical audience. How did you approach that?"

  (Evaluates: communication skills, empathy, ability to translate complex concepts)

- "Describe a project or task where you collaborated closely with professionals from a discipline different from your own. How did you build trust and achieve alignment?"

  (Evaluates: collaborative ability, interpersonal skills, leadership.)

Category 4: Scenario-Based Questions for Critical Thinking and Adaptability

- "Imagine you're leading a cybersecurity project but lack direct expertise in a key technical area. How would you ensure the project is successful despite this gap?"

  (Evaluates: strategic thinking, self-awareness, resourcefulness.)

- "Suppose you discover a cybersecurity compliance issue at your organization. You lack formal authority to directly fix it. What steps do you take?"

  (Evaluates: problem-solving, influence without authority, diplomacy.)

- "You encounter resistance from colleagues when implementing a new cybersecurity procedure. How would you handle that situation?"

  (Evaluates: conflict resolution, interpersonal effectiveness, leadership.)

Category 5: Self-Awareness and Growth Mindset

- "What do you expect will be the most challenging aspect of your career change into cybersecurity? How are you preparing to meet that challenge?"

  (Evaluates: self-awareness, resilience, willingness to grow.)

- "Can you give an example of feedback you received in the past that initially surprised you? How did you respond, and what did you learn from that feedback?"

  (Evaluates: openness to feedback, adaptability, professional maturity.)

Competing Successfully for Established Professionals

For most mid-career professionals, transitioning into cybersecurity is a carefully considered move. By the time they apply for your role, they have likely weighed the risks and trade-offs of leaving behind a stable career, a familiar professional identity, and often a comfortable salary. What they're seeking isn't simply a job; they're looking for a role that feels purposeful, future-oriented, and worth the leap. To compete successfully for these candidates, hiring managers must recognize that job security, role clarity, and flexibility are not perks for this group—they're prerequisites. Offering remote or hybrid work options, predictable hours, and transparent expectations around job duties and growth paths helps reduce uncertainty and make your opportunity feel like a smart, strategic move rather than a risky departure.

But winning over experienced professionals isn't just about offering stability. It is also about showing respect for what they bring to the table. Many mid-career candidates are willing to start fresh in a new field, but not at the expense of their autonomy or ability to contribute meaningfully. When a role offers real ownership, opportunities to lead projects, and a visible path for professional advancement, it becomes far more attractive. Hiring managers who signal a commitment to learning and development—not just in the first 90 days but across the long term—create a powerful incentive for these professionals to join and stay. And when advancement isn't possible immediately, clear communication about how performance is evaluated and how growth is supported goes a long way in building trust.

A key part of competing for mid-career talent is storytelling—framing the cybersecurity role not as a reset, but as a natural next chapter. Many career-changers worry that their prior experience won't be valued or understood in a new field. You can ease that anxiety by explicitly showing how their background connects to the challenges your team is trying to solve. Highlighting past hires who've made a successful transition reinforces that your organization doesn't just tolerate non-traditional candidates; it celebrates and invests in them. Whether it's through testimonials on your careers page, casual conversations during the interview process, or mentor pairing after the hire, reinforcing that their transition is strategic and supported helps close the deal. And if you're looking to reach these professionals in the first place, know that many are not actively job hunting on traditional cybersecurity channels. They are browsing LinkedIn, engaging in industry-specific forums, attending virtual conferences, or participating in alumni networks and professional associations tied to their former careers. Showing up in these spaces with tailored messaging makes it more likely your open role will be seen by the right person at just the right time.

Just as important as what you offer is what you avoid. Subtle signals can easily discourage strong mid-career candidates. Overemphasizing certifications, using overly technical language, or creating overly prescriptive job descriptions can make experienced candidates feel like outsiders. Startup-style language, like requests for "cyber ninjas" or "hackers at heart," may appeal to early-career talent but can unintentionally signal that your culture is geared toward youth and speed over substance and collaboration. And in interviews, even small signs of skepticism about career-switching or age can be enough to push away a candidate who would otherwise bring maturity, insight, and stability to your team. Competing successfully for established professionals means showing, at every stage, that you recognize what they've accomplished and are excited about what they can contribute next.

Onboarding, Retention, and Professional Development

Successfully attracting mid-career cybersecurity professionals is just the first step. How you onboard, retain, and develop these experienced hires determines whether they flourish or struggle within your organization. Unlike entry-level staff, mid-career professionals bring substantial experience and well-established ways of working. Effective onboarding for them must go beyond typical orientation and procedural checklists, focusing instead on rapidly integrating their existing strengths into cybersecurity-specific contexts.

Customized onboarding programs that leverage their prior expertise and clearly acknowledge their professional maturity are most effective. Assigning mentors or guides who have themselves transitioned careers can be particularly impactful. Such mentorships create a comfortable space where mid-career hires can freely discuss challenges, ask questions, and quickly grasp the unwritten norms and expectations within your cybersecurity organization.

Retention is closely tied to meaningful professional development. Career-changers thrive when they feel continually challenged and supported in acquiring cybersecurity-specific knowledge and skills.

Investing in structured professional growth such as relevant training courses, industry certifications, and strategic assignments helps mid-career hires become productive more quickly and stay engaged over the long term. Additionally, since mid-career professionals often have substantial family and community responsibilities, providing flexibility through remote or hybrid work, predictable hours, or supportive family-friendly policies can significantly enhance loyalty and retention.

Managers should also remain actively involved post-onboarding. Regular, informal check-ins, combined with clear conversations about career progression, ensure mid-career professionals understand their trajectory and feel valued as integral members of your team. Recognizing their past professional achievements while offering clear avenues to acquire new skills creates an environment in which they are eager to remain, grow, and meaningfully contribute for many years.

Innovative Approaches to Mid-Career Recruitment

The competitive nature of today's cybersecurity talent market requires hiring managers to rethink traditional recruitment strategies and explore innovative approaches. Mid-career professionals, especially those transitioning from other industries, can be difficult to reach using conventional job-posting methods. To successfully attract and engage this uniquely qualified talent pool, hiring managers must meet mid-career candidates where they are and speak directly to their aspirations and concerns.

One innovative recruitment practice gaining traction is the structured use of "returnships" or apprenticeship-style programs specifically aimed at mid-career professionals transitioning into cybersecurity roles and those who have been away for a while.[95] Unlike standard internships which often cater primarily to students or recent graduates, these paid, structured programs enable experienced professionals to leverage their extensive career skills while acquiring cybersecurity-specific knowledge. Organizations

---

[95] https://hbr.org/2021/09/return-to-work-programs-come-of-age.

such as Amazon, IBM, and Meta have successfully piloted programs that blend targeted training, mentorship, and real-world project experiences, rapidly integrating mid-career hires into impactful cybersecurity positions. These programs not only help candidates quickly build confidence and credibility but also reduce the perceived risk of hiring professionals without direct cybersecurity experience.

Another powerful strategy involves leveraging professional networks and industry associations outside the cybersecurity community. Many experienced professionals who would thrive in cybersecurity roles currently engage with professional organizations in fields like healthcare, law, finance, education, or engineering. Forward-thinking hiring managers have found great success by directly engaging these communities, offering workshops, seminars, or webinars explicitly designed to showcase cybersecurity career opportunities to non-cyber professionals. Such efforts help demystify cybersecurity careers, create direct connections with potential candidates, and provide an accessible entry point for professionals considering a career change.

Additionally, leading organizations are embracing skills-based hiring approaches to evaluate candidates through interactive, practical assessments rather than relying exclusively on credentials or traditional interview methods. This approach includes scenario-driven assessments or small-group simulations where mid-career candidates showcase their transferable skills, professional judgment, and ability to quickly assimilate new information. Skills-based evaluations are especially attractive to mid-career candidates who may find traditional hiring processes overly focused on specific technical experience or certifications they haven't yet acquired.

Finally, storytelling and transparent communication about successful mid-career transitions have become essential recruitment tools. Providing compelling real-world examples and testimonials of mid-career professionals who have successfully transitioned into cybersecurity within your organization helps candidates visualize themselves in similar roles. These stories clearly signal to potential applicants that your organization understands and values their existing expertise, is committed to their professional growth, and genuinely welcomes diverse career backgrounds.

By embracing these innovative recruitment approaches—structured apprenticeships, strategic community outreach, skills-based hiring, and authentic storytelling—you position your organization as a welcoming, forward-thinking destination for exceptional mid-career cybersecurity talent.

Mid-Career Talent Audit Checklist

This checklist is designed to help hiring managers quickly assess whether their current hiring approach effectively attracts and welcomes mid-career cybersecurity candidates. For each statement, evaluate if the answer is Yes, No, or Needs Improvement.

Job Descriptions

- **Clearly indicate openness** to non-traditional backgrounds and transferable skills.
- Use **inclusive language** highlighting collaboration, professional maturity, and strategic thinking.
- Avoid overly technical jargon or **unnecessary certifications** that may unintentionally deter excellent mid-career candidates.
- Clearly communicate opportunities for **professional development and learning.**

Recruitment and Outreach

- Post job openings in places frequented by mid-career professionals (e.g., professional associations, LinkedIn career groups, industry forums).
- Engage with **mid-career networks** or **career-switcher groups,** such as online communities or professional associations outside cybersecurity.
- Highlight stories or testimonials from mid-career hires who've successfully transitioned into cybersecurity within your organization.
- Actively challenge unconscious biases related to age, industry experience, and career transitions within your hiring team.

Interview Process

- Interviews include questions designed to uncover **transferable skills**, potential, adaptability, and motivation rather than purely technical knowledge.

- Interview teams receive clear guidance on **evaluating mid-career professionals**, including awareness of implicit biases against candidates from different professional backgrounds.

- Candidate evaluations clearly value prior professional accomplishments, **leadership skills**, and real-world experiences from outside cybersecurity.

Competitive Positioning

- Compensation packages are **clearly competitive** for experienced professionals (salary, flexible work arrangements, health/family benefits).

- Roles clearly articulate pathways for career growth and professional stability.

- Your organization clearly communicates how mid-career hires can leverage their existing expertise to **add immediate value**.

Onboarding and Retention

- Provide customized onboarding programs designed specifically for **mid-career hires** to rapidly integrate and become productive.

- Assign mentors or guides who have similar experiences or made similar career changes.

- Offer ongoing professional development tailored to mature learning styles, including training, certifications, or leadership growth opportunities.

Regularly seek feedback from mid-career hires about onboarding and team integration, adjusting your processes accordingly.

Chapter Summary

- Mid-career professionals bring maturity, judgment, and a wealth of transferable skills that are often overlooked by traditional cybersecurity hiring practices.

- To attract these candidates, job descriptions should emphasize competencies, adaptability, and impact rather than rigid credentials or narrowly defined experience.

- Effective interviews focus on potential, problem-solving, and learning agility, using scenario-based questions rather than technical trivia.

- Structured onboarding, mentorship, and professional development tailored to career-switchers significantly improve integration, confidence, and retention.

- Competitive organizations offer more than salary. They communicate clearly about flexibility, long-term growth, and meaningful work aligned with the candidate's values.

- Innovative recruiting strategies—such as mid-career apprenticeships, outreach to industry associations, and skills-based hiring—help uncover hidden talent.

- Hiring managers who recognize and embrace the strategic value of non-traditional candidates will build stronger, more resilient cybersecurity teams.

Chapter References

CyberSeek (n.d.). *CyberSeek*. https://www.cyberseek.org

Miller, A. (2022). *Cybersecurity Career Guide*. Manning Publications.

Conclusion

Career scholar Herminia Ibarra reminds people that career change is rarely linear or scripted, especially for mid-career professionals reinventing themselves. Instead of waiting for clarity, she urges action: try out divergent roles, activate dormant networks, and embrace what she calls the "learning plot," where identity is reshaped not through introspection but by doing. This mindset—accepting temporary ambiguity while building toward something new—is essential when moving into cybersecurity's dynamic and evolving landscape.

For people wanting to move into cybersecurity, Ibarra's advice particularly applies: try different cyber roles, activate your networks, and be willing to flex when your original plans don't work out. The immature nature of the cybersecurity industry allows you to find your own path into and through the profession. This can be a blessing and a curse. Be prepared to move with changes in the profession, your industry, and the threat landscape. Know that being a cybersecurity professional requires a commitment to continuous learning and constant change, and that the only way to stay on top of this is to commit to learning from your networks and to practice hands-on experimentation and deep intellectual engagement.

The effort it takes to move into cybersecurity is worth the payoff. You can find meaningful work in a community of people who take care of each other. You will be constantly challenged with new ideas, new ways of working, and new ways to add value. There will always be important challenges that need to be overcome, and problems to solve. Leaders recognize the importance of cybersecurity as a business enabler and are investing accordingly.

As a mid-career jobseeker, there has never been a better time to move into cybersecurity. Your prior work experience with other roles and with professional skills of empathy, teamwork, and communication, are particularly important. Use them to land that first cybersecurity role and advance quickly through the cybersecurity ranks.

Welcome to cybersecurity.

Index

Helen Patton is a long-time security professional, author, teacher and speaker. She is currently a cybersecurity advisor for a security company and was previously a chief information security officer in the technology and higher education sectors.

Helen is a founding member of the Cybersecurity Canon, an industry non-profit that shares cybersecurity wisdom; co-founder and advisor to the Ohio State Institute for Cybersecurity and Digital Trust; and a member of the Forte Group, an advocacy group of women in cybersecurity. She is a university cybersecurity risk management instructor and the author of *Navigating the Cybersecurity Career Path*. Helen holds a Master's Degree in Public Policy from Ohio State University.

Why I chose cybersecurity as my field: I began my technology career in the 1990's and was dismayed to see the impact of computer worms and other attacks on my company, and my own workday. After 9/11 I was asked to create the first disaster recovery plan for my company, and from there I moved into Information Security. I was hooked. Since then, I've continued to work as a defender, helping companies plan for, respond to, and recover from cybersecurity and technology incidents. There is always more to be done.

Josiah Dykstra is a cybersecurity practitioner, researcher, and leader. He served for 19 years as a senior technical leader at the National Security Agency (NSA) and has worked in industry for the past several years. Dr. Dykstra is an experienced cyber practitioner and researcher whose focus has included the psychology and economics of cybersecurity. He received the CyberCorps® Scholarship for Service (SFS) fellowship and is one of ten people in the SFS Hall of Fame. In 2017, he received the Presidential Early Career Award for Scientists and Engineers (PECASE) from then-President Barack Obama. Dr. Dykstra is a Fellow of the American Academy of Forensic Sciences (AAFS) and a Distinguished Member of the Association for Computing Machinery (ACM). He is the author of numerous research papers, the book, *Essential Cybersecurity Science* (O'Reilly Media, 2016), and co-author of *Cybersecurity Myths and Misconceptions* (Pearson, 2023). Dr. Dykstra holds a Ph.D. in computer science from the University of Maryland, Baltimore County.

Why I chose cybersecurity as my field: Cybersecurity is attractive because it helps to ensure that people can feel more confident in their primary goals, from messaging to banking to healthcare. I enjoy the challenge of learning rapidly-changing technology and countering emerging threats. Having seen global-scale threats in government and helped small businesses implement recommended practices, I've come to appreciate the costs and values of cybersecurity. Today, I'm grateful to share my stories and experiences with the hope that they encourage and motivate the next generation.

www.ingramcontent.com/pod-product-compliance
Lightning Source LLC
Chambersburg PA
CBHW061234220326
41599CB00028B/5425